COMING OUT STRAIGHT

Four Stages of Healing Homosexuality

1. Transitioning (Behavioral therapy)

- Cutting off from sexual behavior •
- Developing a support network •
- Building self-worth and experiencing value in relationship with God •

2. Grounding (Cognitive therapy)

- Continuing with the support network •
- Continuing to build self-worth and experience value in relationship with God •
- Building skills: assertiveness training, communication skills, problem-solving techniques •
- Beginning inner-child healing: identifying thoughts, feelings, and needs •

3. Healing the Homo-Emotional Wounds (Psychodynamic therapy)

- Continuing all tasks of Stage Two •
- Discovering the root causes of homo-emotional wounds •
- Beginning the process of grieving, forgiving, and taking responsibility •
- Developing healthy, healing same-sex relationships •

4. Healing the Hetero-Emotional Wounds (Psychodynamic therapy)

- Continuing all tasks of Stage Two •
- Discovering the root causes of hetero-emotional wounds •
- Continuing the process of grieving, forgiving, and taking responsibility •
- Developing healthy, healing opposite-sex relationships and learning about the opposite sex •

Coming Out Straight

Understanding and Healing Homosexuality

RICHARD COHEN, M.A.

• 2ND Edition •

Oakhill Press
WINCHESTER, VIRGINIA

10   9   8   7   6   5   4   3   2   1

Second Edition

ISBN 1-886939-77-2

Cover photo: Richard and Jae Sook Cohen

The Library of Congress has cataloged the hardcover/paperback editions as follows:

Cohen, Richard, 1952–
    Coming Out Straight : Understanding and Healing Homosexuality / Richard Cohen.
        p. cm.
    Includes bibliographical references (p.) and index.
    Library of Congress has previously cataloged this book as follows:
    ISBN 1-886939-41-1
    ISBN 1-886939-47-0 pbk
    1. Homosexuality. 2. Gays--Mental health. 3. Psychoanalysis and homosexuality. 4. Cohen, Richard A., 1952- I. Title.
    RC558.C642000
    306.76'6—dc21   00-021844

Oakhill Press
1647 Cedar Grove Road
Winchester, VA 22603
800-32-Books
Printed in the United States of America

Dedication

This book represents my life's work and my personal journey out of homosexuality. I therefore dedicate this book:

To God, who has always been present, guiding me each step of the way.

To Jae Sook, Jarish, Jessica, and Alfred, my devoted and loving family, who stood with me through it all.

To my parents, Samuel and Lorna Cohen, who did their best and gave their all. Dad, thanks for defending our freedom.

To all the men and women I have had the privilege of assisting on their journey toward wholeness, you have been my teachers.

To all those who have generously contributed to the work of the International Healing Foundation, you are my champions.

To the many men and women who loved me and helped me get this far. So far.

Thank you all, from the bottom of my heart and soul.

Contents

Preface

C oming Out Straight was first published six years ago, and it has been heart warming to hear from thousands of readers whose lives were changed forever. I believe that anyone who desires to heal from same-sex attraction (SSA) may do so. By following this four-stage model of healing, obtaining support from family, friends and mentors, and seeking God's guidance each step of the way, I know that you or your loved one will come out straight. *No one is born with same-sex attraction and change is possible.*

Same-sex attraction is a psychological defense for two basic issues: 1) wounds that have not healed, and 2) needs for love that have not been fulfilled. When these two essential issues are resolved, a profound sense of internal change will occur and heterosexual desires will ensue. *It works if you work the program.*

Since the publication of this book, some have said to me, "When I read the four stages of healing, I felt overwhelmed by all that's required." Here are some strategies for success: *First, take it slow.* Take it one step at a time. Don't think about tomorrow, only today. *Second, be patient with yourself and others.* It took many years to develop SSA, and it will take time to heal the wounds that created the desires in the first place. *Third, you must develop healthy, healing relationships with members of your own gender.* Men must heal with other men, and women must heal with other women.

You will need to heal homo-emotional and homo-social wounds, and then hetero-emotional and hetero-social wounds. Homo-emotional wounds stem from a breakdown in the father-son or mother-daughter relationship. Homo-social wounds originate in lack of peer bonding, boys with boys and girls with girls. In the process of healing, you will need to experience healthy, non-erotic, same-gender relationships. Especially important is bonding with those who do not experience same-sex attraction (SSA), that is, those who have opposite-sex attractions (OSA). Four types of relationships are necessary: 1) bonding with OSA men/women who know about your SSA and are good friends, 2) bonding with OSA men/women who do not know about your SSA and are good friends, 3) bonding with other SSA men/women who are on the same path of healing, and 4) OSA mentors who stand in the gap as paternal and maternal figures. And if you experience SSA, do not think of yourself as less than any OSA person. You are gifted and exceptional, and have much to offer.

It will take time to develop these relationships. Be patient with yourself and others. Healing is a journey, not a destination. Through this process, you will be changed step-by-step, and day-by-day. After healing with those of your same gender, you will need to address the hetero-emotional and hetero-social wounds. Hetero-emotional wounds stem from an unhealthy attachment between mother-son and father-daughter. Hetero-social wounds originate in any disruption between men-women and women-men. This model of recovery works for those who are attracted to the same sex, those who have attractions for both men and women, and those who experience gender-identity confusion. There is great hope for healing and discovering one's true gender identity and coming out straight.

Since *Coming Out Straight* was published in 2000, Dr. Robert Spitzer, professor of psychiatry at Columbia University and longtime member of the American Psychiatric Association, published a study in the *Archives of Sexual Behavior* in October 2003 entitled, "Can Some Gay Men and Lesbians Change Their Sexual Orientation? 200 Participants Reporting a Change from Homosexual to Heterosexual Orientation." This landmark study found that people can and do change their core sexual orientation. For more information about the efficacy of change, please view *www.new direction.ca/research* and *www.narth.com*. There you will find dozens of scientific studies that document the possibility of coming out straight. For wonderful stories of transformation, please view *www.peoplecanchange.com*.

After you finish reading this book for the first time, read it once again. And after you finish it for the second time, read it again. As you grow, the book will change. This is a text to create radical healing. You will not be able to grasp all the concepts in the first or second read. Therefore, begin your personal journey, or begin helping your client or loved one. Then read the book once again to deepen your understanding about the process of change.

Freedom is not free. There is a price to pay to achieve one's goal. Keep going. **Never give up**. Do not worry about what anyone says or thinks. Focus on *your* dream. It is neither popular nor fashionable to explore the possibility of changing from a homosexual to a heterosexual orientation at this time. But be of good cheer. I have worked in this field for over two decades, and I believe that the time is coming when more people will know the truth: *No one is born with same-sex attraction, and change is possible.* So, dig your heels in, roll your sleeves up, and get started. I am praying for you and your loved ones.

—Richard Cohen, M.A.
January 2006

Acknowledgments

I would like to thank my family and friends for standing by me these past years as I fought so many battles to stay alive.

Thank you, Mom and Dad, for your love and openness. I know I have challenged you each step of the way. Thanks for hanging in there with me. I love you both.

Thanks to Jae Sook, my devoted wife, who is the stabilizing force in the Cohen family. Your steadfast love and support have allowed me to write this book. It is laced with our blood, sweat, and tears. It is a gift we return to God and others. It is the result of our victories of love throughout our eighteen years of marriage.

Thanks to Jarish, Jessica, and Alfie, our three wonderful children. You are great. You are the future. Fly and be free! I love you.

Thanks to John, Hilde, Wayne, and Camas for being lifelong friends, for being there, for holding me up when I fell down, for your monthly contributions that helped sustain this healing providence, and most of all, for your love and passion for God and healing humanity.

Thanks to the Wesleyan Christian Community for the years of counseling you willingly and freely gave us. You were precious teachers of many gifts.

Thanks to Phillip, Peter, Russell, Steve, and Gordon, the men who poured into my empty and hungry bucket. Thanks to Nora, Berti, and Victoria who also mentored me, helping me experience healthy women's love. Thanks to Hans, Barbara, Ken, Jackie, Herbert, Helga, Gabriel, Irma, Gert, and Siglinde for your friendship, love, and support.

A special thanks to Joe Nicolosi, Charles Socarides, and Ben Kaufman who created NARTH (National Association for Research and Therapy of Homosexuality). You are truly brave men to stand against the tide. My brothers and sisters and I are deeply indebted to you. Thank you, Joe, for inspiring me to write this book. I appreciate your mentoring me and your constant encouragement and friendship over the past eight years.

Thanks to all the courageous souls who minister to those wishing to exit homosexuality: NARTH, EXODUS, Courage/Encourage, JONAH,

Transforming Congregations, Pastoral Care Ministries, Evergreen International, One by One, HA, PFOX, and others. You are God's champions, and I deeply respect and appreciate you all. Special thanks to Father John Harvey for having the guts to start Courage/Encourage. You are a shining light in the darkness. Thanks to Father Donald Timone for his heart of compassion. Thanks to Dr. Dean Byrd for his pioneer efforts in this field of reparative therapy. Your generosity has touched me and so many others. Thanks to Leanne Payne and her invaluable healing ministry.

Thanks to all the men and women I have had the privilege of counseling over the past decade. You are the salt of the earth. I stand in awe before you. Thank you for allowing me to be part of your journey home.

Thanks to Dave and Joanie Orgon Coolidge, Glenna Dameron, Dean Byrd, Joe and Linda Nicolosi, and my friend Steve, who willingly gave of their time and expertise to help edit this book. I am grateful for your input and heart investment into this project.

Thanks to Joe, Roxanne, Doug, and Maria Miller for your generosity and support. I can't say thank you enough. Your devotion to God is an inspiration.

Thanks to Claude Aubert for your contributing the wonderful charts and graphs.

Thanks to my brother Neal for helping me create a title!

Thanks to the Bonners, the Church of the Holy Spirit (Father Bob and Father George), and Rich and Sue Huggler for giving me room to cloister myself away from the world to finish this book.

Thanks to Ron for helping me find journal articles.

Thanks to Diana for all her service, sacrifice, and support. I deeply appreciate your love and loyalty throughout the years.

Thanks to Clint for your wisdom, mentoring, and healing touch.

Thanks to Rev. and Mrs. Jim Schuppe and BBC, my wonderful and supportive church family.

Thanks to Pastor and Mrs. Ronald Crawford and NVBC, my other wonderful and supportive church family.

Thanks to the wonderful staff at Oakhill Press: Ed Helvey, Paula Gould, Craig Hines, and BJ. Your help and input were invaluable.

Introduction

"In American society, everything is tolerated except those who do not tolerate everything."

—Anonymous

- No one is born with a homosexual orientation.

There is no scientific data to substantiate either a genetic or biologic basis for same-sex attraction.

- No one chooses to have same-sex attraction.

They are the result of temperamental, familial, environmental, and social conditions.

- People can choose to change and come out straight.

No one is born with same-sex attraction; therefore, change is possible.

- What was learned can be unlearned.

When the wounds are healed and the unmet needs fulfilled, gender identity will be experienced and heterosexual desires will ensue.

- It's not gay, nor bad, it's SSAD—Same-Sex Attachment Disorder.

There is nothing "gay" about the homosexual lifestyle; it is full of heartaches and most often an endless pursuit of love through codependent relationships.

It is not bad to have same-sex attractions, as they represent a drive to heal unmet love needs. However, acting upon the desires leads to frustration and pain.

It's a SSAD lifestyle, whereby the individual is disidentified with his own masculinity or her own femininity and tries desperately to fill the deficit by joining with someone of the same sex.

In this book I will present the basic causes of same-sex attractions, a clear model of recovery, and stories of individuals who made the change. Anyone can accomplish whatever he or she wants. With a strong determination, the love of God, and the support of others, healing is possible. Of course, at the present time, many will say that no one can come out of homosexuality. This is a myth. Change is possible.

During summer vacations, while in junior and senior high school, I worked as a volunteer at the Inglis House, "The Philadelphia Home for Incurables." (Since then, fortunately, they have changed the name!) This was a home for people with cerebral palsy, muscular dystrophy, multiple sclerosis (MS), and other physical disabilities. I became friends with a woman named Sarah. MS struck her in the prime of her life. Previously, she had been a concert pianist.

She inspired me to play the piano. In 1968, at the age of sixteen, I began studying with Dr. Nagy. After studying with him for three months, I heard the "Moonlight Sonata" by Beethoven. It captivated me, and I determined to learn it. When I told him of my desire, he said, "No. That's nonsense. You won't be ready to play that piece for years." Well, that was his opinion.

I went straight to the store and purchased the music. It took several weeks for me to wade through the notes, but somehow my hands remembered what my mind could not retain. My fingers knew just where to go, and my heart sang each time I played it.

Finally, after a month or so, I decided to play the piece for Dr. Nagy. Well, you can imagine his surprise. I will never forget the look on his face. "Who taught you to play this?" "I did." That was the beginning of our real work together as teacher and student. He then believed in my talent and helped me learn simultaneously advanced and beginner pieces. After two years of intensive training and diligent practice, I entered college as a piano major.

I learned from this experience that anyone can accomplish whatever he wants, if he has a burning desire and does not let what "they" say stand in his way. For those who always say nay are merely afraid to embark on the journey themselves.

Everything starts from an idea. Then add burning desire, make a plan, and follow through with continuous efforts toward the goal. It does not matter how many times he may fall down or fail. These are merely temporary roadblocks. There is no failure; there is only feedback. Thomas Edison discovered 3,032 ways how NOT to invent the light bulb before reaching his goal. The key, therefore, is to keep going. Just pick himself up and try another way.

The reason I am a good therapist or fellow journeyman is because I have made just about every mistake humanly possible. I am not proud of this. But I didn't let anything or anyone stand in the way of my breaking through and figuring out how to heal homosexuality. For me, it was a matter of life and death. If I died trying, that was enough. At least my life had some meaning as I tried year after year to heal this seemingly bottomless wound in my soul.

I had sexual attractions to men. People told me that I was born this way and the thought of changing was impossible and therapeutically contraindicated. Phooey! Not play Beethoven's "Moonlight Sonata"? Anyone can do whatever he wants if he has a burning desire, makes a plan, gets support, and goes for it. I have been able to guide many men, women, and adolescents out of homosexuality because I didn't listen when people told me, "Be true to yourself, you were born this way, accept it."

I learned where my same-sex desires came from, how to heal those wounds, and how to fulfill the unmet needs of my past. The benefit of reading this book and following this plan is that I am offering a shortcut to coming out straight. I have made so many mistakes, which makes it possible for others to avoid some of the pitfalls on the road to freedom. What took me a decade to do, I have been able to help others accomplish in one to three years.

I wish to thank all the men and women with whom I have had the privilege of counseling over the past twelve years. They have been my teachers. I have included some of their stories in this book. I have changed their names and details to maintain confidentiality. They are all brave souls, swimming upstream, against the tide. God bless you.

I wrote this book for professionals and nonprofessionals alike. I have the unique position of having been the client and now the therapist. I not only struggled with unwanted homosexual desires, I struggled equally in trying to find professionals who understood my condition and how to help me heal. It was so difficult trying to explain myself to therapists who did not have a clue. Now, undergraduate and graduate schools throughout the country and world are teaching "gay affirmative therapy."

The intent of this book is to help therapists, counselors, clergy, and others understand how to assist men and women with unwanted (ego-dystonic) same-sex attractions. It is also a guide for the overcomers. My hope and prayer is that, in time, the stigma of same-sex attractions will wane and understanding will prevail. May this book serve as a stepping stone toward that dream.

In **Part I**, I share my story and describe the root causes of same-sex attractions. I do not concentrate on etiology, because I believe there are many good books written on this subject. For more information on the causes of same-sex attractions, please see the list of references at the back of the book.

In **Part II**, I present a four-stage model of recovery, a step-by-step guide to healing. Then I describe a variety of therapeutic tools and techniques to use in each stage of recovery. I give a general introduction to various approaches to healing but will not detail these techniques as you can read about them through the suggested reading. My intention is to provide the technology for healing homosexuality. The specific techniques may be learned from further study. I also discuss the importance of anger and touch in the process of recovery. Finally, I describe a mentorship model to create secure attachment.

In **Part III**, I offer suggestions for family members and friends who have loved ones experiencing same-sex attraction. There is much that family and friends can do to help those with same-sex attraction become whole and ultimately experience their innate, heterosexual potential.

Laced throughout the book are stories of five men and a woman I have counseled. In their own words, you may further understand how this process of healing works.

In this book, instead of saying *he* and *she* each time, I will use the masculine pronoun. However, this model of recovery applies to both men and women unless otherwise specified.

A Final Note

I have counseled, coached, and facilitated thousands of men, women, and adolescents over the past years. This program for healing applies to those who are gender disidentified, and it also works for the average man or woman. The only difference is that stages three and four, as discussed in chapter 4, are reversed. A brief explanation of how the program works follows.

Stage One: Making behavioral changes by cutting off from unhealthy activities and relationships, building a support network, and developing a sense of spirituality by finding personal value in relationship with God.

Stage Two: Cognitive restructuring, inner-child healing, and continuing with all tasks of the previous stage. Here the individual learns to replace negative self-talk with positive affirmations regarding self and others. Next, an awareness of one's thoughts, feelings, and deeper needs must be brought into conscious awareness. Then the individual learns to live more joyfully in the here and now through healthy self-expression and being assertive in a positive manner.

Stage Three: Healing hetero-emotional wounds. Women need to heal father wounds, and men need to heal mother wounds, or any other wounding incurred by a significant person of the opposite sex. Core wounds need to be revealed and then healed. The final part of this phase is to fulfill unmet love needs in healthy, nonsexual relationships, thus filling in the developmental gaps of yesteryear.

Stage Four: Healing homo-emotional wounds. Women need to heal mother wounds, and men need to heal father wounds, or any other wounding incurred by a significant person of the same sex. Again, core wounds need to be revealed and healed, and then unmet love needs fulfilled in healthy, nonsexual relationships.

When each woman and man learns to increase a sense of self-worth by learning new skills, experiencing value in relationship to a loving God, healing past wounds, and fulfilling unmet love needs, she and he will blossom into the fullness of their original design. My next book will be called *Healing Heterosexuality*. For now, this will do!

PART I:

Understanding

CHAPTER ONE

My Story: Coming Out Straight

"It says that where a man's wound is, that is where his genius will be. Wherever the wound appears in our psyches, whether from alcoholic father, shaming mother, shaming father, abusing mother, whether it stems from isolation, disability, or disease, that is precisely the place from which we will give our major gift to the community."[1]
—Robert Bly

In childhood and adolescence, I remember my father screaming at us and my mother clinging to me. I was quite distant from him and too close to her. When I was five, a friend of the family came to live with us. He gained my trust, won my heart, and sexually abused me. I was also the bearer of a gift—the gift of sensitivity. It led me to experience life quite deeply and made it hard for me to let things go. I was more artistic, whereas my father and brother were more athletic. My dad would emotionally beat my brother Neal, and then Neal would beat on me. These are some of the causes that led to my experiencing same-sex attractions.

I sought refuge in the arms of men. I had several boyfriends in college, and then a lover of three years. However, it was not enough. I wanted to marry and have a family. I had a religious conversion experience that helped me leave the homosexual lifestyle. Eventually, I met Jae Sook and she became my wife. That was not enough. I had repressed my same-sex attractions. I needed to heal my wounds and fulfill unmet needs. I found this through therapy, support groups, mentors, friends, and my faith. In this way, I was able to change and finally come out straight. I share my story to give you some idea of where I have been, where I am, and the knowledge that change *is* possible.

Early Childhood and Adolescence

I grew up in Lower Merion, a suburb of Philadelphia. I was the youngest of three children in a Jewish family. My brother Neal was four and a half years older, and my sister Lydia was two and a half years older. My father was in the shoe business, and my mother was a full-time housewife. Most often, my dad would come home from work and scream at us. Because of my sensitive nature, it felt like daggers piercing my soul. My dad and Neal had a very antagonistic relationship. They fought about everything. When my brother was feeling frustration and pain, he would take his aggression out on me. I tried to fight back, but it seemed futile, as he was so much bigger and older than I. There was constant fighting and tears in the Cohen household. Yet when guests came over, we smiled and acted like a happy suburban family.

I would bounce back and forth between Neal and Lydia. One day I would be in her favor, the next day in his. Fighting between my parents and fighting among us kids was our daily diet. My role was that of a peace-maker. I was always trying to bring order and peace in this chaotic home. I would clown around, trying desperately to relieve the tension that was in the air.

From middle school, I began to experience same-sex attractions. Though girls noticed me, I experienced an ever-increasing interest and desire to be close to guys. From the seventh grade, some of my guy friends wanted to experiment sexually. I went along with it, but what I really wanted was to be physically intimate with them. I wanted to hold and to be held.

I would sleep over at my friend Steve's house. It was great to snuggle up with him. I couldn't get enough, but Steve felt a bit uncomfortable with my continuous overtures for intimacy. My same-sex desires got stronger with each passing year. I had more sexual experiences with school friends. For them it was a novelty, but for me it was a growing obsession. At the same time, I tried to act "normal," so I had girlfriends. In my senior year of high school, I went steady with Maria. Many people thought we would marry. I suppose we did, too, but this growing obsession for a man continued to haunt me.

At seventeen years of age, I ventured out into the world to seek a homosexual relationship. I went to my father's health club and met a man who invited me back to his place. My heart was pounding so loudly that I thought it would burst out of my chest. I had never done such a thing in my life. When we got to his apartment, the seduction began. I was so nervous since this was all so new for me. What he did to me that day, I didn't know two men could do. My body and spirit felt ripped in two. Afterwards, I left his apartment and took the subway home. When I was underground waiting for the train, I walked into a dark corner and deeply sobbed. I felt so violated and disappointed. I was looking for closeness, for a safe place to be held and to hold. What I experienced felt like rape.

I went home and never told anyone about what had happened. Finally, toward the end of my senior year of high school, I told my parents about my struggle with same-sex attractions. My mother said she knew, which made me very angry. From early infancy, I had a love-hate relationship with her. I didn't know where she began and I ended. I knew part of my gender confusion was due to our inappropriate closeness. I embarrassed my father, who had grown up in military school and was a marine in World War II, by my revelation. I requested to see a psychiatrist, which I did, but it was a fruitless experience. He and I didn't connect at all.

College

In 1970, I went to Boston University to study music. I began psychotherapy twice weekly with a traditional Freudian psychoanalyst. This continued over the next three years. It was an excruciating time of pain and little gain. I did learn a bit more about myself; however, I didn't learn about the origins of my desires, nor did I experience any relief from the pain.

During my first year at college, I went to some "gay" bars, but I didn't like the scene. It felt like a meat market, and I didn't want to be a commodity on the shelf. I attended some meetings at my university's "gay and lesbian" student alliance. In my first year of college, I had several boyfriends, each lasting several months.

When I visited home, it was more confrontational, as I would use some of my therapeutic tools to challenge my parents. One time, my dad and I got into a fistfight. During the fight, he was hitting me while I was on my bed. My mom started screaming to my dad, "Stop it! Stop it! For God's sake, stop it!" I turned my head and said to her, "No. This is great. This is the closest we've ever been in my life!" She ran out of the room in tears.

I remember, after one visit, my father wrote a letter that hurt me deeply. At the same time, I felt suffocated by my current boyfriend, Mike. Besides all that, my schoolwork was overwhelming. I decided to take a bottle of Bufferin and end it all. However, I woke up in the middle of the morning sick as a dog, and still alive. I called my sister, who lived nearby. She came over and took me to the emergency room at the hospital where they pumped my stomach and stabilized my condition.

I recovered, continued therapy, went back to school, ended my relationship with Mike, changed my major to theater, and felt a bit more hopeful. In my second year of school, I met Tim, an art major. We would become lovers for the next three years.

Since my early childhood, I had three dreams. First, I wanted to have a best friend, someone with whom I could totally be myself, without apology or excuse. Second, I wanted to perform in a group that would travel the world, both educating and entertaining people. Third, I wanted to marry a beautiful woman and create a loving family.

Tim was my first dream come true. However, there was a price to pay. It was a roller-coaster relationship. I was the pursuer and he was the distancer. This was our continuous dance for three years. The close times were incredible, and the love we shared was wonderful. We were best friends. I learned many things by seeing life through Tim's eyes. He had an affinity for nature, and I learned to see things I had never seen before. He was and still remains an exceptional man.

Spiritual Journey

Another significant event occurred through our relationship. Tim loved Jesus very deeply. I persecuted him for his beliefs until he said, "Richard, stop it. You believe what you want to believe, and let me believe what I believe." I realized he was right, and I apologized. Since I loved Tim, I wanted to see why he loved this Jesus so much. For the first time in my life, I began reading the New Testament. As part of my Jewish upbringing, I was both bar-mitzvahed and confirmed, studying only the Old Testament.

I had always been on a spiritual quest, trying to find the meaning and purpose of life. I tried so many kinds of faiths and ways: Judaism, Buddhism, and therapies. Then I met Jesus. He was a remarkable individual. In fact, he was the kind of man I had always wanted to be myself. What I admired in him was that his thoughts, feelings, words, and deeds were one. He was a congruent man, the same inside as he was on the outside. He spoke of forgiveness and God's grace. These were new concepts for me. I wanted to be like him. This began my journey as a Christian. I joined an Episcopal church in Roxbury and began teaching Sunday school.

More and more, Tim and I knew that homosexuality was not compatible with God's Word, so we eliminated the physical part of our relationship. We both met the Unification Church shortly after that. I believed that God was calling me to explore this faith, and in 1974, I joined. For nine years, I remained celibate. I lived a life of service, trying not to think about myself, but focus on God, His Word, and others. The same-sex desires emerged now and then. I would push and pray them away. I begged God to take them away for good.

I fulfilled my second dream by performing in the church choir, traveling throughout the States and Asia, bringing a message of hope and love. While performing, I met my wife-to-be. We performed together. She was in a Korean folk dance troupe. We spoke very little, but would come to know each other better in the years ahead.

Marriage and Therapy

In 1982, Jae Sook and I married, and I was on my way to fulfilling my third dream. The first few months were wonderful. I told her about what I thought was my homosexual past. Then the problem resurfaced. I felt so much rage toward my wife. I projected onto Jae Sook all the pent-up hostility I had previously felt toward my mother. I started treating her as my father treated us: "Do this, do that." "Why didn't you do it that way?" "Don't you know anything?" I kept ordering her around and insulting her. My rage got so bad that I even felt like killing her at times.

It was a shocking mess, heightened by the fact that I was successful in my business. I was an arts manager, touring classical musicians and ballet companies throughout Asia. Many people loved me and thought I was just the greatest. At home, Dr. Jekyll turned into Mr. Hyde, a rageaholic. I had become what I vowed I would never be—just like my father. My wife soon became pregnant with our first child. I knew I must begin therapy again. So, in May 1983, while living in New York City, I went to see a noted psychologist. For one year, I attended weekly individual and group sessions. It was the beginning of my journey out of homosexuality.

One night, after Jae Sook and I had made love, I turned away from her. I felt exhausted from working two jobs (as arts manager and a waiter in a restaurant) to support us and pay for therapy. Jae Sook put her arms around me. In an instant, it felt as if my spirit had jumped out of my body! I dissociated from my physical self. All of a sudden, I was looking down at my body lying next to my wife. It was much too painful to stay in my body. My heart was screaming. At that moment, I came to realize that I had experienced some kind of abuse in early childhood. My hypothesis was that there was an incestuous relationship between my mother and myself.

It felt like an eternity, which in reality was probably several seconds, before I returned to my body. I asked Jae Sook not to touch me. It was just too painful. I could not wait for the next therapy session. My therapist introduced me to several bioenergetic techniques. I pounded several pillows with a tennis racquet to release pent-up anger and frustration. While pounding away at what I thought was some abuse caused by my mother, I had a flashback. All of a sudden, I saw male genitals coming toward my mouth. I screamed. I felt shocked. I felt horrified.

I cried and the tears flowed for the next few years, as I worked through memories of sexual abuse that occurred when I was between the ages of five and six years old. A friend of the family—we called him Uncle Dave—lived with us while he was in the process of getting a divorce. Dave was a very large, powerful man. He provided for me what my father could not. He spent time with me, listened to me, held me. He gave me the feeling that I mattered and that he cared. He was actually the first adult with whom I had bonded. Then, it began. He started playing with my genitals and had me do the same with his. It was shocking and horrifying. Of course, it felt good, too. God has, after all, designed the human body to feel pleasure in the genital areas. This is one reason that sexual abuse is so confusing for a child. It feels painful and pleasurable all at the same time.

I cried so many tears sorting through the web of confusion and destruction that those experiences caused me. I learned that my neurology was programmed to respond to men in sexual ways. For me, intimacy with a man equaled sex. I learned that to be close to a man, I must give him my body. This was the learning of a child hungry for his father's love. Because of my hypersensitive temperament and my father's rageaholic nature, I never had a chance to bond with him. Uncle Dave was my first male mentor.

Healing and Hell

Working through the effects of the child sexual abuse brought havoc to my life. We were having our first child. I was traveling to Asia for my job every few months, and I was working as a waiter three to four nights a week. We had little emotional and spiritual support at the time. There were few organizations in New York City to help those who desired to come out of homosexuality. I attended one Christian group, but they rejected me because, at that time, I was still a part of the Unification Church. I tried another ex-gay ministry in a nearby state, and the director approached me to have sex with him. This created more pain and feelings of hopelessness.

I knew the wounding occurred because of my unhealthy relationship with Uncle Dave and the emotional detachment from my father. Therefore, I knew that I needed to be close to men in healthy ways to heal and grow. I needed mentoring, corrective parenting to reconcile what had gone wrong so many years before. I reached out to men in my church. I was voracious to experience healthy love, but I scared most of them away. I threatened them with my powerful needs, and they didn't know what to do. I am also sure I must have triggered some issues within them, as most men in our culture carry deep father wounds (one reason for homophobia). I continued to pray, asking God to bring mentors into my life. The more I prayed, the more I sought to find such men, the further away they seemed to be.

Finally, I decided I couldn't take it anymore. I needed touch, to be held, to be mentored, to be initiated into the world of men. So, I told God, my wife, and several friends that if I couldn't find what I needed through godly men, then I would go back into the homosexual world to find someone who was willing to be with me.

It certainly wasn't plan A, not even plan B, but I knew what I needed, and I knew I wouldn't stop until I found it. Back into the sad "gay" world I went. I felt like a complete hypocrite, going against all my religious convictions, but the need for love is more powerful than religion. I shared everything with God. Through that period of my life, I knew He was guiding me.

It was a very bizarre time. It was a most painful and lonely time for Jae Sook and our first son, Jarish. I was out running around New York City with my boyfriend, and she was at home alone taking care of our son, knowing her husband was out with a man. I cry now, as I write these words, realizing again the pain I caused her and our children. I am truly sorry, and I have repented to her, our children, and God for what I did.

I told her of my commitment to our relationship and of my desire for her not to divorce me. I needed to heal with men. I didn't know how to do it. I couldn't find anyone at the time to show me the way, so I had to do the best I could. I prayed the whole way through this unusual course, from start to finish.

It would take volumes to describe what I went through in the next two and a half years. I learned that I was indeed looking for closeness, not sex. I needed to make up for all the times that I had never shared with my dad—just being together, doing things together, talking about life, and learning from him. This I experienced with a wonderful man. I was very honest with him from the start about being married and wanting to heal these same-sex desires. There was no pretense with him, my wife, or God.

Slowly, my heart began to heal as I grieved the effects of the sexual abuse in therapy and I spent time with my friend. However, there was still a deep wound in the pit of my soul. Eventually, this ache turned into an ulcer. I was overworking as an artist manager, waiting tables in the restaurant, desperately trying to heal the same-sex wounds, and be there for Jae Sook and the kids. We had had a second child during all this. Jessica was a beautiful girl.

At that time, I prayed, "Oh God, how terrible to bring children into such a mess. You know how desperate I am to change. I pray that You take care of Jae Sook and the kids, for surely I am unable and ill-equipped at this time."

Finally, I took a one-year leave of absence from my job. More and more, my wife and I were growing distant in our connection to the Unification Church. We were struggling emotionally, mentally, and spiritually. In the years to come, we would eventually resign and return to our Christian roots. (Now we attend a wonderful church in our community. There we find fellowship, support, and love.)

Breakthrough

By the grace of God, I found a Christian friend who was willing to help me heal the homo-emotional wounds of my past. He himself was quite stable and comfortable in his masculinity. I cannot describe everything that took place between David and me. Yes, his name was David. God is just. It was Dave who abused me at five, and it was David who helped me heal at thirty-five!

Together, with the guidance of God, we walked back into the room of my abuse, and there I faced my biggest demon—myself, my accuser. "It was all my fault!" This is how I felt. This is what I thought! "It was all my fault!" David helped the child in me see that I didn't cause the abuse, that it wasn't my "fault." In that instant, the connection between Uncle Dave and I was cut, and I became free for the first time in my life. With that sense of freedom, I sobbed for about an hour in David's arms. It was such a release and relief to know that I wasn't responsible for what had happened and that God had forgiven me. In those moments of release, I found my freedom from same-sex desires. Cutting this neurological connection to the sexual desires freed me from thirty years of relentless pain and an endless pursuit of men.

After that, I needed to do maintenance work to ensure that I was receiving healthy, nonsexual love from other men. I found several men who were willing to mentor me. This was another critical part of my healing. Developmentally, I had to learn the many lessons I missed as a child, adolescent, and young adult. My friends Phillip, Russell, Rev. Hillendahl, Steve, Gordon, and Rev. Schuppe poured and continue to pour into my soul lessons of love, initiating me into the world of men.

More Healing

Jae Sook and I attended an EXODUS Conference in 1987, just after I had my breakthrough with David. (EXODUS is the umbrella organization for the ex-gay Christian ministries around the world.) There I prayed to God to show us the next step—what to do and where to go. Each day at the conference, I prayed for God's guidance, but nothing came. Finally, the conference ended. I walked to a nearby lake. I knelt down and prayed, "OK, God, it's showdown time! I'm not moving from this spot until you tell me what to do and where to go. Even if I die sitting here, so be it. I await your guidance." Then the directions came clearly: "Move to Seattle, receive help for your marriage, get an education, and then reach out to help other people." In amazement, I asked, "Would you please repeat that one more time?" The words came one more time, exactly as I had heard them before.

I told Jae Sook what I had received. We both prayed about this for several weeks until we were certain that this was God's desire for our lives. When it became clear that this was to be, I quit my job. This was very painful to do after ten years and much success in the arts management business. I had decided, however, that I did not want to do as my father and his father had done—be successful in business and miserable at home.

We packed an eighteen-foot truck with our belongings, said good-bye to our friends in New York City, and headed off to Seattle. There we started a new life, not knowing what God had in store for us. I thought we were there to work with the local ex-gay ministry. After several counseling sessions with the director, I realized that it wasn't going to work. He was single and I was married. I also perceived he was struggling with his own issues (later, he left his position to receive more help). Why was I here in this city?

Then we heard about a Christian healing community on Vashon, a small island outside Seattle. We tried several times to get there, but each time some accident or event stopped us. Jae Sook said, "Maybe it's God saying don't go." I realized that it was not God but the other side trying to stop us! Finally, I determined to get there, no matter what. We all went one chilly Saturday afternoon in December 1987. There we met with Rev. and Mrs. Lou Hillendahl, the pastors of the Wesleyan Christian Community. Within an hour, I knew this was why God had brought us to Seattle.

On January 1, 1988, we moved into this healing community. We stayed with them for six months of intensive therapy and received counseling and support from them for the next two and a half years. Their guidance and expertise were invaluable. We grew as individuals, as a couple, as parents, and as a family. They taught us many skills. I learned about mentoring from them. (I will explain about mentoring in chapter 12.) I learned how to be a better husband and father. We are eternally grateful for the love, time, and investment they gave to our family. We have been able to give so much to others because of what they gave to us.

I had another breakthrough experience there. In the summer of 1988, my parents came to visit. We all met with my counselors from the Community. I shared about the past abuse with Uncle Dave and how I walked into the homosexual world, always looking for my father's love in the arms of other men. I told Dad, "You never held me as a child, at least not in my memory. So, even though you are seventy and I'm thirty-six, I need you to hold me now." With that, I jumped on my father's lap! I had to put his arms around me, as he was so stiff and awkward. It felt good, but there was too much performance anxiety as my mother, wife, two kids, and three counselors looked on.

Later that evening, we took my parents back to their hotel room. I asked everyone to leave my father and me alone for a while. Then I said, "Dad, now it's just you and me. I really need you to hold me." I remember so well that room and the chair where he held me. I climbed on his lap and began to weep. He got so nervous, as he is uncomfortable with tears. I told him, "Dad, please just let me cry. It's good. I just need to let go of all the losses of my life, all the times we missed being together when I was growing up. Please just hold me while I grieve." With that, I let go of so many years of pain and disappointment. It was a wonderful moment for both of us. At last, we were bonding as father and son.

Becoming a Wounded Healer

I knew that eventually we were going in the direction of helping others heal out of homosexuality. I decided that, first, I must serve those in the homosexual community without trying to persuade anyone into my way of thinking. For three years, I was a volunteer, working with people who had AIDS. It was a privilege and honor to be with these men and women. I felt humbled and grateful for each relationship and experience. I could see their beauty and raw desire just to be loved.

At the same time, I began graduate school to obtain my master's degree in counseling psychology. Simultaneously, I worked as a waiter in a restaurant and as an AIDS educator for the American Red Cross. Jae Sook worked as a preschool teacher. She was able to keep Jarish and Jessica with her during the days. We continued our healing with other couples who had attended seminars with the Wesleyan Christian Community. We supported each other. It was a blessed time. Even though there were so many ups and downs each day, we still had each other, and that was a lot.

After graduation, through the guidance of God, I founded the International Healing Foundation. My vision was to establish healing centers throughout the world to help men, women, and children to experience their value as children of God. This is still my vision, as we continue our journey.

I worked for the American Red Cross as an HIV/AIDS educator for three years. I worked for Catholic Community Services in Child Abuse Treatment and Family Reconciliation Services. I also had my private practice, helping men and women heal out of homosexuality.

I began to give public presentations on the process of transitioning from homosexuality to heterosexuality. I thought that, because of my heart toward the homosexual community, they would see that I was not their enemy, but just presenting another possibility for those who desire to change. I was naive. We received death threats at our home and at my office! People kept tearing down my nametag on my office door. We received obscene telephone calls at home with angry, venomous words of threat and accusation. The Gay and Lesbian Task Force of the mayor's office in Seattle requested that the American Red Cross fire me from my position as an HIV/AIDS educator. Their reason was that I was homophobic and spreading hate. Many in the homosexual community have felt threatened by my work. I understand their fears and their pain.

Over the past twelve years, I traveled extensively throughout the States, giving presentations about the healing of homosexuality on college and university campuses, in churches, in mental health institutions, at therapeutic conferences, and on TV and the radio. I have also conducted healing seminars throughout the States and Europe on topics such as inner-child healing, marital relations, parenting skills, communication skills, conflict resolution, addictions, sexual abuse, and anger management. For the first six years of my counseling practice, I worked almost exclusively with couples and individuals dealing with all sorts of issues, i.e., couples conflicts, obsessive-compulsive disorders, anger problems, sexual abuse, and addictions. For the past six years, my practice has taken another turn. I counsel mostly men and adolescents coming out of homosexuality. I continue to conduct healing seminars for both healing homosexuality and marital relations. I enjoy the variety of doing both.

I continue to grow into the man that God created me to be. We continue to grow as a family. With the help of Dr. Martha Welch and her practice of holding (see explanation of Attachment/Holding Therapy in chapter 6), I had a significant breakthrough with my mother. I asked my mom to visit us and help me resolve some long-standing issues that I had with her. Over a period of five days, we held each other as I expressed years of pain, anger, and frustration. Mom listened as I detoxed: "Why weren't you there when Uncle Dave was doing those things to me?" "Why didn't you stop him?" "Why didn't you stop Dad from screaming at us year after year?" We cried together as we recalled, relived, and released the past. She apologized for her shortcomings. "I am sorry, honey. I never meant to hurt you." Finally, for me, a miracle occurred—I bonded to my mother's bosom. I bonded with my mom. The walls around my heart came down, and I allowed her to enter. For the first time in my life, I was here! I was alive. I felt bonded and I belonged.

When I took her to the airport and said good-bye, my heart sank. I missed my mother. I missed her. The child within my heart, who finally allowed her love inside, missed his mom. This was a whole new sensation for me. I wept out of sadness and joy.

Another blessing occurred five years ago. God gave us a precious son, Alfie. He came on the foundation of our (God's) battles and victories. Now, Jae Sook and I and our three children are growing more deeply in love.

I love God with all my heart, mind, and soul. I live to end His suffering and pain. I pray the understanding of same-sex attractions and the treatment plan for recovery that I am about to share is a blessing to you and those whose lives you will touch. I have learned over the past twelve years of counseling hundreds of men, women, and adolescents, and working with thousands of people in healing seminars around the world, that no matter what issue or issues we are facing in our lives, our wounds all originate from the same sources. For, as Leanne Payne said, "To write about the healing of the homosexual is to write about the healing of all men and women."[2] We all fall short of our original design for greatness. When we heal ourselves, the world heals a little more. When we help others heal, we heal in the process.

CHAPTER TWO

Definitions and Causes of Same-Sex Attractions

Over the past twelve years, I have been counseling men, women, and adolescents who have desired to come out of homosexuality. For those who wish to make this transition from homosexual to heterosexual, I am certain that it is possible. My personal journey and the experience of the many men and women whom I have had the privilege to assist support this claim.

I would like to share with you what I have discovered over the past thirty years of personal and professional investigation. These insights come from my own course of healing and have been substantiated through the findings and observations of other therapists and former homosexuals. For me, these discoveries meant life or death. I determined to find answers because I knew that God did not create me this way.

Before I begin, I would like to make it quite clear that this is not a blame game. It is naming what occurred for the purpose of healing and restoration. We must uncover what is unseen so that we can become the masters of our own ships. Blaming never healed or restored anyone. It is equally important to place responsibility for others' actions squarely upon them so that we do not carry their burden, i.e., "It's all my fault."

Throughout the book, I will use male pronouns; however, everything applies to both genders unless otherwise stated.

Definitions

"Homosexuality is not about sex. Rather, it is ultimately about rejection of and detachment from self, from others, and one's own gender identity," says Slade, a client of mine whose story you will read in chapter 13.

I will use the terms, *homosexuality* and *same-sex attractions* interchangeably. If one experiences sexual attractions for the same gender, I define him as homosexually oriented. The "gay" man or woman is one who has accepted homosexual desires and reports feeling comfortable with those feelings. The "nongay" homosexual person is one who does not accept those desires and seeks to change. A *bisexual* is one who experiences attractions to both genders. He may choose to accept those desires or seek to change.

I use the term homosexual as an adjective, not as a noun. "Homosexual is not used as a noun for referring to a person, but is used as an adjective to describe a person's thoughts, feelings, desires and behaviors."[1] I do not believe there is any such thing as true homosexuality. I believe that anyone who experiences same-sex attractions is latently heterosexual and merely stuck in an early stage of psychosexual development. When the causes are revealed and healed and the unmet needs fulfilled, gender identity will be experienced and heterosexual desires will ensue.

Biology and Genetics

Over the past decade, there has been much talk about the biologic and genetic predispositions to homosexuality. This concept was posited by three studies. Major newspapers reported that these studies proved homosexuality to be immutable, that people are born homosexual, born "gay."

In this section, I will list these three studies, give a brief critique of each one, and let other social scientists comment on the reliability of their findings. What becomes abundantly clear is that there is no scientific data to support a genetic or biologic basis for same-sex attractions.

Three Studies

LEVAY STUDY

Simon LeVay, "A Difference in Hypothalamic Structure Between Heterosexual and Homosexual Men," reported in *Science* magazine in August 1991. LeVay professed to have found a group of neurons in the hypothalamus (called INAH3) that appeared to be twice as big in heterosexual men than in homosexual men. LeVay theorized that this part of the hypothalamus has something to do with sexual behavior. Therefore, he concluded, sexual orientation is somehow biologically determined.

Brief Critique of the LeVay Study:

- All 19 homosexual subjects died of AIDS, and we know that HIV/AIDS may affect the brain, causing chemical changes. Therefore, rather than looking at the cause of homosexuality, we may be observing the effects of HIV/AIDS.
- LeVay did not verify the sexual orientation of his control group. "Two of these subjects (both AIDS patients) had denied homosexual activity. The records of the remaining 14 patients contained no information about their sexual orientation; they are assumed to have been mostly or all heterosexual."[2] It is poor science to "assume" anything about your subjects.
- Three of the 19 homosexual subjects had a larger group of neurons in the hypothalamus than the average heterosexual subject. Three of the 16 heterosexual subjects had a smaller group of neurons in the hypothalamus than the average homosexual subject. That means 6 out of 35 male subjects disproved his hypothesis. These results, then, are not statistically significant or reliable.
- There is no proof that this group of neurons affects sexuality. Dr. Charles Socarides, professor of psychiatry at Albert Einstein College of Medicine in New York City, said, "The question of a minute section of the brain—submicroscopic almost—as deciding sexual object choice is really preposterous. A cluster of the brain cannot determine sexual object choice."[3]
- LeVay himself stated, "It's important to stress what I didn't find. I did not prove that homosexuality is genetic, or find a genetic cause for being gay. I didn't show that gay men are born that way, the most common mistake people make in interpreting my work. Nor did I locate a gay center in the brain. . . . Since I look at adult brains, we don't know if the differences I found were there at birth or if they appeared later."[4]

BAILEY AND PILLARD STUDY

John M. Bailey and Richard Pillard, "A Genetic Study of Male Sexual Orientation," reported in the *Archives of General Psychiatry*, December 1991.

They studied the prevalence of homosexuality among twins and adopted brothers where at least one brother was homosexual. They found that 52 percent (29 pairs out of 56) of the identical twins were both homosexual; 22 percent (12 pairs out of 54) of the fraternal twins were both homosexual; and 11 percent (6 of 57) of the adoptive brothers were both homosexual. They also found 9 percent (13 of 142) of the nontwin biological siblings were both homosexual. The authors therefore concluded that there is a genetic cause to homosexuality.

Brief Critique of the Bailey-Pillard Study:

- The biggest flaw is the interpretation of the researchers. Since about 50 percent of the identical twins were not homosexual, we can easily conclude that genetics does not play a major part in their sexual orientation. If it had, then 100 percent of the twins should be homosexual since identical twins have the same genetic makeup. We might just as easily interpret the findings to mean that environmental influences caused their homosexuality. Biologist Anne Fausto-Stirling of Brown University stated, "In order for such a study to be at all meaningful, you'd have to look at twins raised apart. It's such badly interpreted genetics."[5]

- This was not a random sample, but a biased sample, as the twins who volunteered were solicited through advertisements in homosexual newspapers and magazines as opposed to general periodicals. Therefore, the subjects were more likely to resemble each other than nonhomosexual twins.

- Dr. Simon LeVay stated, "In fact, the twin studies . . . suggest that it's not totally inborn [homosexuality], because even identical twins are not always of the same sexual orientation."[6]

- Dr. Bailey himself stated, "There must be something in the environment to yield the discordant twins."[7]

- The researchers failed to investigate the roles that incest or sexual abuse and other environmental factors play in determining same-sex attractions. If they had found that incest was more common among identical twins than fraternal twins or nontwin blood brothers, this could have helped explain the varying rates of homosexuality.

HAMER STUDY

Dean Hamer et al., of the National Cancer Institute, "A Linkage Between DNA Markers on the X Chromosome and Male Sexual Orientation," reported in *Science* magazine, July 1993. The media reported that the "gay gene" was discovered as a result of this study. The researchers studied 40 pairs of homosexual brothers and suggested that some cases of homosexuality are linked to a specific region on the X chromosome (Xq28) inherited from the mother by her homosexual son. Thirty-three pairs of brothers shared the same pattern variation in the tip of one arm of the chromosome. Hamer estimated that the sequence of the given genetic markers on Xq28 is linked to homosexuality in 64 percent of the brothers.

Brief Critique of the Hamer et al. Study:

- Dr. Kenneth Klivington, assistant to the president of the Salk Institute in San Diego, states, "There is a body of evidence that shows the brain's neural networks reconfigure themselves in response to certain experience. Therefore, the difference in homosexual brain structure may be a result of behavior and environmental conditions."[8]
- There was no control group. This is poor scientific methodology. Hamer and associates failed to test the heterosexual brothers. What if the heterosexual brothers had the same genetic markers?
- It has not been proven that the identified section of the chromosomes has a direct bearing on sexuality or sexual orientation.
- One of Hamer's fellow research assistants brought him up on charges, saying that he withheld some of the findings that invalidated his study. The National Cancer Institute is investigating Hamer.[9] (To date, they have not released the results of this investigation.)
- A Canadian research team using a similar experimental design was unable to duplicate the findings of Hamer's study.[10]
- Hamer himself emphasizes, "These genes do not cause people to become homosexuals . . . the biology of personality is much more complicated than that."[11]

COMMENTS ON THESE STUDIES BY OTHER SCIENTISTS

"Evan S. Balaban, a neurobiologist at the Neurosciences Institute in San Diego, notes that the search for the biological underpinnings of complex human traits has a sorry history of late. In recent years, researchers and the media have proclaimed the 'discovery' of genes linked to alcoholism and mental illness as well as to homosexuality. None of the claims, Balaban points out, have been confirmed."[12]

—*Scientific America,* November 1995

"Recent studies postulate biologic factors as the primary basis for sexual orientation. However, there is no evidence at present to substantiate a biologic theory, just as there is no compelling evidence to support any singular psychological explanation. While all behavior must have an ultimate biologic substrate, the appeal of current biologic explanations for sexual orientation may derive more from dissatisfaction with the present status of psychosocial explanations than from a substantiating body of experimental data. Critical review shows the evidence favoring a biologic theory to be lacking. In an alternative model, temperamental and personality traits interact with the familial and social milieu as the individual's sexuality emerges."[13]

—*Archives of General Psychiatry,* March 1993

"Reports of morphological differences between the brains of humans with different sexual orientation or gender identity have furthered speculation that such behaviors may result from hormonal or genetic influences on the developing brain. However, the causal chain may be reversed; sexual behavior in adulthood may have caused the morphological differences. . . . It is possible that differences in sexual behavior cause, rather than are caused by, differences in brain structure."[14]

—*Nature,* October 1997

"Upon critical analysis of hormonal theories of homosexuality and transsexualism, there are no robust data to support the role of hormones in the development of these behaviors or identities among humans."[15]

—*Journal of Neuropsychiatry,* Spring 1993

"The myth of the all-powerful gene is based on flawed science that discounts the environmental context in which we and our genes exist. . . . Many modern researchers continue to believe that sexual preference is to some extent biologically determined. They base this belief on the fact that no single environmental explanation can account for the development of homosexuality. But this does not make sense. Human sexuality is complex and affected by many things. The failure to come up with a clear environmental explanation is not surprising, and does not mean that the answer lies in biology. Such studies are bound to come up with plenty of meaningless correlations which will get reported as further evidence of genetic transmission of homosexuality."[16]

—*Exploding the Gene Myth*, 1993

"In the early '90s, three highly publicized studies seemed to suggest that homosexuality's roots were genetic, traceable to nature rather than nurture. . . . More than five years later the data have never been replicated. Moreover, researchers say, the public has misunderstood 'behavioral genetics.' Unlike eye color, behavior is not strictly inherited; it needs to be brought into play by a daunting complexity of environmental factors. . . . The existence of a genetic pattern among homosexuals doesn't mean people are born gay, any more than the genes for height, presumably common in NBA players, indicate an inborn ability to play basketball . . . admits biologist Evan Balaban, 'I think we're as much in the dark as we ever were.'"[17]

—*Newsweek*, August 17, 1998

" . . . Sexual orientation is not under the direct governance of chromosomes and genes, and that, whereas it is not foreordained by prenatal brain hormonalization it is influenced thereby, and is also strongly dependent on postnatal socialization."[18]

—*American Psychologist*, April 1987

"Like all complex behavioral and mental states, homosexuality is multifactorial. It is neither exclusively biological nor exclusively psychological, but results from an as-yet-difficult-to-quantitate mixture of genetic factors, intrauterine influences (some innate to the mother and thus present in every pregnancy, and others incidental to a given pregnancy), postnatal environment (such as parental, sibling, and cultural behavior), and a complex series of repeatedly reinforced choices occurring at critical phases in development."[19]

—*Homosexuality and the Politics of Truth*, 1996

CONCLUSIONS

Repeated sexual behavior and environmental conditions change brain structure and body chemistry, which means the genetic/biological characteristics observed in these studies may be the result of homosexual behavior rather than the *cause* of it.

All of these studies lack consistency and replication. Their results are inconclusive and speculative at best. Simon LeVay, Richard Pillard, and Dean

Hamer are all self-proclaimed homosexual men. Therefore, I suggest that behind their work is a strong motivation to justify their same-sex attractions.

If homosexuality is a normal sexual orientation, why is only 1 to 3 percent of the population homosexual and not 50 percent? Why are there more homosexual males than homosexual females?

Masters and Johnson, leading sex researchers in America, state, "The genetic theory of homosexuality has been generally discarded today. . . . No serious scientist suggests that a simple cause-effect relationship applies."[20]

There is a preponderance of scientific evidence conducted over the past eighty years that shows homosexuality to be an acquired condition. Dr. Irving Bieber, Dr. Charles Socarides, Dr. Joseph Nicolosi, Dr. Elizabeth Moberly, Dr. Lawrence Hatterer, Dr. Robert Kronemeyer, Dr. E. Kaplan, Dr. Edith Fiore, Dr. Gerard van den Aardweg, Dr. Earl Wilson, Dr. Jeffrey Satinover—these are but a few of the psychiatrists and psychologists who have substantiated these findings through years of clinical research and empirical studies.

The best evidence to disprove a theory is experience. Thousands of men and women throughout the world have changed from homosexual to heterosexual. Masters and Johnson claim about a 65 percent success rate in helping people change. Other therapists who report successful treatment are Drs. Bieber, Socarides, Nicolosi, Hatterer, Gershman, Hadden, Hamilton, van den Aardweg, Barnhouse, Ellis, and many others.[21] The National Association for Research and Therapy of Homosexuality (NARTH) conducted a survey of 860 respondents and found that those who want to change their sexual orientation may succeed.[22]

Defining Homosexuality

Since same-sex attractions are not inherently caused by biologic or genetic factors, they are therefore developmentally determined. First, I will give an overview of the basic motivations behind same-sex attractions. Then, I will define ten basic factors that contribute to the development of a homosexual orientation.

HOMOSEXUALITY IS A SYMPTOM.
Homosexual feelings, thoughts, and desires are symptoms of underlying issues. They represent a defensive response to conflicts in the present, a way to medicate pain and discomfort. They represent unresolved childhood trauma, archaic emotions, frozen feelings, wounds that never healed. They also represent a reparative drive to fulfill unmet homo-emotional

Defining Homosexuality

1. Homosexuality is a symptom.

- Defensive response to present conflicts
- Reaction to unresolved childhood trauma
- Reparative drive to fulfill unmet homo-emotional needs

2. Homosexuality is an emotionally based condition.

- Need for same-sex parent's/peer's love
- Need for gender identity
- Fear of intimacy with someone of the opposite sex

3. Homosexuality is a Same-Sex Attachment Disorder.

- Detachment from same-sex parent
- Detachment from same-sex peers
- Detachment from one's body
- Detachment from one's gender

Same-Sex Attachment Disorder (SSAD)

© Richard Cohen, M.A., January 2006

love needs of the past—an unconscious drive for bonding with the same-sex parent. Dr. Elizabeth Moberly[23] coined and Dr. Joseph Nicolosi[24] further developed the term *homo-emotional love need*.

A homo-emotional love need is an *unconscious* drive for bonding between a son and his father, or between a daughter and her mother. This is a hidden and profound wound in the soul of anyone who experiences same-sex attractions. If questioned, the active homosexual would not say he is looking for his father's love in the arms of another man. This is often a hidden, unconscious drive buried deep in the psyche. As Dr. Harville Hendrix states, "Each of us enters adulthood harboring unresolved childhood issues with our parents, whether or not we know it or will admit it. Those needs have to be met, because their satisfaction is equated, in our unconscious minds, with survival. Therefore, their satisfaction becomes the agenda in adult love relationships."[25]

HOMOSEXUALITY IS AN EMOTIONALLY BASED CONDITION.

There are three underlying drives to same-sex attractions:

• Need for same-sex parent's/peer's love

Most case histories demonstrate that homosexual thoughts and feelings originate in preadolescent experiences. Therefore, it is basically a nonsexual condition. *"The homosexual love need is essentially a search for parenting. . . . What the homosexual seeks is the fulfillment of these normal attachment needs, which have abnormally been left unmet in the process of growth."*[26] Therefore, the drive is one of reparation, seeking to fulfill unmet love needs of the past. It is a homo-*emotional* reparative drive.[27]

This drive may also represent a need for bonding with same-sex peers, or a homo-social wound. In preadolescence, he did not bond with other boys, and she did not bond with other girls. After puberty, those needs become sexualized. However, by acting upon those desires the individual's needs will never be fulfilled, simply because they are the unmet needs of a child for parental or peer love. Only through healthy, healing, nonsexual bonding will true and lasting change occur.[28]

• Need for gender identification

The homosexual person feels a lack of masculinity or femininity within himself or herself and seeks to fulfill this need through another man or woman.[29] This resulted from a distant or disrupted relationship between father and son or mother and daughter in early childhood or adolescence.

Gender identity is an awareness of one's masculinity or femininity. In homosexual people, there is a feeling of inadequacy and incompleteness in the inner essence of their being.[30] Therefore, *they search for the missing part of themselves in another person.* Through a sexual contact or union with another person of the same sex, they feel, at least momentarily, whole and more complete.

• Fear of intimacy with someone of the opposite sex

In the case of a homosexual male, there may have been an *abnormally close mother-son attachment.*[31] In a marriage where the husband does not meet the mother's emotional and physical needs, she may turn to her son for emotional comfort and support.[32] This is not done with conscious intent to hurt. Nonetheless, it has a profound and damaging effect upon the psychosexual development of the son. He may overidentify with his mother and femininity and disidentify with his father and masculinity.

Later in puberty, the son may experience sexual attraction toward his mother that leads to extreme guilt and the repression of a normal sexual drive toward women. He might then turn to men for intimacy and sex, not wanting to "betray" his mother or reexperience his guilt. This process may be completely unconscious.[33]

The father or another significant man is usually the abuser in the case of a homosexual female, followed by female sexual abuse.[34] The abuse could have been sexual, emotional, mental, or physical. This leaves her deeply traumatized by men. Not wanting to reexperience the memory of abuse, she then turns to women for comfort, love, and understanding.

HOMOSEXUALITY IS A SAME-SEX ATTACHMENT DISORDER (SSAD). Homosexuality represents an attachment strain, defensive detachment, or defensive exclusion from the same-sex parent, same-sex peers, one's own body, and one's own sense of gender identity.

Homosexuality is an attachment disorder, whereby the individual feels separated from parents, self, body, and others. "I don't fit in," "I don't be-long," "I'm different from the rest," "I'm neither a boy nor girl," are some of the thoughts of those who experience same-sex attractions. The result is a *Same-Sex Attachment Disorder.*

Dr. Martha Welch defines four types of attachment in the parent-child relationship:

- Secure Attachment—Parents are available, responsive, empathic, and effective; the child is competent, self-confident, resilient/cheerful, cooperative, and humorous/playful, and tries harder.
- Insecure Resistant Attachment—Parents are sometimes available, less responsive, less empathic, and less close; the child is clingy, re-buffing, tense, volatile, impulsive, passive, and defeatist.
- Insecure Avoidant Attachment—Parents are rebuffing (having been raised by rebuffing parents), avoid closeness, are inconsistent and am-bivalent, and reject; the child is hostile/bullying, whiny/needy, com-pulsively self-sufficient, distant, and demonstrates little give and take.
- Insecure Disorganized Attachment—Crosses boundaries of all three other types of attachment. Mother is depressed, was abused or ne-glected herself, and is mourning; the child is depressed, anxious, passive-aggressive, inhibited, clingy/tearful, gloomy/joyless, hard to comfort, can't get out of anger, and will perceive the mother as ne-glectful because someone else is abusing him even if the mother doesn't know about the abuse.

All children who suffered the three types of insecure attachment experienced separation anxiety and hyperarousal, and therefore learned to cut off and detach emotionally from self and others.[35]

I submit that anyone who experiences homosexual thoughts, feelings, and desires has a *Same-Sex Attachment Disorder (SSAD)*. Being homosexually oriented is therefore *not gay, nor bad, but SSAD!*

Major Causes of Same-Sex Attractions

There is a constellation of contributing variables that may lead an individual to experience same-sex attractions. The sum is greater than the parts. It is the combination of the following causes that may lead to homosexual ideation in either the male or female. A single factor does not cause a Same-Sex Attachment Disorder. It is the confounding of several variables that will lead an individual to experience same-sex attractions. The ten variables are: 1) Heredity, 2) Temperament, 3) Hetero-Emotional Wounds, 4) Homo-Emotional Wounds, 5) Sibling Wounds/Family Dynamics, 6) Body-Image Wounds, 7) Sexual Abuse, 8) Social or Peer Wounds, 9) Cultural Wounds, and 10) Other Factors. (See the chart on the facing page, Constellation of Potential Variables Creating Same-Sex Attractions.)

There are also differences between male and female homosexuality. In my years of practice, I have observed that many homosexual females are attracted to men, but the majority of homosexual males have no attraction to women. Many homosexual females have been so hurt by men that they turn to women for their affectional needs. However, their attraction to men may still exist. Therefore, the psychology behind male and female homosexuality is different.

HEREDITY

The school of psychology generally accepts the belief that we are born with a "clean slate," born pure. Then our parents (caregivers), siblings, and other environmental influences cause us harm. I believe this concept is an oversimplification and that we are not born with a "clean slate." The school of family systems therapy contributes to the understanding of this concept.

"It is assumed [by intergenerational and transgenerational family systems theory] that relational patterns are learned and passed down across the generations and that current individual and family behavior is a result of these patterns. Thus, accurate assessment of relational patterns, both functional and dysfunctional, not only is the first step in understanding families from an intergenerational perspective, but also is an essential step

Constellation of Potential Variables Creating Same-Sex Attractions

Heredity:
- Inherited wounds
- Unresolved family issues
- Misperceptions
- Mental filters
- Predilection for rejection

Temperament:
- Hypersensitive
- High maintenance
- Artistic nature
- Gender nonconforming behaviors: Male more feminine; Female more masculine

Hetero-Emotional Wounds:
- Enmeshment
- Neglect
- Abuse
- Abandonment
- Addictions
- Imitation of behaviors
- Wrong sex

Homo-Emotional Wounds:
- Neglect
- Abuse
- Enmeshment
- Abandonment
- Addictions
- Imitation of behaviors
- Wrong sex

Sibling Wounds/Family Dynamics:
- Put-downs
- Abuse
- Name calling

Body Image Wounds:
- Late Bloomer
- Physical disabilities
- Shorter
- Skinnier
- Larger
- Lack of coordination

Sexual Abuse:
- Homosexual imprinting
- Learned and reinforced behaviors
- Substitute for affection

Social or Peer Wounds:
- Name calling
- Put-downs
- Goody-goody
- Teacher's pet
- Nonathletic
- No rough and tumble (boy)
- Too rough and tumble (girl)

Cultural Wounds:
- Media
- Educational system
- Entertainment industry
- Internet
- Pornography

Other Factors:
- Divorce
- Death
- Intrauterine experiences and influences
- Adoption
- Religion

The severity of wounding in each category will have a direct impact on the amount of time and effort it will take to heal.

for proper treatment."[36] "Contemporary perspectives on intergenerational family therapy suggest that difficulties and dysfunctions in relationships across generations are frequently replicated in subsequent intergenerational relationships, thereby adding to the complexity and potential trauma for members of those family systems."[37]

I suggest that we are born with two natures. One is our original nature, our God-given authentic self, full of purity, goodness, spirituality, and creativity. We are also born with an inherited nature, consisting of the victories and failures of our ancestors, our people, and our nation. The unpleasant side of this inherited nature may consist of unresolved issues, such as prejudice, addictions, mental disorders, theft, various forms of abuse, hatred of men or women, and sexual problems. It says in the Old Testament, "The Lord, the Lord, a God merciful and gracious, slow to anger and abounding in steadfast love for thousands, forgiving iniquity and transgression and sin, but who will by no means clear the guilty, visiting the iniquity of the fathers upon the children and the children's children, to the third and fourth generation."[38] Other religions call it karma—what goes around comes around.

What is now being described as genetic predispositioning may also be interpreted as transgenerational "sin" or the multigenerational transmission of unresolved family issues. These manifest themselves within the genetic structure of the lineage. "We are born with splits—from ancestors, in our genes—not all from our parents."[39]

Dr. Bernard Nathanson illuminates the power and mystery of the gene. The United States government has sponsored a $5 billion program known as the Human Genome Project. Its purpose is to identify the structure and location of all the genes in our body. Theoretically, by next year, a small sample of blood will be able to determine if someone will get cancer or diabetes, how intelligent he will be, and if he is susceptible to violent crimes or alcoholism, and so on. "Genes are not destiny unaltered and unadulterated. We can have the gene for alcoholism but may never become a drinker, because we can control it. To some extent, you have control of your body. But there is this predilection. The gene gives you the predilection to alcoholism or violent crimes or whatever the behavioral gene happens to be."[40]

I therefore believe that we are not born pure. We are born with mental filters or predilections, which may impact how we view and respond to any given situation. Mental filters/predilections are like looking at life through tinted glasses. We see things from a particular perspective, not necessarily how they are. A mental filter may cause us to misinterpret someone's actions or words. "The concept of filtering or forming a 'cognitive set' is closely related to what is called a 'learning set' or a 'cognitive map.' It is a rule by which a person interprets learning tasks or stimuli from the environment."[41] Bert Hellinger, founder of Systemic Family Therapy in Germany, teaches that we accumulate feelings from family members known and unknown, i.e., grandparents, great-grandparents, divorced mates, and lovers. These feelings and issues are present in the family system and influence all its members.

How this bears on the development of a Same-Sex Attachment Disorder (SSAD) may be unique to each individual depending upon the issues in the family system. At the core of a SSAD condition is a sense of not belonging, not fitting in, and feeling rejected. These feelings and thoughts may already be an inheritable characteristic of the child. Therefore, he is born with a *predisposition for rejection.* He has a propensity to misinterpret his parents' and others' behaviors and words. It is not the event that shapes him, it is his *response* to the event. *Perception becomes reality.* This inheritable characteristic may contribute to feelings of *rejection* and *being different,* which is at the heart of the Same-Sex Attachment Disorder.

Jed grew up in a middle-class family. His father was a pillar of the community. They attended church religiously. Jed's father was very critical and demanding, as his father before him was. Jed always felt insecure and inadequate around his dad, never being able to measure up to his expectations. At a very early age, Jed emotionally detached from his father and aligned himself with his mother. I believe Jed was born with a predisposition for rejection and detachment. Having hailed from a lineage that endured massive persecution, Jed easily experienced a feeling of not fitting in, not measuring up, and being different.

Albert was born into a high-stress family system. His dad was an executive of a large corporation. He would bring home the burdens and worries of his work and constantly complain about life. Albert's mom was very unhappy in her relationship with her husband. She would hold her son and share her pain and sorrow with him. Albert internally detached from both his mom and dad as an infant. He felt unaccepted, like an outsider. He was sure he had been adopted, no matter how many times his parents protested that he was their child. Albert hailed from a lineage that had also experienced intense social rejection and discrimination for many generations. He had a predisposition for experiencing ridicule and rejection, which he then projected onto his parents and eventually his siblings and peers.

TEMPERAMENT

Some of the temperamental characteristics that may lead to a Same-Sex Attachment Disorder are hypersensitivity, a more artistic nature, a more masculine female, a more feminine male, and a "high maintenance" child.

The characteristic of hypersensitivity, or greater sensitivity, may be part of one's original or inherited nature. In this world as it currently exists, I call this a "curse blessing." I have observed that many men and women with a Same-Sex Attachment Disorder also have a greater sensitivity to any given stimuli. Of course, this does not mean that all sensitive children are or will become homosexual. Remember that there is a confounding of factors that will create this orientation; it is not just one variable alone.

The hypersensitive child will react more deeply than the other children within the family system. If his family appreciates and understands his feelings, there will be no danger of the development of a Same-Sex Attachment Disorder. If his family mocks or criticizes his feelings and there are any number of other variables present, this may contribute to a SSAD condition. He may also have a more compliant nature, rather than an aggressive character, whereby there is a tendency to acquiesce and withdraw rather than to stand up and speak out.

Having an artistic nature may also be a burden if the family rejects or misunderstands the child's gifts. The sensitive child in an insensitive environment experiences undue stress on his mental, emotional, and spiritual development.

A more masculine girl or a more feminine boy, by nature, may also be the subject of ridicule by parents, siblings, peers, and society. It is the square-peg-in-the-round-hole effect, causing the child to doubt his or her original nature. These characteristics are defined as *gender nonconforming* behaviors. The child will grow confident in his talents when he is understood, accepted, and encouraged. If he experiences or perceives criticism, the results will be psycho-social-biological damage. "Society's differential response to 'sissies' and 'tomboys' may be one reason for the difference in numbers between male and female homosexuals," says Dr. Dean Byrd.[42]

A brief note: If the child exhibits some of these gender nonconforming behaviors, it is important for parents to encourage same-sex activities. Boys need rough-and-tumble activities, even if they have a more sensitive and/or artistic nature. Girls need to participate in same-sex activities as well, even if they exhibit a more athletic nature. Identification with one's own gender is extremely important in the formative years of psychosocial, psychological, and psychosexual development. Same-sex activities are most important from preschool through high school years.

The "high maintenance" child requires more specialized care and attention. Those who have children like this may understand what I am describing. Each child is born with a completely unique temperament. Some children *require* much attention, others not as much. The "high maintenance" child needs much reassurance, touch, and constant attention. If his needs go unmet, a deficit will develop and a poor self-image will ensue.

Bernard was the younger of two boys. His mother embraced his sensitive nature while his father rejected him. Bernard's father's father was very cold and strict and eventually abandoned his son and family. Therefore, Bernard's dad never experienced the warmth, encouragement, and touch of his father. Consequently, whenever Bernard would display emotions, his dad would mock and criticize him. Bernard soon learned that it was unsafe to express feelings with men. He emotionally distanced himself from his father and then doubted his own masculinity.

Matthew's father grew up during World War II in England. Matthew's grandfather was a casualty of war; therefore, Matthew's father never experienced paternal love. Matthew's stepgrandfather taught his dad that it was sissy and unmanly to show emotions. This was the philosophy that Matthew's dad lived by. Therefore, when Matthew came along and displayed a very sensitive character, his dad was uncomfortable and distressed while in his presence. He would scream at Matthew to stop crying, stop being such a sissy, and stop touching him. Matthew eventually became like his father—a stoic. He also demonstrated oppositional behavior toward his father, doing everything he could to make him upset.

There are numerous stories of men who, as boys, felt their fathers' disapproval because of their sensitivity. They were criticized and mocked instead of being accepted and appreciated. What becomes clear is that their fathers' fathers were rejecting of their own sons' sensitivity, and in order for their dads to survive, they had to bury that part of their personality deep in their unconscious. When the father then observes this sensitivity in his son, he must suppress in him what he had repressed in himself. Otherwise, he will experience much pain, anger, and grief.

HETERO-EMOTIONAL WOUNDS

There has been much literature written about the smother mother, dominating mother, or excessively involved mother. Again, this is not a blame game. I do not know of any parent who sets out to either hurt or damage his or her child. Also, it is not merely the events that shape a child's character, but his response to the situation, influenced by heredity and temperament.

Drs. Bieber et al.,[43] Socarides,[44] Nicolosi,[45] van den Aardweg,[46] Freud,[47] Siegelman,[48] Westwood,[49] Schoefield,[50] Thompson et al.,[51] and Kronemeyer[52] have observed that *homosexual men had an abnormally close mother-son attachment.* This relationship between mother and son represents unhealthy attachment, rather than a healthy sense of bonding. His mother may be distant from her husband and overattach herself to her son. Psychologist Dr. Patricia Love calls this the "Emotional Incest Syndrome." The mother may confide all her pain and problems to her son, making him a substitute spouse. Being so close to his mom, and detached from his dad, he becomes more and more like her. In such instances, the boy overidentifies with his mother and femininity and disidentifies with his father and masculinity.

One client shared, "As a child, I was so confused about my relationship with my mother, I didn't know if I was her lover or son. She confided all her pain and problems to me." I have observed in the majority of my male clients this characteristic—an overidentification with the feminine and a disidentification with the masculine.

The mother may have directly or indirectly criticized the father: "Don't be like him." "He's no good." This also distances the son from his father, his role model of masculinity. In fear of losing his mother's love, he detaches from his sense of masculinity (as the masculine father seems to be the enemy) and becomes a reflection of his mother's character. "Jung said something disturbing about this complication. He said that when the son is introduced primarily by the mother to feelings, he will learn the female attitude toward masculinity and takes a female view of his own father and of his own masculinity. He will see his father through his mother's eyes."[53] Dr. Charles Socarides, in his many studies and articles on homosexual development, has found that there is a *lack of separation/individuation, or differentiation, between the mother and son, which is decisive for gender identification.*[54]

The homosexual female may also have had an abnormally close father-daughter attachment. Dr. Socarides, as well as Drs. Zucker and Bradley[55] talk further about daughters who mold themselves in the image of their fathers. In some cases, the daughter may view the mother as unsafe, ineffectual, or weak, and therefore choose to model herself after the more competent and powerful parent, her father. The father may speak poorly about his wife, further distancing the daughter from her role model of femininity.

The homosexual female may have been abused either by her father or significant men in her life, such as a brother, uncle, grandfather, stepfather, or friend of the family. The abuse could have been sexual, emotional, mental, and/or physical. She then turns to other women for comfort, love, and understanding to prevent her from reexperiencing the memory or memories of abuse.

In other cases, the daughter sees that her distant mother loves Dad. Therefore, she may overidentify with her father, taking on a more masculine nature and appearance in order to win the affection and approval of her mother.[56] The son may take on a more feminine appearance to win the affection and approval of his father.

Another factor in the mother-son or father-daughter relationship is imitation of behavior. This is a very strong learning mechanism for all children. Their first method of learning is imitation of what they see, feel, and sense around them. If a son has an unhealthy attachment with his mother, he will learn a more feminine way of being. If a daughter has an unhealthy attachment with her father, she will learn a more masculine way of being. In both cases, the young child may become more and more estranged from his or her own gender and internalize the nature of the opposite sex. Again, this inhibits normal psychosocial and psychosexual development.

Finally, if a parent expresses disappointment with the child's gender or if the child perceives the parent's disappointment with his gender, he may then take on the characteristics of the opposite gender in order to obtain his parent's love and acceptance. This may become another factor in creating gender disidentification. Here are a few case examples:

> Robert was his mommy's precious little boy, sleeping with her and sharing in all her activities. He was what Dad could not be—an

attentive and perfect gentleman. The problem was, Robert was a child, and Mommy was an adult.

Jim's mother would often criticize her husband for being a failure, being a nothing, and being less than a man. In fear of losing his mother's love, Jim aligned himself with his mother and grew more and more distant from his father.

John's father, an academic and head of a scientific agency, never touched his son. John only experienced his father's critical nature. He longed for acceptance and found that in the arms of his mother. Seeing that his dad loved his mother, he became more and more like her, hoping to attract the attention and affection of his dad. Of course, this never came to pass, as he was a boy and not a girl, even though his actions were more feminine than masculine.

Toni was her father's favorite. She would play ball with him and his friends every weekend. From an early age, she would go to the pub with her dad and sit by as he and his buddies would drink. Mom was always busy working, and when at home she was either cooking or doing house chores. Toni longed for her mother's affection, which she experienced as unavailable. Again, like John, she modeled herself after her opposite-sex parent in order to win the love of her same-sex parent. Toni dressed in boy's clothes, had short hair, and acted more masculine. However, all these ploys were ineffective in winning her mother's love.

HOMO-EMOTIONAL WOUNDS

In the father-son, mother-daughter relationship, a homo-emotional wound develops if the child perceives or experiences his or her same-sex parent as either cold, distant, absent, passive, abusive, or unavailable. This homo-emotional wound is a *key* factor in the development of what may later appear as same-sex attractions. In the heart of every man or woman who experiences same-sex desires is a sense of detachment from his or her same-sex parent. This may be on a very unconscious level, as the imprinting for this condition may have occurred in utero and in early infancy. Ninety percent of the brain develops by the time we are three years of age. Therefore, experiences of detachment, which occurred in the first years of life, are locked deep in the unconscious mind. That is why many homosexual individuals say, "As long as I can remember, I felt different."

Drs. Moberly and Nicolosi found that the prehomosexual boy experienced a hurt or disappointment in his relationship with his father.[57] To protect himself against future hurt, the boy developed a defensive attitude characterized by emotional distancing. Not only did he fail to identify with his father, but also, because of the hurt, he rejected his father and the masculinity he represents. You may read more about attachment disorders in the works of John Bowlby.[58]

The father may have a difficult time relating to his son if he exhibited any kind of gender nonconforming behaviors, e.g., more feminine, more artistic, and nonathletic. The father may be preoccupied with his own problems and have no time for his son. The father may abdicate responsibility for parenting by having his wife raise the boy. He may have left the family, or he may be at home physically, but unavailable emotionally. The boy may then see his father as emotionally distant, perhaps verbally or physically abusive, and unavailable. In some cases, there is an emotional enmeshment between the two, whereby the father enrolls his son into a peer relationship, and the son loses his identity in order to care for his father's needs.

By experiencing his father's disapproval, disappointment, or distance, the son will withdraw from the relationship, feeling hurt and rejected. This leads to a deep sense of ambivalence toward the same-sex parent—"I need you, but you hurt and rejected me, so stay away, but come close and hold me, but it hurts too much." Dr. Moberly calls this a defensive detachment reaction,[59] and Dr. Welch calls it an attachment strain.[60] The child defends himself from future wounding by putting up an imaginary shield around his heart and soul. He then detaches from his same-sex parent, rejecting his father.

This same-sex ambivalence causes feelings of love and hate to occur at the same time. He seeks bonding with a man, but underneath that need is an angry and hurt little boy. This is why homosexual relationships have a short life span. Furthermore, these ambivalent feelings toward men function as a lifelong block against full male identification.[61]

This defensive detachment is generally an unconscious decision. The detachment also prevents him from internalizing his own sense of gender identity. He has cut off psychologically and emotionally from his father, his role model of masculinity. Hence, a Same-Sex Attachment Disorder is created in the child. This leads to alienation from the parent, self, and others, and a feeling of being "different." When he rejects his primary source of masculine identification, he is essentially rejecting his own core gender identity.

On a very deep psychic level, the son feels rejected by his father. This may originate from a deep source within the child—a heritable predisposition for being rejected, or an intrauterine experience of feeling unwanted—not necessarily by the parent's actions or words. (I will explain about intrauterine influences under "Other Factors" below.) Counselor David Seamands said, "Children are the best tape recorders but the worst interpreters."[62]

The boy, from ages one and a half to three, has an added developmental task girls do not have. He must separate and individuate from his mother, and then be initiated into the world of the masculine by his father or another significant male role model. The girl, even though she, too, must separate and individuate in this stage of development, will continue to identify with her mother, her primary role model of femininity. Three things may rob a boy of his masculine role model and his new source of strength: 1) the mother continues to cling to her son, 2) the father is unavailable or abdicates responsibility to the mother, or 3) the son perceives rejection from the father. This is a critical time for the son to bond with his father or other men.[63]

It states in *My Little Golden Book About GOD*, "God is the love of our mother's kiss, and the warm, strong hug of our daddy's arms." Pictured are both Father and Mother holding their children warmly. Parents are God's representatives for children. When children detach from either Mr. or Mrs. God, they are distancing themselves from their role models of gender identification. Therefore, a defensive detachment from father or mother may lead to a defensive detachment toward God.

That is why later on, when the adult tries repeatedly to rid himself of the same-sex desire, it will not go away. This is because the origin of the desire is one of reparation, to make good on past deficits, the need for bonding with the same-sex parent, which did not occur sufficiently in the earliest years of life.[64]

Michael Saia, in his book, *Counseling the Homosexual*, speaks of a five-phase model that leads to the development of a Same-Sex Attachment Disorder:

First: The child feels or perceives *rejection* from the same-sex parent.
Second: The child *rejects* the same-sex parent.
Third: The child *rejects* his gender identity, saying unconsciously, "If men are that way, then I don't want to be like them."
Fourth: The child *rejects* himself because he is the same gender of the parent he just rejected. Again, he unconsciously says, "If Daddy

> is not good, and he is a man, then I am not good, because I am a boy."
>
> Fifth: The child then *rejects* others of the same gender, as a defensive reaction of self-protection against further wounding.[65]

During puberty, the unmet homo-emotional needs are experienced as homosexual feelings. The individual may then spend a lifetime trying to fulfill those unmet needs for attachment through sexual relationships.

Of course, the defensive detachment may occur with the opposite-sex parent. This is why so many marriages break up and so many men and women seek opposite-sex partners but find it very difficult to commit to a truly intimate relationship. The defensive detachment toward the opposite-sex parent lodges deep in their hearts. *They are experiencing an Opposite-Sex Attachment Disorder (OSAD).* Until the individual extracts the wounds, defensive behaviors continue to plague adult attempts at intimacy. (My next book will be entitled *Healing Heterosexuality*.)

> Chris's father was authoritative and punitive. Chris was sensitive and perceived his father's strictness as personal rejection. Because of this, Chris continued to seek refuge in the safety of his mother's world, identifying more with her and his sister than with his dad and brothers. This attitude spilled over into his school-age years. Chris was always the teacher's pet, doing great in academics, yet socially inept in relating to the other boys. In his adult life, Chris fantasized about being sexually intimate with the men he admired. His need for his father's love and approval had translated itself into sexual desires after puberty. Today, Chris is becoming more authentic as a man among men, speaking more openly with his dad, and learning to befriend other men as equals.
>
> Another young man I counseled was Bob. When he entered therapy, he thought his relationship with his father was nearly perfect. It took quite a while to untangle this enmeshed affair, for his father had enrolled him into a peer relationship. Bob spent his life trying to compensate for his father's wounds and weaknesses. His father had shared his problems and pain with him throughout his childhood, adolescence, and early adulthood. His dad isolated himself from the world and had no close friends except his son. In response, Bob had learned to deny his feelings and needs, reinventing himself as his father's savior, best friend, and confidant.

After Bob strengthened his sense of self-worth and developed firm boundaries, he began the process of successfully separating and individuating from his father. This was frightening for Bob. Each time he slipped back into being the good little boy and pleaser, same-sex attractions emerged. When he stood in his power and expressed himself in a healthy, positive, and assertive manner, he experienced a newfound masculinity. When he thoughtlessly acquiesced to his father and other authority figures, his same-sex fantasies blossomed. Again, the Same-Sex Attachment Disorder is a symptom, a defensive response to past and present conflicts.

Bob worked to heal his relationship with his father. He now expresses himself as an adult, rather than a good little boy. He let go of *expecting* his father to change and is making the necessary changes in his life to mature into his God-given masculine identity.

I have counseled several men whose fathers were in the military or government. Because of their service to the country, they were often away for extended periods of time. This left their sons feelings abandoned and alone. Other men had fathers who were physically present, yet emotionally absent. As much as they tried to win their fathers' love, their dads remained distant and unavailable. Another group of men had fathers who were workaholics. Their fathers were never home enough to become seriously involved in their sons' lives. Others had fathers who were alcoholics, drug addicts, sports addicts, and/or rageaholics. They experienced the war of their fathers' mood swings, never knowing when Dr. Jekyll or Mr. Hyde would show up. They had to be on guard 100 percent of the time.

SIBLING WOUNDS/FAMILY DYNAMICS
The prehomosexual boy, who exhibits a character difference or physical disability, may bear the brunt of emotional, mental, physical, and/or sexual abuse by his siblings. If the same-sex sibling, especially an elder, criticizes him, this may contribute to gender disidentification.[66] This may be another factor that reinforces the boy's poor self-image.

The potential homosexually oriented individual may be the oldest, middle, youngest, or only child in the family system. The oldest may become the family hero or parentified child, taking on a more adult role to solve the family problems, thus losing his sense of identity. (The parentified child is one who loses his childlike nature and takes on a more adult persona, thus becoming more like a parent than a child. He knows too much too soon.) The next child may become the rebel, manifesting behavioral problems. The rebel acts out in a negative manner in order to gain attention and affection. The middle child may become withdrawn, not appearing to have as many needs as the oldest or youngest. He becomes invisible, shy, or isolated. His needs seem to be less important than the others. The youngest child may be indulged or spoiled. He may also be the recipient of the unexpressed feelings of the entire family system. When he expresses their repressed feelings, he is then identified as the "problem child." The youngest child may be a performer or clown as a means of obtaining attention and affection.

> Brad was the youngest of four. His older brother, Mark, was the tyrant of the family. Mark and his dad had an extremely antagonistic relationship. Brad's dad would beat on Mark, then Mark would beat on Brad. Mark would physically abuse Brad when no one else was around. He would also verbally abuse Brad, i.e., "sissy," "faggot," "queer." Brad lived in fear of Mark's fits of rage. This relationship caused Brad to further distance himself from his father and men.
>
> One way of coping with the distress of his relationship with Mark, the absence of his alcoholic father, and the unhealthy attachment with his mother, was to be the peacemaker of the family. When the siblings would argue or his parents would fight, Brad would jump right in to make smooth the path between them all. He was the performer and peacemaker, trying to create harmony in the midst of chaos.

Several other men I counseled had same-sex siblings who would chastise and criticize them for their more sensitive nature. Name-calling was a common experience. Generally, the older brothers had poor relationships with their fathers and would take out their frustrations on the younger brothers. Others played the part of the family hero—getting good grades, being the pleaser. However, no matter how hard they tried, they never experienced the love they so desired.

BODY-IMAGE WOUNDS

Late bloomer, early maturation, physical disabilities, shorter, taller, skinnier, or fatter—these are some characteristics that may result in body-image wounds. Bodily attributes may cause pain because of peer or parental reactions. Body-image wounds seem to be quite high on the scale of contributing variables. Many, if not all, whom I have counseled felt a lower sense of self-worth due to feelings of inadequacy about their physical appearance. They detached from their fathers and then detached from their own gender. Finally, they detached from their own bodies, as they were reminders of the masculinity they rejected.

In adolescence, some did not develop as quickly as others and therefore felt inferior to peers. Others were either overweight or extremely thin, which contributed to a sense of low self-worth. Others were shorter, never grew taller like their friends or peers, and were left feeling inadequate and insecure. Still others may have had some kind of physical disability and received or perceived social criticism and rejection. Again, body-image wounds seem to be an important factor with many who have developed same-sex attractions.

> I worked with a tall, handsome man named Dirk. If you saw him, you would never imagine he ever struggled with his body image. Today, Dirk is a bodybuilder and very muscular. However, when in school, he felt athletically incompetent and socially inferior to the other boys. To heal these wounds in adulthood, he engaged in a variety of sports, learned to be one of the guys, and finally learned to enjoy himself. Several organizations that help individuals come out of homosexuality organize sports activities to help them overcome their fear of athletics and competition.

> Dan was a firefighter, the stereotypical image of a macho man: handsome, muscular, athletic, and educated. However, he felt inferior to other men and attracted to adolescent boys. Dan was a late bloomer. He entered puberty around fifteen years of age. When he had to shower with the other boys after gym class, he felt ashamed and embarrassed because of his lack of physical maturity. Dan felt unable to share his pain with his father. His dad was a workaholic and an alcoholic. In addition, he would beat on Dan while intoxicated. Therefore, Dan became developmentally stuck in prepubescent years. Even though he matured and blossomed into a handsome, powerful man as an adult, he still felt inferior to other men.

One group of men I counseled was physically shorter than the average male. This impacted their sense of gender identity. Each was emotionally detached from his father. This detachment, combined with the shorter height, made them feel inferior to other men. Others were overweight, extremely thin, or had some kind of physical disability. This created a sense of gender disidentification in each case.

SEXUAL ABUSE

Childhood sexual abuse occurred in a high percentage of homosexual adults. Research studies and clinical observations support this claim. Men have sexually abused 90 percent of homosexual females, and 75 to 85 percent of homosexual males have been sexually abused.[67]

Patrick Dimock[68] and Mike Lew[69] found confusion over sexual orientation as a result of early sexual abuse. David Finkelhor, leading researcher in the area of child sexual abuse, in his book *Child Sexual Abuse: New Theory and Research* (New York: Free Press, 1984), and Johnson and Shrier, in their article "Sexual Victimization of Boys" (*Journal of Adolescent Health Care*, 1985), both found a statistically strong correlation between childhood sexual abuse and homosexual activity in adolescence and adulthood. "Boys victimized by older men were over four times more likely to be currently engaged in homosexual activity than were non-victims."[70] Johnson and Shrier studied adolescents over a six-year period and found those who had been molested "identified themselves as currently homosexual nearly seven times as often and bisexual nearly six times as often" as those who had not been molested.[71]

Dr. Charles Socarides and other therapists have observed that a high percentage of their clients were sexually abused as children. Wendy Maltz and Beverly Holman confirm, "Studies of boys who were sexually victimized by men do indicate that a high percentage of them relate homosexually as adults."[72] Many directors of ex-gay ministries have reported that a high percentage of men and women seeking help have experienced childhood sexual abuse.

Most sexually abused children had already developed a defensive detachment toward the same- and/or opposite-sex parent. The male child, disidentified with his dad and overidentified with his mom, is more susceptible to abuse by a male perpetrator. Perpetrators easily perceive the child who harbors this unmet homo-emotional need. Most often, the perpetrators are family members or close friends of the family. The insidious nature of abuse is that it first begins as emotional intimacy and later becomes sexual. The perpetrator gains the trust of the child, fulfilling basic unmet homo-emotional love needs. Then he alters the relationship to include sex. This is a very confusing message to a hungry and impressionable child. Here, the psychic wiring and physiology of the child become confused because the messages of love, sex, and intimacy become intertwined, especially when it involves homosexual behavior. "Some survivors may adopt the orientation role of the abuse because they experienced sexual arousal during the abuse, and they may think that this arousal proves the orientation role they had in the abuse."[73] The child starves for the same-sex parent's love. Being emotionally detached from this source of love, he may repeat the learned sexual behavior as a means of fulfilling unmet homo-emotional love needs.

> Steve's father, an alcoholic, was physically abusive toward both his wife and Steve. At the age of six, a neighbor sexually abused him. This occurred again at ages nine and ten by older boys in the community. These experiences, coupled with his detachment toward his father, laid the foundation for homosexual acting-out behavior throughout his adult life. Through successful treatment, Steve was able to grieve the losses of his past and cut the ties that connected him to his same-sex attractions. Today, he is free of homosexual desires.

> Another case is Howard. His father was away on business trips much of the time, and when at home, was quite passive in his relationship with his son. When Howard was four years old, an older schoolboy named Robert sexually abused him. He had known Robert for some time. Howard received attention, affection, and then sexual intimacy from him. This created a pattern in Howard's body, which told him that to receive love from a man, he must have sex with him. As an adult, he continued to act out homosexually whenever pressure built up in his life. This was his outlet, his quick fix for masculine bonding.

I can share dozens of similar cases illustrating that sexual abuse is one more factor that may contribute to homosexual ideation.

SOCIAL OR PEER WOUNDS
Some experiences and characteristics individuals with same-sex attractions have lived through include name-calling, put-downs, goody-goody, teacher's pet, nonathletic, lack of rough-and-tumble for boys, and too much rough-and-tumble for girls.

Social and peer wounds also rate high on the scale of contributing variables. The majority of individuals who experience same-sex attractions have felt socially inept or out of place. There seem to be two polarities involved: inferiority or grandiosity—"I'm better than all the rest of them," or "I'm not as good as them." The individual may flip-flop from inferior to grandiose many times within a day.

"Fathers may influence children in ways that mothers don't, particularly in areas such as the child's peer relationships and achievement at school. Research indicates, for example, that boys with absent fathers have a harder time finding a balance between masculine assertiveness and self-restraint. Consequently, it's tougher for them to learn self-control and to delay gratification, skills that become increasingly important as boys grow and reach out for friendship, academic success, and career goals. A father's positive presence can be a significant factor in a girl's academic and career achievement as well, although the evidence here is more ambiguous. It's clear, however, that girls whose fathers are present and involved in their lives are less likely to become sexually promiscuous at a young age, and more likely to forge healthy relationships with men when they become adults."[74]

Dr. Gerard van den Aardweg believes that lack of peer bonding is a major factor in the creation of a SSAD condition. "The strongest association, then, is not found between homosexuality and father-child and mother-child relationships, but between homosexuality and 'peer relationships' . . . Feeling less masculine or feminine as compared to same-sex peers is tantamount to the feeling of not belonging."[75]

Many prehomosexual boys lack proper eye-hand coordination and athletic inclination and feel inferior to their male classmates. Even those who did participate in athletics may have felt, internally, less adequate or inferior. Still, other artistically inclined boys withdrew entirely from sports, either by nature or as a defensive reaction to the masculine experience of being detached from Dad, brothers, and his own body. To compensate for his low self-worth, he may become a perfectionist. Toxic perfectionism represents the psyche's attempt to obtain acceptance.

"Studies of three- and four-year-old children conducted by Ross Parke and Kevin MacDonald provide evidence to this link between fathers' physical play and how children get along with peers. Observing children in twenty-minute play sessions with their dads, the researchers found that kids whose fathers showed high levels of physical play were most popular among their peers. An interesting and significant qualifier emerged in this study, however: Kids with highly physical dads were nondirective, noncoercive. The children whose dads were highly physical but also highly bossy received the lowest popularity scores. Other studies have provided similar evidence.

Across the board, researchers have found that children seem to develop the best social skills when their dads keep the tone of their interactions positive and allow kids to take part in directing the course of play."[76]

Many athletically inclined women were subject to social mockery as girls because of these innate gifts. Some girls may have been more into rough-and-tumble and less into dolls because of nature and/or nurture. If other elements, such as homo-emotional wounding and/or hetero-emotional wounding, were present, then this characteristic may have just been another contributing factor in the development of same-sex attractions.

In the healing process, it is very important for men to learn to be men among men, and for women to learn to be women among women. Learning to participate in group sports for men and feminine activities for women is an important aspect for healing and experiencing gender identity.

> David was the teacher's pet throughout elementary, junior, and senior high school. He received many awards for high academic achievement and good behavior. However, he never knew how to relate to the other students. He was a little adult, not knowing how to be a child. He knew too much, too soon, as he was his mother's confidant and best friend.

> Chris was a very religious boy. He served in his church's youth group, participated in retreats, studied the Bible, and mentored other children. However, he was extremely distant from his father and believed he was different from the rest of the boys. At school, many called him a "faggot," "sissy," or "queer." He hated himself and longed to be loved by a man.

> Randy was athletically challenged. He did not know how to throw a ball, swing a bat, or run fast. His dad was busy teaching other boys, and Randy felt neglected and inferior. Being more sensitive and withdrawn, he never asked his father for instruction. Instead, he carried this wound throughout his childhood and adolescence. He was never chosen for any of the teams when the kids would play games at school. During recess, he would sit on the sidelines, watching enviously as the other kids played.

CULTURAL WOUNDS

Cultural wounds are experienced from the media, educational system, entertainment industry, Internet, and pornography. These influences lead to the molestation of the mind. Today, people are buying into the "myth" that homosexuality is a natural, normal, innate state of being. This is not true. There is no scientific evidence to prove this theory. Some say that several animals are naturally homosexual. This is a distortion of creation to fit someone's desperate attempt to legitimize a condition born out of emotional brokenness. "Preferential homosexuality is not found naturally in any infrahuman mammalian species. Masculine/feminine differences and heterosexual preferences are quite consistent up through the phylogenetic scale."[77]

Communism and the homosexual movement have both utilized the same strategy, which is known as the Big Lie Theory. It is a very simple principle that works like this: If you repeat anything long enough, and loud enough, over time it will become known as a fact. Some examples of these big lies, turning myths into facts, are: "Homosexuals are born this way"; "Once gay, always gay"; "Homosexuals cannot change"; and "Ten percent of the population is homosexual." These are all myths. They are all false.

If you take a frog and place him in boiling water, he will die immediately. If you take a frog and place him in mild water, he will happily swim. Gradually, you begin to turn up the heat. If you do it ever so slightly, he will not notice the temperature change. Eventually, the water reaches boiling level, and without notice, he dies.

And so it has gone with our cultural attitude toward homosexuality. Years ago, there was outrage and misunderstanding. Now, there is acceptance and misunderstanding. Members of the homosexual movement have planted myths into our culture and continued to repeat these myths over a period of decades. Now, without our noticing it, homosexuality is accepted as an alternate lifestyle. For a more comprehensive overview of how this was achieved, please read chapter 14 about the agenda, strategies, and goals of the "Gay Rights Movement."

Many people believe these myths about homosexuality, which are propagated by the media (newspaper, radio, TV, magazines), the entertainment industry, the educational system, academia, the psychological community, and religious institutions. Through constant repetition of these myths, many intelligent and well-intentioned people have come to believe these lies.

Now most schools, colleges, and universities throughout the world are teaching our children on the platform of human rights and social equality, that homosexual people are born this way and cannot change. The promotion of these myths is another factor that may influence someone to become homosexual, or pull him over the line. This is cultural indoctrination for impressionable youths who are still confused about their sexual identities. There is presently a 50 to 60 percent divorce rate in the United States, which means many children are growing up without a same-sex parent. The National Fatherhood Initiative reported that by 1990, approximately 14 million children lived in mother-only households. This makes these children more vulnerable to cultural influences.

In the words of some homosexual activists, "The first order of business is the desensitization of the American public concerning gays and gay right. . . . You can forget about trying to persuade the masses that homosexuality is a good thing. But if you can get them to think that it is just another thing with a shrug of their shoulders, then your battle for legal and social rights is virtually won."[78]

On the Internet, a young child may download pornography, seeing every imaginable and unimaginable sexual act between two men, two women, two or more of anyone or anything. This is sexual abuse and the rape of our children's minds. Also, in many schools, sex-education curricula are teaching the normalcy of homosexuality, where to get it, and how to do it.

American TV shows, major motion pictures, and local news reports embrace homosexuality and homosexual relationships. In this way, more and more wounded and love-starved children are being deprived of *true* liberation by being enrolled into this big lie. Homosexuality is a developmental disorder that leads to immense "dis-ease" and emotional unrest.

The Gay Rights Movement, the media, the educational system, and the mental-health profession tell us that homosexuality is normal and natural. Let us observe some of the statistics about homosexual behavior and see if this condition is, in fact, normal:

- The Kinsey Institute published a study of homosexual males living in San Francisco which reports that 43 percent had sex with 500 or more partners, 28 percent had sex with 1,000 or more partners, and 79 percent said that over half of their sex partners were strangers.[79]
- An American Public Health Association survey reported that 78 percent of homosexual people surveyed have been infected by a sexually transmitted disease.[80]
- A National Lesbian-Gay Health Foundation report revealed that alcohol and drug abuse were three times more prevalent among homosexual individuals than among heterosexual individuals.[81]
- A report by the U.S. Department of Health and Human Services,

Task Force on Youth Suicide, in 1989 revealed that one-third of all teenage suicides are committed by those who suffer from homosexual problems. This is an extremely high percentage considering that only 1 to 3 percent of the population is homosexual.

- Homosexual men are six times more likely to have attempted suicide than heterosexual men.[82]
- McWhirter and Mattison, both therapists who are homosexual, conducted a survey of 156 male couples. The results were reported in their book, *The Male Couple*. They found that 95 percent of the couples were unfaithful, and the 5 percent that were faithful had been together five or fewer years. This statistic is glaring in comparison to surveys conducted about the fidelity of heterosexual couples. The *American Journal of Public Health* reported a survey conducted with over 2,000 respondents and revealed that during a five-year period, only 6.4 percent of married couples were unfaithful, which means that 93.6 percent were faithful.[83] The National Opinion Research Center in Chicago reported that, from over 3,400 respondents surveyed, about 3 to 4 percent of currently married people have a sexual partner besides their spouse in a given year, and about 15 to 17 percent of married people have a sexual partner other than their spouse while married.[84] These results are opposite to the 95 percent of unfaithful homosexual couples. McWhirter and Mattison themselves state, "The expectation for outside sexual activity was the rule for male couples and the exception for heterosexuals."[85]
- "Homosexuals are at least 12 times more likely to molest children than heterosexuals; homosexual teachers are at least 7 times more likely to molest a pupil; homosexual teachers are estimated to have committed at least 25 percent of pupil molestation; 40 percent of molestation assaults were made by those who engage in homosexuality."[86]

These statistics show us clearly that homosexual behavior is neither normal nor natural. Members of the homosexual community argue that social intolerance and prejudice cause these destructive behaviors. I believe there is some merit to this argument. However, the deeper reason for these unhealthy behaviors is the emotional brokenness that caused the homosexual condition in the first place. The social prejudice merely exacerbates the already-existing pain lodged deep in their souls.

Kurt, an honors student at a magnet high school, became addicted to male pornography on the Internet. His father installed many devices on the computer to keep him from accessing those Web sites. However, Kurt was able to break each code and continued to view pornography regularly. What he saw and what he read enrolled him further and further into the homosexual lifestyle. This led to compulsive masturbation and isolation from his peers.

Nathan's wife sent him to see me in hopes that I could "fix" him. Nathan revealed to his wife that he was "gay" and would seek divorce after twenty years of marriage. Nathan had repressed his same-sex attractions for almost fifty years. Now, he would seek to fulfill those "natural" desires. Having read the media reports about the "gay gene" and the biological explanations for homosexuality, he was convinced that he was born "gay." He eventually moved out, divorced his wife, went into the homosexual lifestyle, and died of AIDS while seeking Mr. Right.

OTHER FACTORS

Divorce, death, intrauterine experiences, adoption, and religion are some other influential factors that may cause a SSAD condition. If the parents divorce, if a parent dies, or another close family member dies, the child may interpret this experience as personal rejection and further detach from others and self.

Children naturally self-blame for their parents' divorce, and may even do so regarding the death of a parent. A harrowing message resonates deep in the unconscious of the child: "If only I was better, if only I had done _____ , then Mommy and Daddy would not have divorced, or Daddy would not have died." This thought may be completely unconscious to the adult-child.

"The fact that most grown children of divorce are alienated from at least one parent and a substantial minority is alienated from both is, we believe, a legitimate cause for societal concern. It means that many of these young people are especially vulnerable to influences outside the family, such as from boyfriends or girlfriends, other peers, adult authority figures, and the media. Although not necessarily negative, these influences are unlikely to be an adequate substitute for a stable and positive relationship with a parent."[87]

Intrauterine experiences may contribute to the child's detaching from one or both parents. If the mother was experiencing difficulty in her relationship with her husband while carrying the child or if she felt rejected, unloved, or unwanted by him or she experienced any other painful feelings during pregnancy, the unborn child within may have experienced these thoughts and feelings as though they were directed at him or her. Psychiatrist Dr. Thomas Verny states, "The womb is the child's first world. How he experiences it—as friendly or hostile—does create personality and character predispositions. The womb, in a very real sense, establishes the child's expectations. If it has been a warm, loving environment, the child is likely to expect the outside world to be the same. This produces a predisposition toward trust, openness, extroversion, and self-confidence. The world will be his oyster, just as the womb has been. If that environment has been hostile, the child will anticipate that his new world will be equally uninviting. He will be predisposed toward suspiciousness, distrust, and introversion. Relating to others will be hard, and so will self-assertion. Life will be more difficult for him than for a child who had a good womb experience."[88]

Dr. Verny cites study after study conducted throughout the States and Europe, showing clearly that the first life experiences in the womb shape a child's personality. The results of his investigation were the following: 1) The fetus can see, hear, experience, taste, and feel; 2) What the child feels and perceives begins to shape his attitude and expectations about life; 3) The chief source of those shaping messages is the child's mother; and 4) The father's feelings toward his wife and unborn child also influence the fetus.[89] Dr. Verny calls this field prenatal psychology. You can read case histories and numerous studies that describe the effects of prenatal and birth experiences upon the personality of the child in his book, *The Secret Life of the Unborn Child* (New York: Dell, 1981).

Dr. Monika Lukesch, a psychologist at Constantine University in Germany, studied two thousand pregnant women. She concluded that the mother's attitude toward her unborn child had the single greatest effect on how the infant matured.[90] Dr. Dennis Stott studied over thirteen hundred children and their families. He estimates that a woman involved in a stormy marriage runs a 237 percent greater risk of bearing a psychologically or physically damaged child than a woman in a secure relationship.[91]

Leanne Payne, a noted pastoral therapist, speaks about assisting several individuals heal from the effects of painful intrauterine experiences. "It is no small thing, for example, to see a person healed who has been hospitalized, perhaps several times, due to rejections they experienced *before* birth."[92]

Adoption may also contribute to an attachment disorder with either the same-sex and/or opposite-sex parent. If the child does not securely attach with his or her same-sex adopted parent, then a Same-Sex Attachment Disorder may ensue.

> Sarah clung to her adopted mother. She was constantly needy and at other times rebuffing. After high school, she sought other women to fulfill her constant need for attention and affection. Her relationships were short-lived. Beneath her homosexual desire was an ambivalent child who felt unloved and rejected by her birth mother.

Another contributing factor may be religion. Particular religious beliefs may impact the child in a negative way if there is already a detachment from either one or both parents. Parents are the first representatives of God for children. They are the visible manifestation of an invisible God. They symbolize our role model for masculinity (Mr. God) and our role model of femininity (Mrs. God). God represents an extension of the father figure. If the child rejects his parents, it follows that he may easily reject his parents' religious beliefs. This distances him from God, parents, authority figures, and a sense of belonging in the world. Dr. Nicolosi states that the "coming out" process is actually the manifestation of a defensive detachment on a social scale.[93]

> Alan never bonded with his father or mother. He never felt as if he belonged to his family. In his therapy, he eventually retrieved an intrauterine memory of experiencing intense pain and anguish. He grieved as he reexperienced those dark memories. He was born feeling unwanted and unloved: "I don't belong here. Why did you have me?" Later, he spoke to his mother and asked her what she experienced during those nine months while she carried him in her womb. She told him that his dad was having an affair with another woman at that time, and she felt unwanted and unloved. In an instant, Alan realized that he had internalized and personalized her feelings.

> Ivan's mother attempted an abortion while in her second trimester. The attempt failed and Ivan was born. He always felt an animosity toward his mother and distance from his father. Similar to Alan, he felt as if he did not belong, did not fit in, and was not meant to be alive. Until he questioned his mother about his birth experience, he never knew about her attempt to abort him.

Jerry was perfectionistic. If only he got it right, then he would be accepted and loved. After receiving Communion at church for the first time, he went home and broke a vase that meant so much to his mother. He never forgave himself for that mistake, and consequently grew more distant from God and his parents' religious beliefs. He felt inadequate, no matter how hard he tried to succeed. Jerry was hypervigilant in his efforts to be the perfect little boy. Being more sensitive and withdrawn, he never shared with his parents how bad he felt about himself. To him, God became his ultimate accuser and judge.

Summary

These ten influences—*heredity, temperament, hetero-emotional wounds, homo-emotional wounds, sibling wounds/family dynamics, body-image wounds, sexual abuse, social or peer wounds, cultural wounds,* and *other factors: divorce/death/intrauterine experiences/adoption/religion*—represent major factors that contribute to the creation of same-sex attractions in men and women. By addressing each one of these issues, by uncovering their meaning and impact, the individual may heal and fully recover the ability to experience his own gender identity and a sense of self-worth.

A final observation I have made in working with clients over the past years is this:

> *The greater the detachment from feelings, thoughts, and needs in the present, and the greater the detachment from the unresolved wounds and unmet needs of the past, the greater or more intense the desire will be for homosexual relations.*

The more a person is unaware of his thoughts, feelings, and needs in present relationships, the stronger the need and energy attachment will be to engage in or fantasize about homosexual behavior. Sex then becomes a way back to the body and soul, either through masturbation (self-sex) or sex with another person. He is trying to obtain his lost self or disassociated parts. Therefore, seeking sex or compulsive masturbation represents a reparative drive to restore the broken self. The frustration is that this never works!

CHAPTER THREE

Steve

I asked several individuals that I have had the privilege of counseling to share their stories with you. In their words, you will further explore and understand the process of healing. I am deeply grateful to each one of them for their courage to heal and reveal themselves before you. I am confident their words of hope will bless you. Names, dates, and other details have been changed to maintain confidentiality.

Both of my parents were born during the Depression. They entered into a life of fear, desperation, and pessimism. The shadows from my ancestry passed from my grandparents to my parents to me. My father attempted to resolve his problems, unsuccessfully, during his mid-twenties. My mother lived with her parents for a few years after graduating college, thinking that she'd never marry. When my father was twenty-eight and my mother twenty-five, they met and soon married. Five years later, my sister was born. After another four years, I was born. My birth was difficult for my mother. I weighed ten pounds, and my mother is a small woman—not an easy task for her. I entered the world with difficulty.

When I was only ten months old, I got sick, and the doctors hospitalized me for one week. For the next several years, I found myself visiting doctors often, with various respiratory problems. From my early years, I carried a feeling that I was close to death, that I was weak, and that I would not survive. I became very disconnected from my body and felt as if it were a foreign object. I avoided sports, roughness, and other physical activities that might make me feel as if I would die and cause me to feel unsafe.

Early in my life, I shut down emotionally. For whatever reason—possibly misperception or lack of skill—my needs were often not met. I had problems connecting with my father. Because of his problems that precluded him from fully connecting with me, I was not able to fully internalize his masculinity. Most boys go through a phase in their toddler years in which they become more independent from their mothers and identify more with their own gender—their father or some other masculine role model. My father and I never connected. He, unknowingly, may have rejected me, and I, in turn, rejected him. I figured if males treat me that way, I don't want to be like them. I quickly began to close myself off from others. I sought my mother out for comfort. When I began school, I soon realized that if I brought home good grades, my parents might notice me and give the attention I wanted, needed, and craved. At the time, I thought that what I did constituted how good a person I was. I worked very hard to do well academically, to be the best student, and never misbehave. When I was seven, I began playing the violin. I soon had two oppressive teachers: one, a tyrannical man, prone to violent outbursts; the other, a stiff, elderly German woman who was very demanding. I shut down more. My life was one of school, practice, study, and pursuing adult events, such as attending concerts. I further buried my longing for Dad's love and affection, Mom's acceptance of me as a male, and my desire to just be and live.

I always felt as if something horrible was just around the corner: death, injury, accidents, and the list goes on. I continued to build my isolated life with more academics, more concerts, more practicing. I wanted to be seen! I thought it was the key to my happiness. Deep down, I longed to fit in as one of the guys—to play sports, to have fun, to throw away the coat and tie and be a boy! On the outside, to my parents, family, and teachers, I was the perfect little boy with good grades, a gifted talent with an interest in academics. In a few instances, I experienced belonging with my own gender: when I visited my outgoing, loving uncle or when I got the courage to play rough with other boys. Inevitably, something always happened that made me run back into my isolated life: sickness, a "bad" test score, or getting yelled at in school. I thought that the cause of these "misfortunes" was that no one was disciplining me enough—because I wasn't *doing* enough. I had some friends in school. They were mostly those who were in the same boat as me: overachievers and other "doers." I found solace listening to music, which warmed my soul. What my soul really wanted was to be a boy, to be loved by Dad, accepted by Mom, and able to make mistakes and break beyond my safe world.

My self-worth was very low. I thought that everyone else was better looking, richer, smarter, and faster than me. My sister became rebellious in her search for love and approval. I saw how her forcefulness caused my parents pain. I did not want to cause such turmoil in the family. After all, I heard my mother say, "What would the neighbors think?"

I began to enter puberty around age twelve or thirteen. I didn't want to begin to shave, to have a lower voice, or to have hair around my penis. My father advised me that if I had any questions about sex, there was a book in the den I could read. So, the inevitable happened: I became an adolescent. The other boys seemed excited about it, but I wasn't. I noticed that I was idolizing older boys at school and wishing that I were them. When some tried to make a connection with me, I got scared and pushed them away.

I noticed some attraction to women. I bought some posters and pornography of women. My sister and my mother found the posters one day and both made comments, which I heard as an, "Oh, no. He's sexually attracted to women?" I became scared of being intimate with women and avoided going beyond a friendship level with them, for fear of rejection and out of shame for being interested in them.

I noticed that I began feeling sexually attracted to other boys and to young men. I denied it and thought it was just a phase. When I was about fifteen, I befriended another needy boy my age. We were both musicians and began to spend time together. He started asking me questions about things like masturbation and sex. He slowly, but surely, began to seduce me. One day, we had sex. The drive to do it and the neediness were too great to say no. I can remember that very first time as if it were yesterday. I didn't really want to do it, but I didn't say no. The faded voice in my mind that didn't want it went away at that point. We began to have sex on a regular basis. He began to get pornography and exposed me to it.

Our "relationship" continued for a few years. He would coax me to his house by saying he would give me sexual favors, just to satisfy his hunger. I didn't say no. I let the need for male attention and touch drive me. He soon began telling me about places where men got together to have sex: in bathrooms, in parks, in bars. I began to explore this world when I entered college. On the surface, I was still the calm, intellectual musician. On the inside, I became a raging sex addict, seeking out sexual contact with men, often a couple of times a week. It was so invigorating, so energizing, and so *rebellious!* I wasn't anything but nice to people on the outside, and on the inside, I was having anonymous sex. This continued for a year or two.

When I was nineteen, I decided I didn't want to continue this lifestyle. I began to look for answers. I didn't want to be gay. I didn't want to have sex with men. Something was missing. It just didn't fit for me. I started writing to many different organizations. I contacted priests, religious groups, and psychological groups. Many answered back with their answers: Accept yourself as you are, or just accept Christ and you'll heal. Neither seemed to be the answer I was looking for. Then, I saw an article in a major American magazine about homosexuality. It discussed the possibility of genetic causes and of how many lived happily in that lifestyle. At the very end of the article, there was a brief discussion of psychological professionals who assist people in exploring why they have homosexual attractions and how to work through them and meet the needs that are underneath the attractions. I quickly wrote to one of the psychologists. He quickly answered my letter, and I soon began sessions with him. He taught me many valuable cognitive tools, including how to make friends, gain more self-worth, etc. His theory was that making nonerotic friendships with other guys and men would cause the homosexual attractions to greatly decrease. I began to feel better about myself. I hung out with other guys and became obsessed with being with guys as much as possible. I idolized them. I sought the best-looking ones to befriend. I wanted them for *me.* I was looking for my masculinity in them.

I was happier for a few years. Then, when I was twenty-two, I moved to a big city after college. All of a sudden, I was alone again—no friends, no access to masculinity, and no one to notice me. I started sexually acting out again. Being in a big city was not helpful! So many bathrooms, parks, and bars! I began to go home with guys, thinking that maybe if the sex was not anonymous, it wouldn't be so emotionally painful. It still hurt my soul. I thought I could continue that life and still marry a woman. Maybe I could marry a bisexual woman. That way, I wouldn't have to stop my behavior, and I could still have the coveted life: a wife and kids and a nice home and live a double life. Something in my soul said, "NO. It's not what I want." I terminated sessions with my therapist.

I began the search again for more help. I tried to avoid acting out, knowing that it was too painful, but I was not always successful. I joined a national religious group that claimed to heal people out of their homosexuality. Discipline, prayer, and "white-knuckling it" seemed to be their motto. I began to realize that many in the group really didn't heal their homosexuality; they just suppressed it and tried to pray it away. It didn't work for me, and I felt very oppressed and afraid to talk about the attractions and behavior. I continued to act out.

My deepest hurt and shadow, the acting out, became my strongest impetus and ally for seeking more help. I thought that if I joined a therapy group, I would grow much more. I found a group with others working on transitioning from homosexuality to heterosexuality. Because the acting out continued, I also started individual therapy with Richard. I also became involved in men's work, including an initiating weekend with New Warrior, a group that helps men find and care for their souls. The tide in my life began to change. At this point in my life, I started to switch from living in my mind to living with my heart. This was one of the most important moments in my life.

I started an intensive healing plan. I attended two healing groups, attended therapy, and began to seek out help from others who were in various forms of recovery. So many of the techniques I used were new and so much more powerful than anything I had ever experienced: emotional processing, psychodrama, nonerotic touch with other men, and focusing on emotions. I began to get to know the little boy inside me that felt so hurt and longed so much to feel loved by me and by others. I spent many nights, days, hours, and sessions crying, getting angry, and learning how to father myself and to love myself. It was crucial for me to investigate further what was beneath the homosexual attractions and feelings. I uncovered more issues that had caused me to never identify with my gender: body wounds, fear of death, sexual abuse, an abdicating father, an emotionally needy mother and sister, and many other issues. Once I began a solid program of bioenergetic work, nonerotic holding with other men, and emotional awareness, the acting out stopped. For a while, I thought it was just a temporary occurrence, like it had been before. The freedom lasted! I have been sexually sober since October 1996. I know now that underneath the urge is a much deeper, nonsexual need. Now I meet those needs in healthy ways.

There was more to work on than just the behavioral change. I wanted to heal more of what was causing the homosexual feelings. Currently, in my healing plan, I am becoming more in touch with and comfortable in my *healthy* body. I am processing feelings I have for things that went wrong in relationship with my dad and mom and continuing to receive healthy touch from others, and many other things. Although I have not fully healed my same-sex attractions, the strength and power of the feelings have diminished as a result of the consistent work on my heart. If homosexual feelings do come up, I search inside for what is ailing me. The attractions might arise when something from my past gets triggered: abandonment, sexual abuse, feelings of sickness and death, or inadequacy with women. I also notice, to my delight, that as I identify more with my own masculinity, I feel more sexually attracted to women. I know and am confident that continuing my healing plan will lead me to further freedom and internal healing.

While doing healing work with others, I have realized that many people have different symptoms of their pain: alcoholism, drug abuse, sexual issues, etc. Down deep in each and every one of us is a golden child just waiting for healthy love and healing. For those of us healing homosexuality, we have the added burden of societal pressures. Political correctness and pressure have made it unpopular to seek change from homosexuality to heterosexuality. We often get shunned by some for having homosexual feelings and by others for not "accepting" our sexuality as it is. I have witnessed it within myself and in others that for those who want to heal from homosexuality, it is possible. Yes, this idea is new and for the most part unaccepted and uncharted territory, but we can do it. The gift of freedom is available for those who wish to take it.

Comment

Today Steve is married and creating the family of his dreams.

PART II:

Healing

CHAPTER FOUR

Process of Healing: Four Stages of Recovery

"The descender makes an exit—from ordinary and respectable life—through the wound. The wound now is thought of as a door. . . . The way down and out doesn't require poverty, homelessness, physical deprivation, dishwasher work, necessarily, but it does seem to require a fall from status, from a human being to a spider, from a middle-class person to a derelict. The emphasis is on the consciousness of the fall."[1]

—Robert Bly

Through my own journey of healing, and through twelve years of helping others, I have developed a four-stage model of recovery. It has proved successful for those who sincerely desire to change. This process applies to those who have been actively homosexual as well as those who have not engaged in sexual activity but are experiencing same-sex desires.

Marriage is not the solution for anyone who has homosexual feelings, because a woman can never meet the homo-emotional needs of a man, and a man can never meet the homo-emotional needs of a woman.[2] In the process of recovery, first a man must heal with other men, and a woman must heal with other women.

Before I sought help, some of my well-intentioned friends told me, "Richard, just find the right woman and she'll straighten you out," or "Just pray hard enough, and God will take it all away. If not, then you're doing something wrong." Well, I wish it would have been that simple, but it was not. I prayed and prayed for God to take the desires away, but He did not. I married, hoping it would straighten me out, but the same-sex desires only intensified. I came to understand that I had been praying the wrong prayer for nearly twenty years. What I needed to pray was: "God, please show me the meaning of my same-sex desires." Later, I understood that God would never take them away, because they had a deeper meaning that I needed to discover, heal, and ultimately fulfill in healthy, non-sexual relationships.

I have divided the process of healing into four stages:

Four Stages of Healing Homosexuality	
Stage One:	Transitioning
Stage Two:	Grounding
Stage Three:	Healing the Homo-Emotional Wounds
Stage Four:	Healing the Hetero-Emotional Wounds

This is a linear and developmental model. However, it does not work as neatly and cleanly as I am about to describe. The individual in transition may jump from Stage One to Stage Three, back to Stage Two, then to Stage One again. It all depends upon the growth, maturity, and needs of the individual in recovery.

The benefit of having this four-stage model is that it represents a road map of recovery. If someone jumps from Stage One to Stage Three, he will eventually need to return to the previous stage and continue to work on and work through those necessary tasks. It's like taking a trip by car from New York to California. Somewhere around Chicago, he remembers a very painful experience he had as a child while living in Wisconsin. So he boards a plane, goes to Wisconsin, takes care of healing that wound, and gets back on a plane, returning once again to Chicago. Then he continues on the road from Chicago to California.

You may think, if he could fly from Chicago to Wisconsin, then why can't he just fly from New York to California and do away with the road trip altogether? There are no shortcuts in life when it comes to matters of the heart. In the process of healing, he is reclaiming his lost self, those parts of his character that he has either buried or not even met yet. This takes time, patience, and diligent effort. The price is high to get one's life back, but the rewards are well worth the efforts. Without such efforts, I would not be alive today. Those who try to fly without doing their groundwork may end up crashing in mid-air.

The following parallel stages summarize this treatment plan:

Four Stages of the Therapeutic Treatment Plan	
Stage One:	Behavioral therapy
Stage Two:	Cognitive therapy and inner-child healing
Stage Three:	Psychodynamic therapy: Healing same-sex wounds
Stage Four:	Psychodynamic therapy: Healing opposite-sex wounds

Often "the process of healing goes from bad, to worse, and then better."[3] People come into counseling in crisis when they feel bad. As they discover the source(s) of the problem(s), things get worse as they experience the pain. Finally, things get better when healing occurs and they experience love.

Four Stages of Healing Homosexuality

1. **Transitioning (Behavioral therapy)**
   - Cutting off from sexual behavior
   - Developing a support network
   - Building self-worth and experiencing value in relationship with God
2. **Grounding (Cognitive therapy)**
   - Continuing with the support network
   - Continuing to build self-worth and experience value in relationship with God
   - Building skills: assertiveness training, communication skills, problem-solving techniques
   - Beginning inner-child healing: identifying thoughts, feelings, and needs
3. **Healing the Homo-Emotional Wounds (Psychodynamic therapy)**
   - Continuing all tasks of Stage Two
   - Discovering the root causes of homo-emotional wounds
   - Beginning the process of grieving, forgiving, and taking responsibility
   - Developing healthy, healing same-sex relationships
4. **Healing the Hetero-Emotional Wounds (Psychodynamic therapy)**
   - Continuing all tasks of Stage Two
   - Discovering the root causes of hetero-emotional wounds
   - Continuing the process of grieving, forgiving, and taking responsibility
   - Developing healthy, healing opposite-sex relationships and learning about the opposite sex

© Richard Cohen, M.A., January 1999

Stage One: Transitioning (Behavioral Therapy)

In Stage One, the individual realizes that he has a problem and wants help. Perhaps he tried to suppress his homosexual feelings unsuccessfully. Perhaps he married, hoping his same-sex desires would disappear, but they have not. Perhaps in the midst of many relationships, he feels empty, hurt, and frustrated. Perhaps he is very young and confused about his sexual orientation. There are many different scenarios, but the underlying common denominator is a deep desire to change. It does not matter if the individual is thirteen or seventy-three. Change is possible at any age. A key factor for change is personal motivation. Without a deep-seated commitment to change, the process of healing is virtually impossible.

In Stage One, there are three tasks:

1. Cutting off from sexual behavior
2. Developing a support network
3. Building self-worth and experiencing value in relationship with God

FIRST TASK: CUTTING OFF FROM SEXUAL BEHAVIOR
In the transitional phase, the individual needs to cut ties with old playgrounds, playmates, and playthings:

1. Playgrounds—Not go to the places where he associated with homosexual men or homosexual behavior, such as bars, bathrooms, pornographic movies, and parks (anyplace he could engage in homosexual activity).
2. Playmates—Cut ties with homosexual friends and partners. Not associate with anyone who will tempt or seduce him into homosexual activity.
3. Playthings—Not purchase pornography or any other homosexual paraphernalia associated with homosexual behavior.

It is equally important to cut ties with sources of negative influence in the world. He may temporarily avoid reading papers and magazines and listening to news reports that support and encourage homosexuality. He needs to surround himself with voices of affirmation and hope. This may seem quite radical to some. Later, I will explain more clearly why it is necessary to separate from these external activities and negative influences.

SECOND TASK: DEVELOPING A SUPPORT NETWORK
The central organizing factor(s) in the life of anyone experiencing same-sex attractions may be homosexual relationships, sexual fantasies, compulsive

masturbation, hangouts (bars, baths, parks, restrooms), or pornography. It is insufficient to tell someone to cut off these relationships and behaviors. It is important to realize that these people, places, and things represent a legitimate need for the individual. The drive for bonding is genuine. However, only healthy, healing, loving, nonsexual relationships will fulfill the deeper needs. A support network must be developed to provide the nurturance and healing environment in which he may heal from past wounds and receive proper love, guidance, and encouragement. Healthy relationships and healthy behaviors replace sexual behavior or fantasies.

The support network may consist of, but not be limited to, family, friends, and spouse; spiritual community; support groups; telephone, e-mail, visiting people, mentors; exercise, diet, sports, therapeutic massage; study of literature; and counseling. Meditation, prayer, and spiritual food will be discussed in the following section.

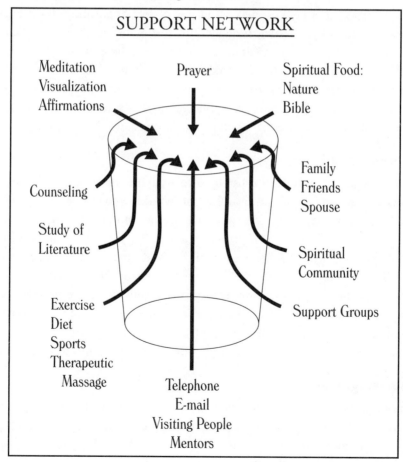

SUPPORT NETWORK

Meditation
Visualization
Affirmations

Prayer

Spiritual Food:
Nature
Bible

Counseling

Family
Friends
Spouse

Study of
Literature

Spiritual
Community

Exercise
Diet
Sports
Therapeutic
Massage

Support Groups

Telephone
E-mail
Visiting People
Mentors

© Richard Cohen, M.A., January 1999

Family, friends, and spouse

Support from parents, brothers or sisters, relatives, spouse, and close friends will aid in this process of change. When the channels of communication are open, it is good for him to share about his situation and needs. If communication is difficult at this time, perhaps in the future he may create that opportunity.

There are basically four types of friendships that will aid in the process of healing:

1) Heterosexual friends that know about the struggle and are supportive;
2) Heterosexual friends that do not know about the struggle and are good friends;
3) Mentors who assist in the process of reparenting the individual; and
4) Fellow strugglers who are coming out of homosexuality.

An attraction to a heterosexual friend is a perfect opportunity for healing and growth. "Heterosexual, sexually attractive male friendships with men for whom the client feels an erotic attraction offer the greatest opportunity for healing. Only through such associations can there be the transformation from erotic attractions to true friendship—that is, the demystifying of the distant male. . . . This transformational shift from sexual to fraternal (i.e., eros to philia) is the essential healing experience of male homosexuality."[4]

Spiritual community

The spiritual community must involve itself in the healing process of these brave men, women, and adolescents who wish to change. Those who wish to come out of homosexuality may not accomplish this without the help of others. They need *time, touch,* and *talk.* True and lasting healing will take place when God's love is manifest and experienced through people. The 12-step movement has developed so powerfully because of the inability of the religious community to successfully solve the problems of men, women, and children. Therefore, the time is overdue for children of God to stand up for each other and be honest about their heartaches, headaches, and pains. We must reach out and put our faith into practice.

Support groups

Transitioning support groups: These are support groups of individuals involved in the same process of healing. It may be a gender-specific group—all men or all women—but this is not necessary. It is important that this group be facilitated by either 1) someone who has transitioned successfully and has been "sexually sober" for at least three or more years; and/or 2) someone who understands the process of healing homosexuality.

Twelve-step support groups: Other support groups that may be helpful if there are any other addictive behaviors include:

- SA—Sexaholics Anonymous
- AA—Alcoholics Anonymous
- NA—Narcotics Anonymous
- CODA—Codependents Anonymous
- SIA—Survivors of Incest Anonymous
- HA—Homosexuals Anonymous

Make sure that any recovery group under consideration is not a group specifically for "gays and lesbians." The person in transition should be aware that the prevailing attitude of the mental-health profession and recovery movement is "gay affirmative therapy," or in support of being homosexual. In some of these 12-step groups, many members or their leaders will say to the individual, "It's OK, just accept who you truly are, just be gay, stop fighting it." This is the danger of attending other recovery groups. The individual must bring his own agenda into the group. He must state clearly his personal desire to come out of homosexuality, asking the group members to support him in this quest. If the group cannot honor and support this desire, then it is not a safe place for him to be. The issue here is *self-determination* versus *social advocacy*. Any individual coming out of homosexuality must be clear about his intentions, rather than following what others think he should or should not do.

I have a great appreciation for 12-step groups. I do, however, have one bias. In the beginning stages of group work the individual is asked to identify with his presenting problem. For example he repeats, "Hello. My name is Richard, and I am a rageaholic." I understand the psychology behind this methodology is to bring someone out of denial and into the light. However, after some time in recovery, after he accomplishes some stability and works through the denial phase, I believe it is important to make a shift in identification. He then says, "Hello. My name is Richard, and I am a son of God." Now, the focus is not on *behavior* but on *being*, on inherent value.

Religious-based support groups include:

- EXODUS International—Umbrella organization for Ex-Gay Christian Ministries

- Homosexuals Anonymous (HA)—Christian-based recovery network
- Courage/Encourage—Catholic Ex-Gay Ministry/Parent's Ministry
- JONAH—Jews Offering New Alternatives to Homosexuality
- Evergreen International—Mormon Ex-Gay Ministry
- Transforming Congregations—Methodist Ex-Gay Ministry
- One by One—Presbyterian Ex-Gay Ministry
- PFOX—Christian ministry for parents, spouses, family members, and friends
- Pastoral Care Ministries—Recovery through healing prayer*

Men's or women's groups: Joining a same-sex group will help those in recovery relate with members of their own gender in healthy, nonsexual ways. They will learn new ways to be with men and women, gaining more confidence in themselves. There may be a men's council and women's support groups in the area. Many religious organizations have same-gender support groups.

Telephone/E-mail outreach

There will be many ups and downs along the way. Discontinuing old behaviors, relationships, and hangouts will leave him feeling insecure, lonely, and vulnerable. Therefore, when in need, he must be able to reach out to any number of people. The recovering person must develop a phone/e-mail list consisting of people in his support network. The support network constitutes his new family of choice.

Exercise, diet, sports, and therapeutic massage

Physical exercise is important for individuals coming out of homosexuality. Many are quite disassociated from their bodies. Exercise, diet, and sports help to heal many body-image wounds and peer wounds. It is important for the person in recovery to learn to be at ease with himself among peers through related same-sex activities.

"Abstaining from caffeine is helpful. Caffeine is a psychomotor stimulant and causes the hypothalamus to increase fear, anger, and sexual drive. Drinking decaffeinated beverages in recovery is helpful because any feelings may lead a sex addict to act out. Not drinking caffeine will heighten emotional well-being and a feeling of emotional stability," according to Dr. Christopher Austin.[5]

---

*See the list of National Resources at the back of the book.

Working with an experienced massage therapist may accelerate the healing process. Therapeutic massage is a tool to release and heal the pains locked in the musculature of the body of a physically or sexually abused person. It is important that the individual ground himself in the first two stages of recovery before using this method of healing. It is equally important to work with the right massage therapist—someone who is safe, sensitive, knowledgeable, experienced with survivors of abuse, and secure in his own gender identity. It may be helpful for the mentor to accompany the individual to his session and/or make sure the therapist is safe.

Study of literature

Bibliotherapy is the study of related literature. There are excellent books on the causes and treatment of homosexuality. Reading such books will help him understand what he is going through and help him identify causal factors that lead him into sexual behavior or fantasies. Studying appropriate literature on healing homosexuality is extremely helpful. (See References at the back of the book.)

Counseling

It is important to find a therapist who understands the nature of homosexuality and the process of healing. Such a counselor needs to establish a very close relationship with the client. Maintaining a distant or aloof therapeutic relationship merely exacerbates the already-present defense detachment in the individual. A Same-Sex Attachment Disorder contraindicates the use of authoritarianism.

I strongly recommend a same-sex counselor during the first three stages of healing. A counselor of the opposite sex will be appropriate in the final stage. First, men need to heal with men, and women need to heal with women. The therapist must be firm and embracing, teach many skills, and assist in the process of grieving. "Be more than a therapist and less than a friend."[6]

The best therapist is one who has done his own work, healing past and present wounds. One can only take someone as far as he has gone himself. One cannot give or share what he has not experienced personally. It is unnecessary for the therapist to have been a former homosexual person. However, he needs to have dealt with his own issues and achieved some success and victories in his personal life. Murray Bowen, the father of Family Systems Therapy, said he believed no one should earn a degree in counseling until healing with one's family members, becoming a mature adult with both Father and Mother.

These activities and relationships from the support network make up the new central organizing factors in the life of the individual coming out of homosexuality. For those with a strong will and ability to self-discipline, developing this support network may be difficult yet achievable. For those with a weak will and a more fragile ego structure, developing this support network may be too difficult. They will need more assistance and community support to supplement their lack of discipline and lack of willpower. They will not be able to make it alone. It takes a family and a community to raise a child. It also takes a community to heal one.

THIRD TASK: BUILDING SELF-WORTH AND EXPERIENCING VALUE IN RELATIONSHIP WITH GOD

Today significant emphasis is placed on sexual identity and sexual behavior. One primary cause of this preoccupation is the lack of intimacy within the family. The pursuit of sex then becomes a substitute for love. If children are deprived of their parents' attention, affection, and affirmation, they will *compensate* for those losses in a variety of ways: performance-based behavior and/or workaholism, overachievement, over-responsibility, codependent relationships, rebelliousness, and drug/alcohol/sexual/gambling/religious addictions.

Another important reason for increased emphasis on sexual activity is a lack of spirituality, a lack of relationship with God, our vertical parent. Without experiencing parents' love, and without experiencing God's love, an individual will never experience or understand his value. "It is an established fact that nobody is born with the ability to love himself. . . . Self-love is either acquired or it is nonexistent. The one who does not acquire it or who acquires it insufficiently either is not able to love others at all or to love them only insufficiently. The same would be true for such a person in his relationship with God."[7]

Value comes from being loved, not from doing, not from accomplishments, and not from physical appearance. True and lasting value comes from simply *being* loved. One of the first tasks of recovery is to de-emphasize either homosexual or heterosexual identity and emphasize true identity as a son or daughter of God.

Beneath these man-made terms relating to sexual behavior is the essence of life: a child's longing for love. It is imperative to reinforce on a daily basis the individual's value that comes from God, the source of life and love.

Meditation, study, prayer, and affirmations are tools to assist in this process. They are explained in more detail in chapter 6. Wounding programs the mind, heart, body, and spirit with unhealthy and destructive messages. We are constantly being bombarded by negative messages around us. We have all heard, "You can't," "You shouldn't," "You won't," "It's impossible," "People are born this way," and so on. The news, reported on TV, in newspapers and magazines, and on the radio, revolves around the misfortune of others, not the noble or uplifting qualities of life. The talk-show format exemplifies the exploitation of the pain and suffering of others. Today, the media and entertainment industry promote the acceptance of homosexuality. Cutting off these sources of negativity is important in the beginning stages of healing, i.e., do not watch particular TV shows, do not attend particular movies, do not read particular magazines and newspapers. Through meditation, study, prayer, and affirmations, we infuse our body, spirit, and soul with positive messages of truth and love.

We must emphasize inherent value as a child of God in this and the subsequent stages of healing. " . . . Every homosexual is a latent heterosexual."[8] Those who find themselves experiencing same-sex attractions are merely late bloomers. They are latent heterosexuals stuck in an early stage of psychosexual development. When the mental and emotional walls break down, the natural process of growth will ensue, and so will heterosexual desires.

In summary, the three main tasks that need to be accomplished in Stage One are: 1) cutting off sexual behaviors; 2) developing a support network; and 3) building self-worth and experiencing value in relationship with God. It is important for all involved to realize that in this stage, and the stages to follow, the person in recovery is likely to become very dependent. A lack of healthy attachment with parents creates the Same-Sex Attachment Disorder (SSAD). Therefore, in the first few years of recovery, there will be a great need for the active participation of others. It is important to build a strong support network and not just rely on one person.

Alex was the youngest of four children. His older brother was Jason, and his older sisters were Becky and Sarah, respectively. He lived in Ohio where his father worked for a large corporation and his mother was a housewife. Alex never got along well with his dad. His father was prone to outbursts of anger, especially when he drank, which increased as Alex got older. His mother would lament about her disappointments with her husband while holding Alex in her arms. A sensitive child by nature, Alex experienced her pain and suffering as though it were his own. More and more, Alex aligned himself with his mother and grew to hate his neglectful and abusive father.

Jason was the athlete of the family. He was a natural at baseball, basketball, and football. Alex felt that he could not measure up to Jason's athletic prowess. As his mom's favorite, he was more inclined to the arts and reading. He would watch as Jason and his friends played sports, wishing that he, too, was just one of the guys. Alex played with his sisters and felt more comfortable in their world. When his dad saw him playing games with his sisters, he called him a "faggot" and "sissy." "You're going to grow up to be one of the girls," his dad would comment. He never spent any quality time with his son. When at home, his dad hid behind the newspaper or watched TV. Often he would not come home until late. He was out drinking with his buddies.

Alex began to experience same-sex attractions in the last few years of elementary school. He always envied the boys who were more athletic and competent. He longed to be just like them. During puberty, those feelings became eroticized as he imagined having sexual relations with the classmates he admired. He dared not share those thoughts and feelings with his family. His dad already considered him a sissy, and his brother would frequently beat him up. Jason and Alex's dad had an antagonistic relationship. They related through arguments and fistfights. Alex wanted no part of that, so he remained an outsider, alone in his fantasies about men.

A neighbor introduced Alex to masturbation, and eventually they became frequent sex partners. Alex felt ashamed of these activities. He and his family attended church weekly. He knew that homosexuality was wrong, but his feelings were so powerful. The guilt was tremendous, but his need for male intimacy was even greater. The relationship with the neighbor continued throughout junior high school until he moved away. Then Alex found male pornography and began to masturbate several times a day.

Alex had sex with several other classmates while in high school. They were all short-term relationships, as Alex continued to battle these desires. In college, he began to have anonymous sex with men in parks, bathrooms, and bathhouses. He was an honors student majoring in business and eventually law. Alex had a very sharp mind and was admired by most of his classmates, but no one knew that Alex led a double life. By day, he was the clever, brilliant student. By night, he was a sex addict, seeking yet another man to fill his loneliness and pain.

When I began to counsel Alex, he was in his late twenties and a very successful lawyer making a handsome income. But Alex was miserable. His colleagues admired his brilliant mind, his way with words, and his successful trial skills. But Alex hated himself. He longed to be one of the guys. He felt like he was on the outside looking in. He felt ashamed of his addictions to anonymous sex, male pornography, and compulsive masturbation. He wanted out, but he did not know how to change.

At first, I had Alex fill out all the questions about his family of origin (all questions are listed in chapter 6). After reviewing his history, I gave him an evaluation and treatment plan. We then began our therapeutic relationship. I had Alex read several books about the etiology of same-sex attractions. Gradually, he began to understand where these desires originated. He understood that he had emotionally detached from his father and had an unhealthy attachment with his mother. Being more sensitive, he feared his father and the strength that he represented. Rather than standing up to his dad, he ran for safety in the arms of his mother and sisters. He came to see that his sexual exploits were a mask for the unobtained love and affection from his father and his inability to communicate his needs in a positive and assertive manner.

Alex was hungry to learn and grow. The next task was to help him build a strong support network in order to replace the sexual addictions and to assist him in the re-creation of his character. He was fearful about sharing his struggle with others. He had managed to isolate this part of his life since he began experiencing same-sex attractions. I gently encouraged him to join a support group of other men in the process of transitioning. He resisted until I told him that in order for me to help him, I needed him to join such a group. Finally, he agreed to attend a meeting. There, to his great surprise, he met other men just like himself who had suffered their entire lives with similar feelings and experiences. He was so relieved and so grateful to learn that he was not alone. He met others who understood him.

Alex began an exercise program. He joined an athletic club and found several men to work out with. He began making friends with men who were secure in their sexuality. As Alex had always been on the sidelines watching his brother and other boys, it was scary for him to participate in group sports. He sought a mentor to teach him basic athletic skills: throwing the ball, hitting the ball, catching the ball, and shooting hoops. Over a period of time, he began to experience his own strength and power. (A word of caution: I encourage those coming out of homosexuality to find *family-oriented* health clubs and exercise with healthy friends.)

I had him begin a regimen of meditation every morning and evening. He listened to messages of affirmations. He began to redefine himself. No longer was he a homosexual man, but a precious son of God. Gradually, Alex began to understand that he did not have to earn love and acceptance through appearance or outward success. He was simply loved just for who he was. This was a revelation for Alex. This internal transformation, combined with new social skills, his support group, and weekly counseling, gave him the strength to stop acting out sexually. Occasionally, he would have a sexual experience, but they were decreasing each week.

Stage Two: Grounding
(Cognitive Therapy/Inner-Child Healing)

I have observed that the individual who experiences same-sex attractions is not grounded in his body and soul. He must learn skills of self-knowledge and fulfillment before healing the wounds of the past. This stage is one of creating inner contentment and peace, a new sense of being centered in his heart, mind, body, and spirit.

In Stage Two, there are four tasks:

1.	Continuing with the support network
2.	Continuing to build self-worth and experience value in relationship with God
3.	Building skills: assertiveness training, communication skills, and problem-solving techniques
4.	Beginning inner-child healing: identifying thoughts, feelings, and needs

FIRST TASK: CONTINUING WITH THE SUPPORT NETWORK

It is important for the individual to develop, participate in, and strengthen his support system. This is a vital part of the recovery program. The support system stands as a container, a safe space around the individual. The support system represents an external form of an internal reality. It is re-creating the family and community in a healthy, positive, loving, and supportive manner. Later, he will internalize all the love received through the support network.

There is a strong need for involvement by the entire support system. Discontinuing sexual activity or fantasies causes the individual to experience feelings and thoughts more intensely than before. Repeated sexual behavior in the past helped the individual to medicate uncomfortable feelings and negative thoughts by numbing the mind, heart, body, and spirit. Sexual behavior or fantasies are escape mechanisms, like a drug to avoid pain, hurt, disappointment, and any other unpleasant feelings. The components of the support system stand as a fortress of strength for the individual in recovery. This is the holding environment, the fertile soil in which to spring forth and grow.

SECOND TASK: CONTINUING TO BUILD SELF-WORTH
AND EXPERIENCE VALUE IN RELATIONSHIP WITH GOD

Meditation, prayer, study, and affirmations are essential to building a strong spiritual foundation and a skin touch relationship with God. Meditation is listening. Prayer is speaking. Meditation creates a safe space for quieting the soul and learning to listen. Prayer is communication between the body, soul, spirit, and God. Study of inspirational words renews our hearts and minds. Affirmations are a way of re-educating our unconscious minds, helping us to develop faith, hope, and self-confidence.

THIRD TASK: BUILDING SKILLS—ASSERTIVENESS TRAINING,
COMMUNICATION SKILLS, AND PROBLEM-SOLVING TECHNIQUES

With a strong support system intact, and through the practice of meditation, prayer, study, and affirmations, the individual enters into the Grounding phase of recovery. A person experiencing homosexual feelings is often unable to regulate his emotions and thoughts. He needs instruction and coaching on how to manage present-day relationships before he is able to go back and heal the wounds of the past.

During this phase, he must learn to cope with uncomfortable feelings and thoughts, dealing with them in more responsible ways. By learning basic cognitive-behavioral skills, he learns to identify negative self-talk, or stinkin' thinkin', and ways in which to untwist these negative thought patterns.

He may need to learn more about the art of self-expression, learning communication skills and assertiveness in a healthy and positive manner—in short, getting his voice back. I use several workbooks that teach about these techniques and skills. Chapter 6 on therapeutic tools and techniques will give more specifics on how to acquire these skills.

A man with same-sex attractions may have a chameleonlike nature, changing color and character to become what others expect of him, or what he thinks they expect of him. This personality trait may be an asset or liability. In the present character of a gender-detached individual, it serves to further distance him from his true self. The use of this and other defense mechanisms creates a false self, character armor to protect a wounded heart. Another characteristic I have observed in the gender-detached individual is impatience or lack of self-discipline. Therefore, he needs to learn how to cope with painful feelings in present-day relationships and situations. Not running away from or trying to medicate uncomfortable feelings is difficult for many in recovery. The first response may be to act out sexually or escape into fantasy. For this reason, he must learn new patterns of behavior. Many times, homosexual desires arise after feeling rejected, frustrated, lonely, angry, or overtired.[9] The individual needs to develop tools to more effectively deal with these unpleasant feelings. There are a number of methods to assist the individual in this task, including:

- Reaching out for help within the support network
- Prayer, meditation, and affirmations
- Bioenergetic/core energetic exercises—pounding, anger release, working through the feelings to get down to the core issues
- Focusing—a technique used to first identify the cause of distress, and second, to create relief in the body and mind
- HALT*—a technique for identifying the cause(s) leading to sexual lust
  Hungry—There is physical hunger and/or feeling of rejection and wanting to fill up with another person or substance.
  Angry—Unexpressed feelings may become eroticized.

---

*See chapter 6 for a more detailed explanation on the use of HALT.

Lonely—Legitimate needs for intimacy that go unmet later are experienced as sexual desires.

Tired—Stress factors kick in and the desire to take care of oneself by using old sexual habits may arise.

- Journaling—Writing on a regular basis helps him understand his inner thoughts and feelings and learn about the triggers that may stimulate inappropriate behaviors. A trigger is any activity, event, or situation that will lead the individual to act out or become emotionally distressed. Many addicts have an obsessive-compulsive (personality) disorder. Writing helps get him out of his head and achieve some distance from the intensity of the experience.

FOURTH TASK: BEGINNING INNER-CHILD HEALING— IDENTIFYING THOUGHTS, FEELINGS, AND NEEDS

To understand the more emotional part of his being, I introduce the use of inner-child work. I assign several workbooks and the use of different inner-child techniques to assist the individual in getting in touch with his deeper feelings and needs. Through inner-child work, he will begin to understand the origins and meanings behind these powerful forces within and around him.

There are three stages of inner-child work: self-parenting, spiritual parenting, and mentoring.

First, he must become his own mentor, the ideal mom and ideal dad for which he always longed. Second, through creative visualization, he may have his spiritual mentor or other mentors mentor his inner child, visualizing wonderful, healing activities together with his mentors. Last, he will heal with and in the presence of others, mentors who can teach him about the ways of men. The individual does this third stage of inner-child work on the foundation of self-parenting and spiritual parenting; otherwise he will develop an unhealthy dependency on the mentor.

I also teach him to get in touch with his body through several techniques: bioenergetics, core energetics, role-play, voice dialogue, and focusing. All these methods will help him get deeper into his body, and more grounded in his character. In this way, he learns to solve his problems, rather than seeking to have a sexual relationship, overworking, or escaping into a fantasy world.

Before going into the psychodynamic aspects of treatment in order to uncover and heal the root causes of these desires, he must become more stable in present-day relationships. He needs to learn how to sustain pain, "ride the wave," as I call it, and not act out inappropriately. Unresolved trauma of the past caused the homosexual disorientation. However, unless he successfully manages his relationships and circumstances in the present, and learns to be an effective communicator, he will be neither able nor equipped to contain the pain that emerges when he begins the process of healing the root causes. He may run away, terminate treatment, start acting out, or feel hopeless that change is impossible.

In summary, the four tasks to be accomplished in Stage Two are: 1) continuing with the support network; 2) continuing to build self-worth and experience value in relationship with God; 3) building skills such as assertiveness training, communication skills, and problem-solving techniques; and 4) beginning inner-child healing to identify thoughts, feelings, and needs.

In the first few stages of my healing, the therapist helped me get in touch with the profound and painful causes of my homosexual feelings without helping me build any support system. He never checked if I had friends, family, and other means of support to help me contain the tremendous amount of pain I was about to experience. Consequently, I ran back into the homosexual world because I felt continuously frustrated from reaching out to friends in my spiritual community who could not understand my pain or need for intimacy. I cannot describe the hell I experienced, nor how lonely I felt during those years. Having no one who understood my situation merely exacerbated the wounds. I learned in a profound and painful way how necessary it is to first help the individual gain stability in the present, develop a strong support system, and learn new coping skills for current problems.

Therapists must be wise in assisting their clients. If you are a therapist, please do not take your client into his deeper pain until he has the resources to deal with it. If you are the client, do not allow the therapist to take you into your deeper pain until you are more stable in your present-day life.

Alex attended his support group weekly. It gave him a sense of stability and comraderie that he needed as he continued on his healing journey. Alex always told me that a life-changing concept for him was that homosexuality was not the problem but a *symptom* of unresolved issues. He stated that this concept freed him to take the focus off of his sexuality and to deal with the underlying causes of his same-sex attractions. We continued to meet for our weekly counseling sessions. I had him begin using Dr. David Burns's book, *Ten Days to Self-Esteem*. Reluctantly, he began doing the assignments. Like many others that I have counseled, Alex did not like this workbook. "It reminds me of all the homework assignments I had to do for school." I told him, "I understand your resistance, and it's fine to hate it. Just do it anyway." And he did.

By practicing Burns's methods, Alex learned to identify his negative self-talk, cognitive distortions that led him into a vicious cycle of depression and sexual addiction. By doing the daily mood logs and other activities suggested by Burns, he gained a greater sense of self-control. Then, instead of getting upset with himself and others, he took the time to reflect on his negative thinking and transform those thoughts into positive energy. This was yet another way in which he gained greater self-awareness and power over the addictive cycle. Dr. Douglas Weiss describes the addictive cycle by the following six stages: 1) pain agents—emotional discomfort, unresolved conflict, stress, or a need to connect; 2) disassociation; 3) the altered state; 4) pursuing behavior; 5) behavior; and 6) time between acting out.[10]

He continued to meditate on a daily basis using several of the tapes that I provided. We also made a tape specifically to reinforce his sense of self-worth. I had him write a list of affirmations, things that he wished his dad and others had said to him while growing up. I asked him if he wanted me to record the tape or if he wanted to do it himself. He requested that I do it, and together we made the recording during our session. I wanted to make sure it was done in a way that was pleasing to his soul. The tape was just about five minutes in length with soothing music in the background. Some of the affirmations were: "Alex, I love you for who you are." "You are my precious son." "You are enough." "You are talented, gifted, and strong." "I believe in you." By using these affirmations on a daily basis, Alex began to believe in his value and self-worth as a loved son of God.

By participating in sports and exercise, Alex was strengthening his masculinity as well. After working with his mentor for months, he finally built up the courage to begin playing basketball with some other men. It was very frightening for him at first. He used the cognitive techniques, slaying negative self-talk with positive and rational responses. It was very hard for him to do this. He used creative visualization, imagining that he was a competent, accomplished basketball player already. He would practice seeing this in his mind several times throughout the day. He made a goal each time he played basketball. One time his goal was to just have fun, no matter how he played. Another time his goal was to focus on skill building—dribbling and passing the ball. Another time his goal was to be as assertive as possible. He also asked a friend to practice with him. Through his continued efforts, his game gradually improved and he learned to have fun.

After completing Burns's cognitive therapy, he began inner-child healing. Alex did the assignments in Dr. Lucia Capacchione's book, *Recovery of Your Inner Child*. As a lawyer, he found this approach ridiculous and stupid. "What does drawing pictures with my opposite hand have to do with healing homosexuality? This seems absurd!" Again, I told Alex, "It's fine to hate it. Just do it." And so he did. At first, the inner-child drawing and dialogue exercises were very difficult for him. It was slow going. Getting in touch with the inner voice was a painstaking adventure for Alex. For so many years, he had buried that hurt little boy beneath all the good grades, smiles, pleasantries, and sexual activity. But through his consistent and concerted efforts, eventually the child within began to speak.

Alex was shocked at what began to emerge—a very angry and raging little boy. He was not nice. He was not sweet. He was hurt, and he wanted to be heard. And so Alex completed many drawings and allowed the little boy within to voice his feelings. During several sessions, I created exercises for that particular inner child. He did some bioenergetic work, pounding on pillows with a tennis racquet. No longer was Alex the sweet, submissive child, but a strong and powerful, masculine force.

He also tapped into other parts of his inner family—the protective parent, the frightened little boy, the critical parent, the playful child. Alex was awakening parts of himself that had been dormant for years. He was learning to access feelings, thoughts, and needs he never knew he had. Alex used the meditation tape, *Healing Your Inner Child*, several times a week (see Resource Materials for a list of audio tapes). Through these inner-child healing activities, he began to find his emotional center and become more powerfully aware of who he was rather than seeking to define himself in response to how others thought and felt about him.

Stage Three: Healing the Homo-Emotional Wounds (Psychodynamic Therapy)

"Those who cannot remember the past are condemned to repeat it."

—George Santayana

Stage Three is emotional, mental, and spiritual surgery through deep grieving and inner healing. First, the causes of same-sex attractions must be illuminated. Next, the wounds need to be healed. Finally, the unmet love needs will be fulfilled in healthy, healing same-sex relationships. Through this process, the individual will naturally come to experience the fullness of his gender identity.

In Stage Three, there are four tasks:

1. Continuing all tasks of Stage Two
2. Discovering the root causes of homo-emotional wounds
3. Beginning the process of grieving, forgiving, and taking responsibility
4. Developing healthy, healing same-sex relationships

FIRST TASK: CONTINUING ALL TASKS OF STAGE TWO
- Continue with the support network: This is critical, as the individual is about to enter psychodynamic work, uncovering the pains of the past. The support network surrounds him with love, understanding, and support.
- Continue building self-worth and experiencing value in relationship with God: It is important for him to continue developing a spiritual connection with the Creator, the inner voice of guidance and support. A personal relationship with God will give greater strength to begin the process of grieving.
- Continue building skills: assertiveness training, communication skills, and problem-solving techniques. Continue to challenge faulty thinking and negative self-talk, and to stretch in new ways. As a more authentic man, he then becomes more responsible, fulfilled, and empowered in everyday relationships.

- Continue inner-child healing by learning to identify thoughts, feelings, and needs. The inner-child work serves as fertilizer for the soil of deeper work to come—the discovery and healing of the root causes of same-sex attractions. By learning to listen to his body and soul, he prepares himself to handle the heartaches and pains as they emerge in this third stage of healing.

SECOND TASK: DISCOVERING THE ROOT CAUSES OF HOMO-EMOTIONAL WOUNDS

In this stage, he must uncover and discover what took place in his past that cut him off from his own gender identity. The primary cause of homosexuality is not an absent same-sex parent, but the child's defensive detachment toward that parent. The child first perceived rejection, from either Dad or Mom, or both, and then self-protected and created an emotional wall around his heart.[11] In the process of healing, this wall must come down. Same-sex desires represent alienation from the true self. He seeks in another man what is lacking within himself.[12] The *false self* is an adaptation of one's character in order to obtain love. Other names for the false self are masks, defensive mechanisms, and character armor. The *true self* is one's inherent God-given nature—pure, loving, spiritual, forgiving, and understanding.

Explanation about "Layers of Our Personality"

At the core of one's being is his God-given true self, full of love, understanding, and forgiveness. He also has an inherited self, with a predilection to misinterpret or misperceive the words and deeds of others, especially his primary caregivers.

If he experienced or perceived any kind of abandonment, neglect, abuse, or enmeshment, as an infant, child, or adolescent, his first feeling response is *fear*. Because children always self-blame, underneath psychological fear is *guilt* and *shame*. Guilt comes from behavior: "I did wrong." Shame comes from being: "I am wrong." If he is allowed to express his feelings freely, and if his feelings are heard and honored by his parents, healing will take place at that time. If his feelings are not expressed or received, he then represses them. "Repression is a state of emotional numbness. . . . It occurs when you are so tired of resisting, resenting, and rejecting that you successfully repress all of your negative emotions to 'keep the peace,' for the sake of the family, or to look good to the world."[13]

If the abandonment, neglect, abuse, or enmeshment continue, the next feeling response will be *anger*. Dr. Steven Stosny describes the physiological component of anger as the following: "Anger comes from a small region of the brain called the limbic system, also known as the mammalian brain, because we share it with all mammals; is part of the survival-based fight or flight instinct we share with all mammals; mobilizes the organism for fighting—the only emotion that activates *every muscle group and every organ* of the body. The chemicals secreted in the brain during anger arousal,

LAYERS OF OUR PERSONALITY

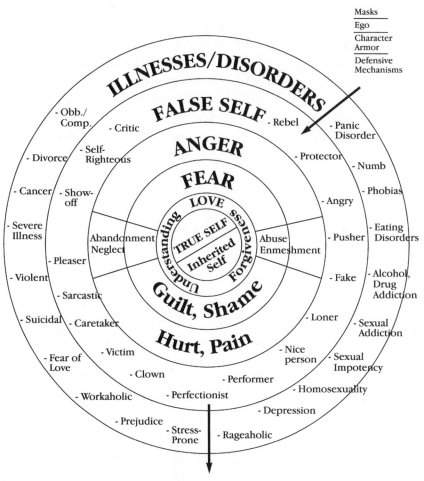

Affection, Affirmation, Acceptance

Developed from an idea by Dr. Robert Kronemeyer
(*Totally Fit Living*. Deerfield Beach, FL: Health
Communications, Inc., 1996, xxvi.)

© Richard Cohen, M.A.
January, 1999

epinephrine and norepinephrine, feel much like an amphetamine and analgesic—they numb pain and produce a surge of energy."[14]

Anger is a physiological response to danger and a psychological response to hurt and pain. Psychologically, anger is always a coverup for hurt and pain. If he expresses his anger, and his parents allow him to do so in a constructive way, then he will be able to heal his hurt and pain. If his family does not receive his feelings of anger, or if he represses them, then he swallows the hurt and pain. *Feelings buried alive never die. Time does not heal all wounds. It just buries them deeper.*

Finally, he will develop many coping skills, defensive mechanisms, and character armor to survive in an environment where his thoughts and feelings go unheard and basic love needs go unmet. These coping skills, defense mechanisms, and character armor then represent the *false self*. These coping skills/defenses are based on his original nature, his inherent God-given gifts. However, these gifts are used for a dual purpose: 1) to mask the hurt, pain, guilt, and shame, and 2) to obtain the affection, affirmation, and acceptance never perceived or received.

The layer of the false self contains the many masks he wears, the dramas he plays, the character armor he puts on, and the defensive mechanisms he uses to shield his wounded heart from further hurt and pain. The problem is, no matter how hard he works to gain the scraps of affection, affirmation, and acceptance he wants or needs, it will never soothe his soul. The reason is that his behavior is driven by a need for recognition—being loved for what he does, *not* for who he is. A primal need we all possess is to be accepted for who we are, not for what we do or what we look like.

I did not include "approval" on the list of three As, because approval is behavior-based. It is okay if a parent, spouse, boss, coworker, friend, or God does not approve of his behavior(s). Behavior has to do with his doing, not his being. Therefore, he can still be loved (for his *being*), even if someone does not approve of his behavior (his *doing*).

The layers of the personality widen until he develops *illnesses/disorders*. Many healers believe that most illnesses and disorders have a psychological base, the result of a broken or lost heart and negative attitudes and beliefs. He is syntonically connected as each part affects the other: spirit, body, heart, and mind. This is why recovering and discovering his child(ren) within (both wounded and golden children) takes time. He must peel away the layers, like an onion, one by one. He cannot move right into the core of his being and blow up his personality. He must remove defensive layers systematically and replace them with healthy ways of being and behaving. When he has gained a sufficient sense of self-worth from his relationship with God, self, and others, then he can move deeper into the well of recovering his lost soul.

I use several techniques to help the individual get in touch with past memories: inner-child drawing and dialogue, memory healing, bioenergetics, core energetics, role-play, psychodrama, focusing, and voice dialogue. In these ways, he will get in touch with lost or repressed memories.

It is critical to understand the origins of the desires; otherwise, mere behavioral attempts to "control" the homosexual drive will create a lifetime of frustration and guilt. Getting to the root causes will allow the defensive shields to come down and love to come in. Without removing these barriers, other techniques will stand as a superficial means of controlling thoughts, feelings, and behaviors.

I believe in complete and total liberation of the soul. The man in transition will at last find his way back home and be able to move on with his psychosexual, psychological, and psychospiritual development by discovering and healing the root causes, including: wounding by the same-sex parent, wounding by a same-sex sibling, body-image wounds, peer wounds, sexual abuse, divorce, or death of a parent.

THIRD TASK: BEGINNING THE PROCESS OF GRIEVING, FORGIVING, AND TAKING RESPONSIBILITY

The stages of healing in this task are recall, release, relief, realize, and responsibility.

- Recall: The first step is to recall the events that created the same-sex detachment, such as wounding with the same-sex parent, abuse, peer wounds, and sibling wounds.
- Release: Next, he must begin the process of grieving. This may consist of tears, rage, anger, laughter, and other emotions. *If we can feel it, then we can heal it.* Without moving through the feelings, the defensive blocks will remain in place and healing will not occur.
- Relief: After releasing the emotional toxicity, he will experience a great sense of relief. The same-sex attractions are connected to the wounds. When the walls come down, then love comes in, and the individual experiences his gender identity.
- Realize: After grieving the homo-emotional wounds and experiencing relief, the individual realizes the need for forgiveness—forgiving self, others, and God. Forgiveness releases him from bitterness and

the need for revenge. When he holds onto his anger and resentments, he will project those feelings onto other relationships, especially those who want to be close to him. Furthermore, if he cannot forgive, he still harbors unconscious guilt. Beneath the blame and anger is the voice of his inner child, "It's all my fault."

There are two kinds of forgiveness: one from the head and one from the heart. The first kind of forgiveness is a decision one makes to let go of the bitterness and pain. He gives the gift of forgiveness to the one who hurt him. It is a conscious choice. The second kind of forgiveness comes from the heart. It flows from understanding. Finally, the wounded child's heart has been heard. Now he can see the same woundedness in the heart of the one who either purposely or unknowingly inflicted the wound. This second kind of forgiveness occurs after grieving the losses of the past.

Forgiving does not mean that all the painful feelings will go away. That takes time. Forgiveness takes place through many stages in life. Healing is like peeling an onion. As he heals and grows, he peels away the layers around his heart. The individual may administer forgiveness at each new stage. A principle of growth is that the closer he gets to others, the more he may hurt. Intimacy is feared because of the original wounds that were experienced with primary caregivers. Being close was not always safe and satisfying. Within the context of intimate relationships, those primary hurts will naturally resurface. That is why there are many stages of grief and loss through which one must work.[15]

Forgiveness is a gift. It sets him free. It helps him let go of the past and move into a brighter present and future, opening him up to greater possibilities of love.

- Responsibility: His mind is able to understand more clearly what occurred after working through the process of grief and forgiveness. Childhood core beliefs, which were developed in response to parents and events, will now come into focus. He might believe, for example, that "I shouldn't say what I think or feel; otherwise, people will reject me"; "Smile and be nice, don't show my feelings, because nobody really cares"; "Don't trust men, they are all uncaring and unfeeling"; "I'm unwanted, and I don't belong here."

In this stage, he begins to see his part in the drama, how he could have handled or perceived the situation differently, even as an infant, child, or adolescent. Therefore, it is important for him to identify his core beliefs and misinterpretations that led to his feeling rejected or allowed him to allow others to hurt him as they did. This may be a radical concept for many that I, as a child, played an important role in how things occurred. This will become clearer after having worked through the stages of grief and forgiveness. Unless you have been there, this may be hard to swallow. I know it was for me.

Once he identifies the distortions and misinterpretations, he experiences an even greater freedom. He can let his parents, his siblings, or the perpetrator off the hook. He sees how he helped create his own defensive detachment and pushed the possibilities of love out of his life, even as a child.

This final phase is extremely empowering and liberating. By taking responsibility for his part in the drama, by understanding his misinterpretations, he may stop blaming others and thereby begin recreating himself as a whole man. Robert Bly speaks about making two rooms in our heart for our father: "The son who always knew about his father's cruel and destructive side will find it easy to furnish one of these dark rooms. . . . But that very same son needs to build a second room to house the generous and blessed side of his father. . . . If we haven't yet made two rooms, and furnished them, we can't expect our father, living or dead, to move in. Those men who have made both rooms inside their souls could begin to think of inviting in a mentor. He will also need two rooms."[16]

FOURTH TASK: DEVELOPING HEALTHY, HEALING, SAME-SEX RELATIONSHIPS

That which was born out of broken, unhealthy relationships needs to be healed in loving, nurturing relationships. Heterosexuality blossoms after a person fulfills homo-emotional needs and experiences gender identity. That is why marriage will never solve same-sex attractions.

Heterosexual men and women are the transmitters of God's love to help provide homo-emotional love needs and successful bonding.[17] Without experiencing the true masculine or true feminine love from another person, the individual in recovery lives a life of frustration and yearning. God's love is experienced through people. We must be true and ideal parents for one another.

Men must heal with other men, and women must heal with other women. Activities such as talking, walking, hiking, camping, fishing, sports, and just being together will provide the environment in which change may take place. In such a safe setting, in safe relationships, the wounds of the past will emerge and healing will occur.

Another therapeutic method I promote and teach is *Mentoring*. This is like planting seeds after pulling weeds. I believe this is an essential element for true, lasting, and organic healing to occur. Mentoring is a profound relationship between two people: the mentor and the adult-child. "If you are a young man and you are not being admired by an older man, you are being hurt."[18] The mentor becomes the surrogate father to the man in recovery. The mentor will be able to provide the unmet homo-emotional love needs that the recovering person never experienced in childhood or adolescence.

When they develop a deep bond, the adult-child may begin to get angry and resistant. When he gets close to someone and starts letting his walls down, primal emotions begin to emerge. Through grieving with the mentor, the pains of his past will heal and successful bonding will occur. It takes time to build trust. First comes honesty: sharing himself with his mentor and feeling accepted. Second comes trust: knowing the mentor will be there rather than run away and judge him. Finally comes love: exposing the ugliest parts to his mentor who still embraces and cares for him. These relationships work, aided by prayer, patience, and persistence.

His defensive shields will break down and healthy bonding will occur as he learns to trust the mentor. In this way, he fulfills homo-emotional needs and experiences his gender identity. If the same-sex parent is alive and willing to engage in this process, he is the best person for the job. Coaching most parents in effective ways to mentor their children is important. (See chapter 12 on mentoring for suggestions.)

In summary, the four tasks to be accomplished in Stage Three are: 1) continuing all tasks of Stage Two; 2) discovering the root causes of homo-emotional wounds; 3) beginning the process of grieving, forgiving, and taking responsibility; and 4) developing healthy, healing same-sex relationships.

> Alex understood the root causes of his same-sex attractions and was ready to face the past, heal the wounds, and fulfill unmet needs. His sexual addictions to anonymous sex, male pornography, and compulsive masturbation were no longer a part of his daily life. He had friends, played sports, prayed and meditated, and had developed a strong sense of his inherent value as a beloved son of God. He practiced good communication skills in his personal and professional life. Whenever someone spoke words that hurt him, he could either take care of himself or he would share honestly with the other person. *Going straight is about being straight with self and others.*

Now it was time to delve into the past. Through voice dialogue, bioenergetics, and memory healing, we began to explore the pain Alex experienced in relationship to his father and brother. *Restoration works in reverse to the way in which the original wounding occurred.* First, one must deal with the lesser wound before facing the more profound wound. Alex sensed that, first, he needed to heal with Jason. Through role-play and voice dialogue, he allowed his wounded inner child to come forth and share with Jason how he felt when attacked and beaten. Frozen tears and primal emotions were released as Alex's inner child spoke about his pain. "Why did you hit me? Why did you beat me? I needed your love so bad, but all I felt was your anger."

We also used bioenergetic exercises to allow his inner child to express his anger and pain. I had him imagine Jason standing on the other side of the pillows as he screamed, pounded, and eventually took back his power. Alex had, in a most unhealthy manner, submitted to Jason and his dad. He abdicated responsibility by shutting down emotionally, thus becoming a "victim." During several sessions, while utilizing memory healing, Alex was able to grieve the loss of a close relationship with his brother, experience relief, and ultimately forgive Jason. Through bleeding his own wound, he was able to see the common wounding in Jason, who was equally deficient in experiencing healthy Father's love. Through role-play, voice dialogue, bioenergetics, and memory healing, Alex was able to reclaim a part of his masculinity.

Next, it was time to investigate his relationship with his father. Alex allowed his inner child to share with his dad how he felt when he was verbally, emotionally, and mentally abused. Through role-play, voice dialogue, bioenergetics, and memory healing, Alex grieved about the pain and loss of Father's love. "Why weren't you there for me? Where were you? I needed you. I'm not a sissy. I'm a boy, and I am deserving of your love." Alex pounded so hard, screaming, shouting, reclaiming his power, and taking back the male energy he abandoned so many years ago. "I am a boy. I am a man. I am deserving of love. I won't take your verbal abuse anymore. I give you back all your shame, all your name-calling, all your fears and guilt."

Alex learned to stand in his power, *transitioning from a victim to a victor of love.* As he let go of his anger, frustration, and pain, he began to experience more power within himself. Through memory healing, he was able to forgive his father and see the wounded child within his dad. Realizing that his dad did not experience the warmth and encouragement of his father, Alex was able to feel more compassionate and forgiving toward him.

Simultaneous with this process of inner healing, Alex was being mentored by an elder in his church. He met weekly with his mentor, Rich. They spent time together sharing. Rich was a good listener and a strong role model for Alex. When Alex was grieving, Rich would hold him in his arms, allowing him to feel loved as he detoxed from years of repressed anger and pain. Rich was very patient and loving toward Alex. In this way, Alex's neurology was being reprogrammed. The pain was being weeded out of his system and love was being poured in—pulling weeds and planting seeds. Alex and Rich also went to games together, played ball, and took walks. Alex was making up for all the times he had missed with his dad.

Alex also maintained close friendships with several guys from the gym, his support group, and his church. He was able to freely share with them what he was experiencing in his emotional and mental reprocessing work. His support network surrounded him as he released the past and reclaimed his masculinity. More and more, he felt grounded in his power. His same-sex attractions waned now that he experienced his own sense of gender identity.

Stage Four: Healing the Hetero-Emotional Wounds (Psychodynamic Therapy)

In the last stage of recovery, the individual will address hetero-emotional wounds. Again, as in Stage Three, the causes must be identified, the wounds healed, and the unmet hetero-emotional love needs fulfilled. The final task will be to learn about the character differences of men and women.

In Stage Four, there are four tasks:

1. Continuing all the tasks of Stage Two
2. Discovering the root causes of hetero-emotional wounds
3. Continuing the process of grieving, forgiving, and taking responsibility
4. Developing healthy, healing opposite-sex relationships, and learning to understand and appreciate the opposite sex

FIRST TASK: CONTINUING ALL THE TASKS OF STAGE TWO

Work with the support network; continue to build self-worth and experience value from God; continue building assertiveness, communication, and problem-solving skills; and continue to identify thoughts, feelings, and needs in the present.

SECOND TASK: DISCOVERING THE ROOT CAUSES
OF HETERO-EMOTIONAL WOUNDS

Finally, and in some cases even more difficult, will be healing the hetero-emotional wounds, i.e., unhealthy mother-son attachment, unhealthy father-daughter attachment, sexual abuse by someone of the opposite sex, women experiencing rejection by men, and men experiencing rejection by women.

There may have been an excessive and/or abusive attachment between the child and parent or significant person of the opposite sex. Sometimes, the meaning of homosexuality is a flight from intimacy with members of the opposite sex to avoid the profound trauma experienced in infancy, childhood, or adolescence. Simple science demonstrates that opposites attract and like polarities repel each other. If a man feels repulsed by a woman, perhaps he is overidentified with the feminine. As he increases his sense of masculine identification, he will be attracted to his opposite, a female. "The purpose of life is to unify the masculine and feminine within, creating a proper balance. It affects all of our behavior and relationships if we are missing one part, or are at odds with one part."[19]

The individual in recovery must uncover the root causes that prevent him from relating intimately with someone of the opposite sex. He must identify and heal these issues.

THIRD TASK: CONTINUING THE PROCESS OF GRIEVING,
FORGIVING, AND TAKING RESPONSIBILITY

The stages of healing are recall, release, relief, realize, and responsibility. The individual must work through hetero-emotional wounds on an emotional level. Afterwards, he processes on an intellectual level, taking personal responsibility for his part in the drama.

FOURTH TASK: DEVELOPING HEALTHY, HEALING OPPOSITE-SEX
RELATIONSHIPS, AND LEARNING TO UNDERSTAND AND
APPRECIATE THE OPPOSITE SEX

In this phase, it may help to have a therapist of the opposite sex. This will allow transference to occur, projecting repressed feelings toward the opposite sex onto the therapist. This will expedite the healing process. Healing the mother-son and father-daughter relationship is crucial for successful transitioning into healthy heterosexual relationships. The individual projects past resentments onto the future spouse unless the wounds heal. This makes the spouse constantly pay for the hurts and wounds received in the past. This is happening in many heterosexual relationships, which is one reason for the high rate of divorce.

To assist in this process, it is important for the individual to establish healthy, healing, loving, nonsexual relationships with members of the opposite sex. The best person for the job is the mother or father. I recommend the use of *Attachment/Holding Therapy* as taught by Dr. Martha Welch. My family and I did some healing work with Dr. Welch. If I had experienced holding time with my parents several decades ago, I would not have needed to process through my thoughts and feelings with so many therapists and groups. I could have taken care of them at the source, with my mom and dad. If the parent is alive, I strongly recommend healing with him or her, if they are willing to engage in the process. (*A warning:* It is important to accept the fact that some parents are too unhealthy and incapable of participating in the healing process. Trying to force or coerce a parent into the healing process may rewound the adult-child.) I will share more about Attachment/Holding Therapy in chapter 6.

In this final stage, it is also important for men to learn more about women, and for women to learn more about men. The works of Deborah Tannen, John Gottman, John Gray, Harville Hendrix, Pat Love, Ellen Kreidman, Barbara De Angelis, Gary Smally, and others will help the person in recovery better understand and appreciate the opposite sex. (See References for a suggested reading list.) If the man in recovery was close to his mother, and more into his feminine nature, he knew women as a woman, not as a man. The same holds true for the woman coming out of homosexuality. She may have known men from a more masculine point of view, not from a woman's perspective. Therefore, it is important to learn about the opposite sex in a healthy way, from one's own gender's point of view. This is a healthy and radical shift in perspective for the person in recovery. "If the son learns feeling primarily from the mother, then he will probably see his own masculinity from the feminine point of view as well. He may find his masculinity fascinating, but still frightening. He may pity it and want to reform it, or he may be suspicious of it and want to kill it. He may admire it, but he will never feel at home with it."[20] The converse is true as well. He will see femininity from the eyes of a woman until he experiences his own gender identity and then learns about women as a man.

Natural desires for opposite-sex relationships often emerge as he experiences his gender identity, heals the hetero-emotional wounds, and establishes healthy attachment relationships with members of the opposite sex. A married man will experience greater intimacy with his wife once he has healed the hetero-emotional wounds.

The individual's true gender identity will emerge after breaking down the defensive detachments between men and men, women and women, men and women, and women and men, bonding with both the same and opposite sexes. Natural attractions and feelings for the opposite sex arise out of this process of healing. There is no magic except for the profound relationships of love that arise during this process of transformation and the freedom experienced by lifting the walls of detachment.

In summary, the four tasks to be accomplished in Stage Four are: 1) continuing all the tasks of Stage Two; 2) discovering the root causes of hetero-emotional wounds; 3) continuing the process of grieving, forgiving, and taking responsibility; and 4) developing healthy, healing opposite-sex relationships, and learning to understand and appreciate the opposite sex.

> Alex needed to work on his relationship with his mother. He had been enmeshed with her since he could remember. (*Enmeshed* describes an unhealthy attachment in an intimate relationship, whereby the proper boundaries between Mother and son have been violated.) He was her precious little boy, sweetheart, and substitute spouse. He carried the scars of this unhealthy attachment through his adolescence and adult life. He feared intimacy with women, afraid he would be consumed by their demands. It was time to face the mother of his past that lived deep within his soul. We used role-play, psychodrama, inner-child healing, voice dialogue, bioenergetics, memory healing, and holding therapy. In sessions, Alex debriefed about how he felt when his mom would share her burdens with him. Through role-play and bioenergetics, he expressed much sadness, anger, and pain. In our support group, he created a psychodrama, having different people play the roles of his mother, father, brother, sisters, and himself. This was a very powerful method for him to recall the family system and see what part he played in the drama and how each family member must have felt.
>
> Alex began a mentoring relationship with Elizabeth, Rich's wife. In this way, he began to know women from another perspective.

Elizabeth was neither clinging nor demanding. She simply embraced him and allowed him to be a part of her and her husband's world. This was a great healing for Alex. He had never experienced what it felt like to be close to a woman in a nonthreatening way. His inner child was scared and excited to know a woman without fear of being consumed by her needs. Elizabeth was a very refreshing influence in Alex's new life.

We arranged for Alex's parents and siblings to attend a holding session that lasted all day. My wife helped me, as she does with each holding session. In this way, both men and women feel represented and safer. First, Alex's parents held each other. I had them express how they thought and felt about one another, the good points as well as the bad points. In the beginning, they were quite superficial, playing the sweet and loving couple. Then, Jason, Alex, and their sisters ganged up on each side of them and began screaming, "Stop acting so sweet. We know that each one of you is so hurt by the other. Let it out and stop making us feel like we have to take care of you!" This was a wake-up call to Alex's mom and dad. While holding her husband, his mother began to express years of pain and disappointment. She cried and screamed how lonely she was while he was out drinking. She told him how hurt she was that he had neglected and abused the children. She mourned in his arms as all the children were crying.

Next, it was Dad's turn. Still an alcoholic, he was unable to access his deeper feelings. For so many years, he had repressed his wounded self. He recalled to his wife and children how his own father had beat him senseless, day after day, year after year, and never gave him one word of encouragement. He told them that he knew he had failed them, but at least he didn't hurt them as badly as his father had hurt him. They were all silent and shocked, as he had never shared about his family before. They could see that he had masked his own pain through alcohol and overworking.

We then had Mom and Dad hold the children—first was Jason, then Becky and Sarah. Finally, it was Alex's turn. He held with his dad. Alex screamed and cried, as this was the first time for him to touch and be touched by his father. He cried out, like a child, "Dad, I missed you my whole life. Do you think I wanted to have sex with other men? I was always searching for you in their arms. I need you, Dad, I need you. Where were you? Why did you always criticize me and call me names? Please hold me and tell me that you love me." On and on he went, letting his dad know how much he was hurt by his actions and words. Alex did not want to let go of his dad since this was their first bonding experience. His father apologized for his critical nature and verbal abuse. He told Alex he was sorry that he had not been a better dad. Finally, he told his son, "I love you, Alex."

Then Alex held with his mother. He screamed and cried, telling her how disgusted he was when she would share her misery with him. "I felt like your husband, not your son. Why did you share that crap with me? I didn't want to know your pain; I just needed your love. I never felt safe with you, only burdened and pained." He continued, "Mom, I am now establishing a new relationship with you. I need clear boundaries. I do not want to hear about your pain, your problems, and your issues. I am your son, not your friend. Please get a life. Find others your own age who can help you. That's not my role. I'm your son. I need you to care for me." Alex felt relieved after sharing these thoughts, feelings, and needs with his mom.

She was deeply saddened by his sharing. She had no idea that he felt so hurt and betrayed. She thought she had done the best for him and the other children. She cried and apologized for any hurt she caused her son. She told him that she loved him and that she would try not to share her burdens with him. She then went into a "poor me" mode, saying that no one is there for her. All the kids held her and screamed, "Mom, get a life. Find friends that can help and love you. Stop leaning on us!" This was very hard for her to hear.

Last, we had the kids hold each other and debrief about unresolved issues they had with one another. Jason and the girls held and cried as they recalled many episodes. Alex held with Jason and told him how hurt and offended he was by the verbal and physical abuse. Jason apologized, knowing that he had passed on to Alex what he felt about his dad. They held each other, cried, and forgave one other.

I would like to say that they all lived happily ever after, but change takes place over a period of time through practice, practice, and practice. Alex had to keep reminding his mom not to share her heartaches with him. He requested that his dad spend some time with him. His father agreed and thus began a new phase in both of their lives. Jason and Alex agreed to talk on the phone frequently, getting to know one another as adults.

Alex's father was still emotionally unavailable, so Alex needed to continue receiving from his male friends and mentors. He eventually accepted the fact that his father could not give him all that he needed. This realization created a peaceful state in his heart and soul. No longer did he look to Dad for the love he was unable to give. Alex saw his father for who he was and learned to be grateful for what he could give. Alex's love for his father was now one of gratitude and maturity.

Alex began dating. His attractions for women began to emerge after healing the homo-emotional wounds and fulfilling the unmet needs. After a year of dating several women, Alex met Christina. She was a very lovely and open woman. He shared about his past and his healing journey. She was very moved by his commitment to change, his perseverance, and his deep faith in God. Eventually they married and had two children. Now, Alex is a good father to his children and a better husband than his father was able to be. Of course, the road is not always easy, as shadows of the past reveal themselves. However, Alex and Christina have tools to use as they work through their respective issues. She, too, has done much healing work to restore her past. They continue to grow individually, as a couple, and as a family.

Alex's therapy lasted a little over three years. It took approximately one year for him to break his addictive cycle. Through that time period, he built a solid support network and learned many skills to gain a better sense of self. Through the passageway of his inner child, the wounds of his past emerged. Healing took place through many methods, as I have already described. Alex experienced his own gender identity as he removed the shields of detachment between himself and his father and brother. His needs were fulfilled through healthy male bonding. He learned more about women by being mentored by a generous woman. Attachment/holding therapy with his entire family helped create an opening to establish new relationships with his father, mother, and siblings. Alex continues to grow each day as a son of God, husband, father, and powerful man in the world.

A brief note about the role of the therapist

This plan of healing out of homosexuality is not exactly a linear model. During the first two stages, the individual may need to heal from profound wounds of the past. Bringing relief to those wounds in the early stages of healing is very important. However, it is vital that the therapist encourage the client to develop a proper support system that will provide the necessary holding environment while he works through the four stages of recovery. I see the role of the therapist as a guide, facilitator, midwife, teacher, mentor, and parent. However, the therapist must direct the client through each stage of recovery, assisting him in accomplishing the developmental and social tasks at hand. The client will experience much transference as a natural part of the therapeutic relationship. However, the therapist should not be the main source of love or the main mentor. The therapist must encourage the client to develop healthy and healing relationships outside the context of therapy.

Conclusion

Of course, this description is very brief and simplistic. In chapter 6, I will discuss more "how to do it," with tools and techniques to be used in each stage of recovery. Healing same-sex attractions is possible. I have done it, and I have assisted many clients as well. Seeing individuals come to understand the deeper meaning of their desires, and seeing them become freed from those chains that bound them for years, is both moving and gratifying. This process takes years. There is no quick fix in matters of the heart.

One client came to me in desperation, having sought help from psychiatrists and psychologists over twenty years of his life. No one could relieve the pain lodged deep in his soul. No one could help him stop acting out. After several initial sessions of assessing his background, I took him back, through a deep state of relaxation, to the key events that created his same-sex attractions. Finally, he was able to face his father, grieve his losses, and offer forgiveness. This was the breakthrough he long sought. He said, "A wall has been lifted," and his acting-out behaviors ceased completely. He came to understand that the desires were merely a cover-up for much deeper emotions that resulted from wounds he never knew existed. Of course, this was an exceptional case, as most do not heal so quickly. He also had done much therapy before our sessions. Today, seven years have gone by and he is blossoming!

Understanding the origins of the homosexual condition is imperative to aiding any man or woman who is trying to exit from this state of "dis-ease." I encourage all therapists to learn more about the process of healing. To those who wish to change, please know that you are not alone. You can do it.

Additional Note

Some strugglers with unwanted same-sex attraction may be unable to stop having sexual relations with others in the first stage of healing. It is important to realize that they are seeking either parental or peer bonding through these "acting out" activities. Gradually, they will need to develop a strong support network of healthy relationships in order to substitute platonic for sexual relations. This may take time. Be patient with oneself. Be patient with your clients or loved ones. Remember, he or she is merely seeking to fulfill basic love needs. Sex will never fulfill those basic needs because they are those of a child, and children do not need sex. They need healthy, healing, and loving relationships.

CHAPTER FIVE

Christian

It was July 1995 and I had come to the end of a very long, long road. I was gay—a homosexual. It was time to give up the charade I had been playing for forty-four years. It was a deep, dark secret I had hidden from everyone. This feeling of gayness had been a part of every aspect of my life, and I could no longer tolerate the incredible pain. I supposedly had it all. I had a great job and social life. I had the suburban lifestyle. I had a beautiful, devoted, loving wife of over twenty years and the greatest daughter and son a father could ever hope for. Ultimately, however, I always felt trapped as a homosexual pretending to be a straight man in a straight world where I just didn't belong. It was time to come out as a gay man.

I grew up as a kid in the 1950s and went to college in the late '60s. I was not part of the pre–"coming out" acceptance of gays in the 1970s. As a child, teenager, and college student, there was no one available in the public sector to openly go to for support. "Queers" and "fags" was the terminology I knew, and I certainly felt I fit the mold. It was always too frightening as a kid and young adult to actually admit I was a queer. I thought if I just play the part of a straight man, maybe it will all go away. The general public did not accept gayness; it was definitely taboo.

With the 1970s a flood of information came to me from strong, openly gay men and women. The media blitz and the changing world were letting me know that, "Hey, you're gay, and it's okay." It was not okay with me. I had already married and started a family. I ached to be a part of the gay scene, but I also ached for my sexual feelings for men to just go away. I was upset with and jealous of gay men because I felt alone, isolated, and detached from any identification with heterosexual or homosexual men.

Up to the early 1980s, I had only once gone to a Christian counselor about my "depression." He informed me I was a latent homosexual, probably should break off my engagement and look at nude pictures of women to get the "cure." Needless to say, I dismissed his advice and pretended this counseling had never occurred.

By the early 1980s, I was like a volcano ready to explode. I had never had a sexual encounter with a man. I had lots of fantasies and wet dreams, but never actual physical encounters. Theater had been a way for me to be around and near gay men. It was after a theatrical performance I confessed to a friend, who was gay, that I had sexual feelings for men. Soon after this confession, I got invited to his apartment where he introduced me to homosexual sex. It was like thirty years of dead, suppressed weight lifted from me. I soon found another cast member who was more than willing to engage in sex with the new gay on the block. I thought I was in heaven, but it quickly turned to hell for me. I felt empty, alone, frightened, deceitful, guilty, dirty, and ultimately, heading in a direction where I did not want to go.

I was living a double life. I confessed to my wife I was gay. She did not accept this as truth. She knew I was not gay, but her ability to help me was just not there. A straight psychologist tried to help me, but he had no clue what to do. He knew I wanted to stay married, but did not know how to help me. I read some literature and got the idea that this was genetic and that was that. To help support the genetic theory, my sister had confessed to the family that she was gay! I dropped the psychologist, and my wife and I pretended that the problem went away. I hated myself.

A few years after this in the mid 1980s, I had again stayed away from gay sexual encounters. However, my wife's and my sexual life was a shambles. I hated sex with my wife. This was not the best criteria for wedded bliss. She sent me off to a New Age encounter with some guru who could "zap" the homosexuality out of me. I was desperate and scared, so I agreed to go. It was horrific. I question if this man was possessed by some demon that really wanted to suck out my soul. He worked by intimidating and humiliating me in front of hundreds of his followers. He pronounced I was the devil and for his followers to shun and stay away from me. I fled this scene and was sure any hope of ridding myself of gayness was totally unrealistic. I again began to periodically engage in sexual encounters with men. It became an addiction and short-lived fix. I could go months without having sex with a man, but then if something happened in my life that was stressful, I would flee for a homosexual encounter. I realized I kept searching for the perfect man, and if I found him, he would be strong enough and love me enough to take me away from the straight world. I would then be safe, warm, and loved. As the years passed, I realized that this was a fantasy that just was not going to come true.

So, I take you back to July 1995. My anxiety level was about to explode. With deep regret, I had secretly begun to see a counselor for gays to transition out of my marriage to the gay community. I felt thoroughly depressed, but felt I had *no other choice* for the sake of my wife and for my survival. At the same time, my wife presented me with a book written by Richard Cohen entitled *Alfie's Home*. She had seen Richard on the *Ricki Lake* show many months before. She had diligently tracked down this book. On this TV show, Richard claimed he could transition men from homosexuality to heterosexuality. I was furious and very skeptical. I decided no more wacko gurus for me. It was garbage. My wife then gave me the best ultimatum of my life: "Go see Richard, or move out and get a divorce." I loved her enough to try one more time, but felt it was another hopeless course.

I was totally and utterly skeptical of therapy that gave me a choice to be straight. I was too old at forty-four to change. There could be no magical "hocus-pocus." I had my feet firmly planted in the genetic theory. My childhood encounters and my parents had nothing to do with this gayness that I felt. Richard Cohen's therapy *would not work*.

I wish there were a way to convey true gut feelings. It was a dark, broken individual who had his first therapy session with Richard. For me, building a trusting relationship with him was the key that began to open the door of healing for me.

Being able to pour out my true feelings to someone who was really listening was an important first step for me. He had walked the walk, so I could accept what was truth for him. His living example gave me the initial prospect that healing just might be possible. I knew I wanted to transition, so I would take it one day at a time.

I began to learn that there were major key factors that contributed to my homo-emotional feelings. It was important for me to learn that my same-sex attractions were the sum of these key factors. My childhood, in my eyes, had been perfect. My parents had provided me with a beautiful home, clothes, food, and social and travel experiences. An incredible realization was that neither of my parents was demonstrative in physical touch or verbal affirmations. I have no memory of either of my parents ever telling me they loved me. I have one memory of my mom hugging me. My father never hugged me. I realized how devastating this was for me. I had no healthy touch experience from my parents within my childhood memories to the present. I clearly remember fantasizing, as a young child, about my dad's friends holding me and having sexual fantasies about them. I was not getting healthy touch from anyone.

I believed that the only time one touched was for sex, so I would dread any touch by anyone, as it would lead to sex. In therapy, mentoring sessions where men and women held me safely brought incredible healing and my biggest breakthrough. I felt like a little child being loved by a parent in a very healthy way. I discovered quickly that I could get healthy touch. I knew I had been seeking out touch with men in an unhealthy way. I just wanted touch and would have sex to get it.

Memory work of the inner child was also another key factor in my transitioning. When Richard asked me to draw pictures with my non-dominant hand and write down feelings and experiences, I truly thought this was a crazy and a stupid task. However, I quickly had clear memories of childhood. It came out on paper about how I left myself wide open for inappropriate touch by one relative and sexual abuse by teenage boys who would baby-sit and take me on outings. This helped to peel away more layers of what had felt like, "I'm gay."

Having group sessions with people who were working towards healing was incredibly supportive. It was another key to my healing to have a support group and individuals with whom I could say whatever I needed to say. Sometimes it was to tell them how I was healing or to tell them I was having a bad time and felt like acting out. It could be to tell them I had sexual feelings for them and to discuss why those feelings were there and how to resolve them in a healthy way.

My pastor and great friend is very secure in his heterosexuality. We get together to talk about anything and everything. He can support me in mentoring and we go to the gym, play tennis, get together for lunch, and just hang out. I am totally comfortable with him in a mutual heterosexual friendship.

Massage therapy really helped me to accept appropriate touch. Having deep pressure applied to my muscles felt as if my body was transitioning from a sexual touch to the acceptance of normal, healthy touch.

In July 1995, I started a therapy course that changed my life. I had individual therapy, sometimes twice a week, for a little less than two years. I was in a support group for the same amount of time. At the end of this time, it became apparent that I was living a wonderful, productive life with my wife, children, and friends. I had and have the tools necessary to continue to grow as the man I have become. My darkness and anxiety are completely gone. I really enjoy sex with my wife. I do not have homo-emotional feelings for men. I am not, nor ever was, gay. I had addictive homo-emotional feelings for men. I feel fantastic because I had a choice made available to me. I believe strongly that I had to make a choice for me. A choice I believe. I chose to transition, and *it is possible*.

I no longer identify with the man I was before July 1995. That was a lifetime ago. I feel reborn. At the beginning of my therapy, I felt so alone. A friend in my support group said, "If you think you're alone, then you are wrong. You are not alone anymore." I have God, my wife, my two children, and the great prospects of what life holds for me each day!

CHAPTER SIX

Therapeutic Tools and Techniques

I believe God designed humankind as complementary opposites. Men and women fit together as the fulfillment of creation. Simple science demonstrates that opposites attract. When you have two magnets of opposite polarities, they naturally gravitate toward each other. If you have two magnets of the same polarity, they naturally repel one another. If a man feels an attraction to another man, then he is internally seeking that which is lacking within himself. He seeks to incorporate the lost, or missing, part of his psyche. If a man experiences his own masculinity, then he is naturally attracted to his opposite, a woman.

I would like to share with you—whether you are a professional therapist, pastor, rabbi, parent, spouse, friend, family member, a concerned loved one, or an overcomer—some of the tools and techniques that may

In this chapter, I address many of my comments to the therapist or helper. I believe there is a great need in the mental-health profession and religious community to understand how to help men and women come out of homosexuality. This is a general introduction, not a detailed explanation, to various therapeutic modalities. My intention is to provide the technology of change; the various tools may be learned by studying the suggested reading and through further education.

facilitate change along the road of restoration. I have complete confidence that by using these skills, together with the four-stage model of recovery, any man, woman, or adolescent who desires to come out of homosexuality may do so.

Every wounded person needs to recover in four areas—intellectual, emotional, physical, and spiritual. To successfully heal, the individual must give attention to each one of these areas. Talk therapy will only address certain issues. Therefore, he must use a variety of techniques in the four stages of recovery. The treatment plan is tailor-made to meet his specific needs. There are assignments that he is required to do for skill building, problem solving, and getting in touch with his thoughts, feelings, and needs. Other therapists and I have found that those who participate in their own recovery by doing homework and other assignments grow and heal much quicker.

A word of warning to therapists, counselors, pastors, and caregivers: If you ever find yourself working harder, or being more invested in the therapy than your client, then something is wrong. Your job is to be the pick. Your client must take up the shovel and do his own work if he is to heal. A Same-Sex Attachment Disorder is an indication of delayed development, being stuck in some earlier stage or stages of psychosexual, psychosocial, psychospiritual, and psychological development. Therefore, much of the work will be identifying where there is developmental arrest, helping the client heal wounds, and assisting in the fulfillment of unmet needs. For this to occur, instruction, guidance, and proper parenting will be necessary.

Those working with the overcomer need to understand: 1) the nature of the homosexual condition; 2) the four stages of recovery; and 3) the need for the fulfillment of developmental tasks in each stage. Here is where the therapeutic tools and techniques are important. It is necessary to follow the four stages in proper order to ensure that the individual does not omit developmental tasks and jeopardize his success. (Again, if necessary, one may need to jump from one stage to another to take care of some immediate business, e.g., deep grieving or facing a critical situation. After this is complete, he returns to the previous stage of healing.)

A Brief Summation of the Four Stages of Recovery

Stage One: The individual needs to cut ties with homosexual fantasy, stop homosexual behavior, terminate relationships with friends in the homosexual community, and build a support network of healthy love. He needs to build a sense of self-worth by developing a personal relationship with God. This is behavioral therapy, modifying inappropriate behavior and replacing it with positive, healthy sources of love.

Stage Two: The individual needs to develop skills for creating happiness in his present life. This is cognitive therapy, teaching communication and problem-solving skills, assertiveness training, and correcting faulty thinking. Here he begins inner-child work, learning about feelings and needs. If an individual bypasses this stage, chances are that he will terminate treatment, give up, and/or go into the homosexual lifestyle.

Stage Three: The individual needs to identify the homo-emotional wounds, heal them, and then fulfill them in healthy, nonerotic same-sex relationships. This is the psychodynamic work of recovery, exposing the wounds, grieving the pains and losses of the past, learning to forgive, and finally moving on.

Stage Four: The individual needs to identify hetero-emotional wounds, heal them, and then fulfill them in healthy opposite-sex relationships. He needs to learn about women from a man's perspective, and she needs to learn about men from a woman's perspective.

People always ask me how long this will take. It all depends on the severity of the wounds and the amount of time and energy the individual is willing to invest in his healing. One to three years is the average time of treatment.

There is one thing that I would like to make clear before presenting the tools and techniques: **The tools and techniques to be used in each stage of recovery may change, but the tasks will remain the same.** Those in the mental health profession know we are always evolving in gaining a better understanding of intrapersonal and interpersonal relationships as well as learning new methods of healing. Even though the methods may change, the tasks that one must accomplish to heal out of homosexuality will always remain the same, as this is a developmental disorder. The wounding occurred in specific ways and in specific times in the individual's life. The individual must identify, understand, and heal those wounds. These tasks will remain constant, as the individual must address them regardless of the latest therapeutic technologies.

The Initial Session

When someone comes for help and shares about the nature of his situation and current conflicts, the first thing I ask is: "What are your goals for our work together?" Quite often, many who seek counseling are not clear about their goals. However, they must address this question. It makes them think about what they want and need, and it gives the client and the helper a clear direction for the work.

When we decide to work together, I begin by taking a thorough history. Generally, this takes from two to three hours, sometimes more. During this time, the client has an opportunity to share much about his life, many things he has never shared with anyone before. It gives the therapist/helper a bird's-eye view of the family system and many other contributing factors that the client will need to address along the road of recovery.

I generally give the client a sheet of questions to take home. I ask him to respond to each question clearly, in outline form. I also ask him to draw a genogram, or family tree, of three generations (see page 113 for an example of a genogram). Of course, I show him how to construct the genogram: beginning with paternal and maternal grandparents, the client's parents, siblings, and the families of siblings (if they exist).

It is very interesting to see how much the individual does or does not know about his grandparents. This in itself may be very revealing about family relationships, or lack thereof. A good book about developing genograms and family histories is *Family Ties That Bind,* by Dr. Ronald W. Richardson.[1]

Here is the list of questions regarding the genogram:

1. Please describe the relationship between your father and his father, your father and his mother, your father and his siblings (if he had any), and your father and any other significant people in his life while he was growing up.
2. Describe the relationship between your father's parents—past to present.
3. Where did your father's family live? Where did he grow up?
4. What was their ethnic background? What was their religious background?
5. Please describe the relationship between your mother and her father, your mother and her mother, your mother and her siblings, and any other significant people in her life growing up.
6. Describe the relationship between your mother's parents—past to present.
7. Where did your mother's family live? Where did she grow up?
8. What was their ethnic background? Religious background?

9. Please describe any major issues or events on both the paternal and maternal sides of the family, such as war experiences, immigration, sexual abuse, physical abuse, emotional-mental abuse, drug/alcohol/sexual addictions, gambling addictions, eating disorders, sexual problems, major depressions, divorce, suicide, rape, murder, theft, abortions, homosexuality, adoption, moving, etc.

The second list of questions is about the immediate family relationships:

1. Describe your relationship with your father—past (from your earliest memories) to the present (current-day relationship).
2. Describe your father's personality—past to present.
3. Describe your father's education, employment history, and religious history.
4. Describe your relationship with your mother—past to present.
5. Describe your mother's personality—past to present.
6. Describe your mother's education, employment history, and religious history.
7. Describe the relationship between your father and mother—past to present.
8. Describe your relationship with your siblings (if you have any)—past to present.
9. Describe your siblings' personalities.
10. Describe your relationship with any other significant people in or out of your family system, i.e., grandmother, grandfather, uncle, cousin, neighbor, and stepparent.
11. What was your role in the family system? (e.g., hero, pleaser, clown, rebel, substitute spouse, golden child, caretaker, loner, scapegoat, peacemaker.)
12. Describe your school history—academically and socially, past to present.
13. Describe your sexual history—from your earliest memories to the present. Include all references to sex and sexuality, in or outside of the family. When did the homosexual feelings and desires begin?
14. Describe your sexual fantasies—from past to present, as they may have progressed over time. What kind of person are you attracted to? What are his or her characteristics: physical attributes and personality traits? What activities are performed and in what environment?
15. Describe your religious history—past to present.
16. Describe yourself—how you see yourself today.

17. List any other significant issues about your life or your family that were not covered in these questions, such as health issues, marriage issues, extramarital affairs, career issues, money issues, and previous treatment or therapy.
18. Please list your goals for therapy.

I will comment on a few of these points from the list of questions:

One thing that becomes apparent while doing this family history or reviewing the family history is the generational detachment between same-sex parents and their same-sex children, e.g., the distance between fathers and sons, and mothers and daughters. I have observed in many of my male clients weaker paternal figures and much stronger maternal figures. This leads a male to identify more easily with the feminine, the stronger of the sexes in the family system.

While giving his family history, one man said, "I wanted to be a girl because my father liked my sister more than me. He was always angry and critical of me. Also, my mother had more fun, could speak her mind, and was more loving."

It is important to have him share about his earliest childhood memories because it is the fertile soil that cultivates the homosexual disorientation. Pay close attention to any memory lapses—there is much useful information in those yet empty spaces. The conscious mind cannot hold that which was too painful to remember. These places will be important to revisit when working through stages three and four of recovery.

When reviewing the individual's social life during school years, I most often hear about a sense of being "different," not fitting in with the other kids, feelings of being less than or better than the others.

Inquiring about sexual fantasies is very important. There is much useful information here since the homo-emotional wounds hide beneath the homosexual fantasy. There is generally a progression of sexual fantasies as well. Sometimes it starts out by just looking at naked men or women, and then progresses to sexual activity, first viewing others doing it, and then putting oneself in the picture. Of course, this will be unique to each individual, depending upon the specific needs and the intensity of detachment from parents and self.

Some feel attracted to older men, displaying a need to be taken care of or fathered. Some adolescents/men feel an attraction to peers, seeking in other men what they feel lacking within themselves. Most men feel drawn to muscular, strong, and confident men—all the qualities they wish to

Genogram of David's Family

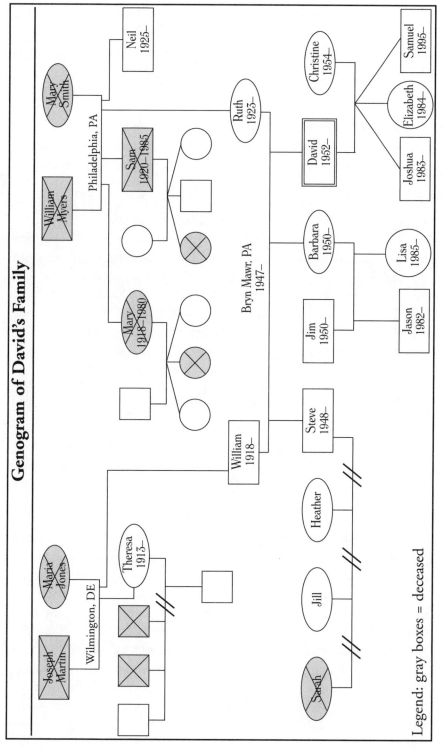

Legend: gray boxes = deceased

© Richard Cohen, M.A., January 1999

possess. Some want to feel dominated, held, cared for, or mentored by the men they admire. Others have an attraction to younger boys or teens. This may represent several things: 1) unresolved trauma at that particular age; 2) unmet needs in that stage of development; or 3) a connection to some form of abuse at that age (oftentimes a repressed or suppressed memory of sexual abuse).

It is important to realize that sexual fantasies are always a coverup for basic unmet homo-emotional love needs or fear of intimacy with someone of the opposite sex. I have also found that these fantasies may hide repressed anger toward one or both parents, anger that the child felt unable to express which is now being manifest as sexual desires. Still others, disconnected from their own sense of gender identity, want to watch heterosexual men having sexual relations with women. In this way, they find their lost identities in the men they wish to be. There are many variations of sexual fantasies. It is important to find out as much detail as possible in order to understand the deeper meanings behind the SSAD condition.

It is important to see what part religion has played in the client's life and what role it now plays. Many experience hurt by the slings and arrows of persecution they experienced in their particular faiths. I have heard horror stories of how they sought help from their clergy and were then asked to leave the congregation. Others feared to reveal their struggle because of the strong judgmental attitudes they found in their faith. In other cases, if they have strongly detached from their parents, then they may easily detach from their parents' religious beliefs. *Oppositional behavior is an integral part of homosexuality.* One young client shared with me, "I consciously chose to be different from my father. If he liked country music, I chose rock. If he liked white, I chose black. This was my way of telling him that I didn't like him at all."

After reviewing the family history, I take time to write a review of each relationship and each area of the client's life. I give my observations and opinions about how these have impacted his growth and development. When I give the client this evaluation, I invite him to first listen and take it in. If I have made a mistake or misperceived something, I ask him to correct me. This is generally a very good experience, for he gets another perspective of the family system and how it has affected his life.

After completing the evaluation, I go over the four stages of healing, thereby giving him a treatment plan, a road map of recovery. Then we begin our work. If a client is in extreme pain at the initial session or sessions, please give him time to express his feelings and thoughts before doing a thorough history. This may be the first time for him to have found a safe and secure place to let go and release his pain and frustration. The helper must create a sacred space that is safe, secure, and nonjudgmental.

Questions to Ask a Prospective Therapist

Nemo Dat Quod Non Habet—You cannot give what you do not have.

I have had many individuals ask me to refer them to a local therapist. Many did not have a clue as to what to look for in a therapist or the appropriate questions to ask. Therefore, I include this section for those seeking counseling.

If you are the prospective client, realize that you are about to share your heart and soul with a stranger. It is therefore important for you to interview him or her. Chemistry is important, as well as the background and skills of the therapist. Here are some questions you might consider asking:

- Please tell me about your education and training in this area of sexual reorientation therapy
- What therapeutic modalities do you use? Please explain them in simple layman's terms. (You will understand more about these modalities after reading this chapter. I recommend finding a therapist who is eclectic, knowledgeable, and proficient in many different schools of therapy.)
- Have you worked with others who have transitioned out of homosexuality?
- What is your success rate in doing this kind of work?
- Do you believe in God? (If important to you: "What is your religious faith?")
- Have you done your own healing work?

The therapist may feel shocked or insulted by this last question: "Who are you to ask me about my personal life?" You are the potential buyer who will be paying lots of bucks for therapy, spending lots of time trying to heal. Surely you do not want to cast your pearls before a swine who does not have his own house in order. *Healing is a journey, not a destination.* We are all on the road somewhere trying to reach our ultimate destination. A therapist can only take you as far as he has gone himself. If he has not healed his own life, how can he help you heal yours?

Again, the therapist does not need to come from a homosexual background. However, he needs to have worked on and through his own issues. The best mentors are those who are victorious and successful in their personal lives. Otherwise, they are talking from their heads, not their hearts or experience. Someone who has been through the war and won the battle can teach well how to fight.

Tools and Techniques

I will now list some of the tools and techniques that may prove useful in the four stages of recovery. This certainly is not an exhaustive list of approaches. They are merely some that I have used and found to be effective. Following is a brief description of each technique. Later in this section, I will recommend books that will describe how to implement these tools and techniques in the therapeutic process. Again, my intention is not to give an in-depth explanation of each approach, but to provide ways and means of healing.

1. *Family Systems Therapy:* Building a family history, seeing the bigger picture, how the individual relates to and is influenced by the entire family system.
2. *Bibliotherapy:* Study of literature, e.g., causes of same-sex attractions, healing of homosexuality, nature of sexual abuse, cycle of sexual addiction, issues in recovery.
3. *Education:* I assist the client in building a support network and teach social skills, communication skills, assertiveness, men-women differences, and problem-solving techniques.
4. *Cognitive Therapy:* It is important to understand faulty thinking and negative self-talk and to learn new skills to correct these cognitive distortions.
5. *Meditation and Affirmations:* I teach clients to meditate, use creative visualization, and work with affirmations on a daily basis. All these help to build self-worth, enhance spiritual growth, and achieve goals.
6. *Inner-Child Healing:* I give many assignments to help him get in touch with his inner child, his inner soul—learning to identify thoughts, feelings, and needs of the present and past.
7. *Bioenergetics and Core Energetics:* Through methods of therapeutic body work, the individual will learn to express anger in a healthy way, release pent-up bodily tension and pain, get down to deeper emotions and needs, and become more grounded and centered in his body.
8. *Role-Play/Gestalt Therapy:* Through role-play and other similar processes, the individual may speak to parents, siblings, perpetrators,

himself, and anyone that caused him pain.

9. *Psychodrama:* This is used in group sessions, recreating the family system or any other situation that caused him harm. Here he relives the experience and then is able to release repressed/suppressed emotions.

10. *Memory Healing and Neuro-Linguistic Programming:* This is a process of going back into past memories, re-experiencing what happened, and this time reframing and healing the experience. This helps him disassociate from the problem and associate with the solution.

11. *Family Constellation:* Based on the work of Bert Hellinger, the individual develops a family constellation in a group setting in order to discover the hidden symmetry of love. The constellation may consist of, but not be limited to, members of the immediate family, people from the lineage, and others who may have impacted relationships and decisions of love.

12. *Mentoring:* This mentoring model helps the individual fulfill unmet homo-emotional and hetero-emotional love needs. Through mentoring, secure attachment is achieved and love restored.

13. *Attachment/Holding Therapy:* This is a method to work with couples, parents, children, siblings, and other relatives. Through holding with family members, a person can heal past wounds and develop or restore healthy attachment.

14. *Voice Dialogue:* A way to discover one's inner family, or subpersonalities. It is also a great method to uncover lost, or disowned, parts of the self.

15. *Exercise and Sports:* For many men, athletics and exercise are a great source of pain. Participating in group sports is very healing and an important part of socialization.

16. *Therapeutic Massage:* This helps release many repressed wounds in the body and brings healing and openness.

17. *Behavioral and Gesture Re-Education:* It is important to help men inherit more masculine behaviors and women more feminine behaviors.

18. *Making Contracts:* Discipline is an area of weakness for many coming out of homosexuality. Making contracts to do homework assignments and other tasks is very useful. Accountability is important.

19. *Friendships:* Establishing healthy same-sex friendships is critical to healing out of homosexuality.

20. *Transactional Analysis:* This is a paradigm of ego structure incorporating the adult, parent, and child.

21. *Journaling:* Writing down thoughts, feelings, and experiences as a means of understanding oneself and the process of healing.

22. *Recording Sessions:* A useful tool for many of my clients is to record each of their individual sessions. Afterwards, in the quiet of their homes or while driving in their cars, they are able to review the lessons that were learned, the skills that were taught, and ways to heal their wounds.

Four Areas of Healing

I will divide each stage of recovery into the four areas of healing—intellectual, emotional, physical, and spiritual (see chart—Therapeutic Tools and Techniques):

- *Intellectual*—The individual needs to re-create himself, developing a positive self-image. Formation of negative thoughts about self and others occurred as a result of unhealthy relationships in the past. The individual must identify negative thought patterns and replace them with positive thoughts and attitudes about self and others. The individual needs to practice positive, assertive behaviors, learning to express thoughts, feelings, and needs in all relationships.

- *Emotional*—The wounds of the past must be healed. You cannot heal it if you cannot feel it. The individual must identify and expose the root causes of present difficulties. He must grieve the wounds of the past. He can only heal the deeper, more severe memories in the presence of others who genuinely care. Forgiveness is also an important part of this process. After grieving has taken place, forgiveness comes naturally, understanding the commonality of our brokenheartedness. He needs to learn forgiveness for himself, others, and God. Many times, the inner child blames God for the abuse and neglect that occurred. When he does not forgive, he gives energy to his pain and projects it onto others. Finally, he learns to take responsibility for his part in the drama by identifying the distortions and misinterpretations that led to his detachment from his primary caregivers.

- *Physical*—Experiencing his masculinity and (lost) gender identity is critical for healing. This is achievable through regular exercise, proper diet, and participating in sports and other same-sex social activities. He needs to heal body-image wounds. He also needs to fulfill unmet love needs in healthy, healing, loving, nonsexual relationships with members of the same and opposite sex. This will be

Therapeutic Tools and Techniques

	Stage I	Stage II	Stage III	Stage IV
Intellectual	Bibliotherapy Education Behavioral Therapy	Cognitive Therapy Communication Skills Problem-Solving Techniques	Understanding Root Causes of Homo-Emotional Wounds	Understanding Root Causes of Hetero-Emotional Wounds Learning About: Men/Women Differences Marital Relations
Emotional	Good Rapport: Client/Helper(s) Building Support Network	Inner-Child (IC) Healing Three Stages of Healing IC Support Network	Grieving/Forgiving/ Taking Responsibility Techniques: Memory Healing/Voice Dialogue/ Role-Play/Psychodrama/ Holding/Mentoring/ Inner Child Support Network	Grieving/Forgiving/Taking Responsibility Techniques: Memory Healing/Voice Dialogue/ Role-Play/Psychodrama/ Holding/Mentoring/ Inner Child Support Network
Physical	Exercise/Diet/Sports/Fun/ Same-Sex Social Activities	Exercise/Diet/Sports/Fun/ Bioenergetics/Breathwork/ Therapeutic Massage	Exercise/Diet/Sports/ Fun/Bioenergetics/ Breathwork/Therapeutic Massage	Exercise/Diet/Sports/ Fun/Behavioral Reeducation/Bioener- getics/Breathwork/ Therapeutic Massage
Spiritual	Building Self-Worth Experiencing Value from God Meditation/Prayer/Affirmations/ Study/Spiritual Community	Building Self-Worth Experiencing Value from God Meditation/Prayer/Affirmations/ Study/Spiritual Community	Building Self-Worth Experiencing Value from God Meditation/Prayer/Affirmations/ Study/Spiritual Community	Building Self-Worth Experiencing Value from God Meditation/Prayer/Affirmations/ Study/Spiritual Community

accomplished by cutting off from the old lifestyle and developing a new support system. He finds committed people who are on the same path and forges new friendships. In this way, he can fulfill homo-emotional needs and experience gender identity, and then heterosexual desires will emerge.

- *Spiritual*—The individual needs to develop a personal relationship with God, experiencing value for being loved as a child, not for talents or tasks, just for being a precious son. He bases his identity not on sexuality, but on being a child, loved for who he is, not for what he does. Finally, he must learn to understand God's heart, how God, as his Heavenly Father, has suffered along with him. God knows his pain and heartaches. God is always there, ready to nurture and embrace him. The individual in recovery experiences this through meditation, prayer, study, and affirmations.

Now, the four stages of healing using these various tools and techniques:

Therapeutic Tools and Techniques
Stage I: Transitioning

Intellectual	Bibliotherapy Education Behavioral Therapy
Emotional	Good Rapport: Client/Helper(s) Building Support Network
Physical	Exercise/Diet/Sports/Fun/ Same-Sex Social Activities
Spiritual	Building Self-Worth Experiencing Value from God Meditation/Prayer/Affirmations/Study/Spiritual Community

© Richard Cohen, M.A. January 1999

Stage One: Transitioning

1. Cutting off from sexual behavior
2. Developing a support network
3. Building self-worth and experiencing value in relationship with God

INTELLECTUAL

• Bibliotherapy

The individual in recovery must understand the causes of same-sex attractions and the process of healing. I assign him books to read on etiology and treatment. Some of the books I recommend for men are: *Reparative Therapy of Male Homosexuality* and *Healing Homosexuality,* by Dr. Joseph Nicolosi; *Homosexuality: A New Christian Ethic,* by Dr. Elizabeth Moberly; *Cleaning Out the Closet,* by Dr. Christopher Austin. And for the woman: *Female Homosexuality: Choice Without Volition,* by Dr. Elaine V. Siegel, and *Out of Egypt,* by Jeanette Howard. For a more extensive book list, please call Regeneration Books for a catalogue at (410) 661-4337. (See References at the back of the book.)

• Education

The helper (counselor, therapist, pastor, and rabbi) needs to assist in teaching about the etiology of homosexuality and the process of healing. Therefore, helpers need to read books and become well versed in understanding this condition.

• Behavioral therapy

It is critical that the individual disassociate himself from playgrounds, playmates, and playthings that are part of the homosexual milieu. He must stop going to places where he has engaged in such activities. He must stop seeing his homosexual friends. He must stop buying homosexual literature or pornography—anything that stimulates homosexual thoughts and fantasies.

Unless the individual begins to get clean and sober, he will not be able to gain greater awareness of himself. The homosexual activities and fantasies continue to keep him disidentifed with and detached from his deeper thoughts, feelings, and needs. For some in recovery, abstaining from same-sex activities might be extremely difficult. This task is not for the purpose of punishment. The purpose is to help the individual reclaim his soul. If he has been sexually active, this will not be easy. That is why a strong support network is necessary.

Dr. Christopher Austin uses a "Daily Rating Sheet" to assist his clients in achieving healthy behaviors. Each day, the individual uses the sheet to help him accomplish a variety of activities. Dr. Austin explains as follows:

Daily Rating Sheet

Name _____   **Week of** _____

Did you do your homework?   Yes   No

Rate yourself on a scale of one to ten each day on the following categories:
(One = needs serious work / Ten = did excellent)

Daily Work	Mon	Tues	Wed	Thur	Fri	Sat	Sun
No Caffeine							
Eating Healthy							
Sleep							
Exercise							
Prayer							
Gratitude							
Inspirational/Scripture Reading							
Meditation							
Visualization (of goals)							
Journaling							
Accountability/Confession							
Healthy Risk Taking							
Emotionally Expressive							
Openness							
Honesty							
Serving/Giving							
Socially Connected							
Recreation							
Sexual Purity							
Homosexual Arousal							
Other							

What have been your personal goal(s) for the week? _____
_____

What has helped you the most this past week? _____
_____

What have you learned about yourself this week that will aid in your recovery?
_____

What have been your strengths this week? _____
_____

© Dr. Christopher Austin, 1999

"The daily rating sheet is one tool to help bring change into your life by reminding you to do the work of recovery throughout the week. Filling it out helps you become accountable for the actual work you do day to day. This is one of the most valuable tools you can use to bring about positive change in your life.

No Caffeine. The goal is to cut out caffeine completely. Caffeine, even in small amounts, can increase anxiety, anger, and fear, and accelerate the number of dysfunctional thoughts. Drink water as a healthy replacement. It is recommended that we drink between 64 and 128 ounces of water per day. Water is a natural flush for the body, keeping the body hydrated.

Eating Healthy. The goal is to eat to fuel and increase functioning of the body. Unhealthy eating can cause your body to feel rundown, tired, or sluggish, as well as increasing your body fat, which has been shown to increase your risk of heart problems, stroke, or disease. It is recommended that you eat five to six smaller, well-balanced meals per day. A good resource is *Lean Bodies, Total Fitness* by Cliff Sheats (1995, Summit Publishing Group, Arlington, TX). I recommend you eat at least 50 to 90 percent of your meals according to this plan.

Sleep. Make time available to get eight hours of sleep.

Exercise. The goal is to increase your body's stamina, burn calories, and cope with stress. I recommend doing aerobic exercise (walking, jogging, aerobics, cycling, swimming, running) every day for thirty minutes and anaerobic exercise (weight lifting, muscle toning) at least two times a week for thirty minutes.

Prayer. Prayer is your way of connecting with God. Requesting God into your life is acknowledging your faith, trust, and hope that God can be in control so you don't have to be. Prayer is a way to acknowledge your thankfulness and express your concerns. I recommend at least five to fifteen minutes daily.

Gratitude. The goal is to recognize the pleasant and pleasing things going on in your life. Gratitudes help you create a sense of well-being and contentment no matter what your circumstances. This is an effort for you to 'notice the small things going right in your life.' Examples: air in tires, car starts, gas in tank, urinating, health, tasty food, beautiful landscapes, funny billboards, meaningful contact with people, beautiful music, comfortable furniture, job, friends, family members, pets. Eventually, the goal is to be grateful regardless of the circumstances. When illness, death, or catastrophes strike and they always do, viewing them as bad only enhances their life wrecking ability. See life's inconveniences as part of growth, which will teach you something valuable. Trials develop courage, character, patience, endurance, and strength. I recommend you do from fifty to five hundred gratitudes daily.

Inspirational/Scripture Reading. Receiving positive messages in our lives is very important, even more so if negative messages were prevalent in childhood. Inspirational reading is a way of receiving new messages about your worth, hope for the future, goal setting, dealing with emotions, or understanding your spiritual relationship. I recommend at least five to fifteen minutes daily.

Meditation/Relaxation. Meditation is used for receiving God's will through quiet reflection. Meditation is also a method of receiving new messages about your worth. Progressive relaxation helps you manage stress levels and lower anxiety about everyday life. I recommend at least five to fifteen minutes daily.

Visualization. You can't go to a place you can't see. Visualization will help you become familiar with the outcome of goals before you achieve them. Spend at least five minutes per day picturing positive outcomes of reaching your recovery goals.

Journaling. A journal helps you process the raw emotion before you try it out on another person. Refer to the journaling section in your treatment program for tips on writing (see References for Dr. Austin's book, *Cleaning Out the Closet*). I recommend writing at least five to fifteen minutes daily.

Accountability/Confession. Accountability/confession serves the purpose of keeping you on the path of recovery. Try to talk to two or three friends on a rotating basis, whether you are healthy or have been acting out sexually. The purpose of two or more friends for accountability is to avoid emotionally dependent relationships with only one person. Talk to these people about how you are doing on this list.

Healthy Risk Taking. Fear limits our ability to enjoy life. Taking risks to overcome fear is vital in being able to live life to the fullest. Do one thing every day to challenge fear in your life.

Emotionally Expressive. Openly expressing emotional responses is healthy. This includes laughing out loud, crying, cheering out loud at sporting events, or any expression of emotion.

Serving/Giving. Performing senseless random acts of kindness, helping or giving to others, gets us out of ourselves. Loving your neighbor is the second greatest commandment because it promotes spiritual well-being and mental health. I recommend two to six acts of kindness daily.

Socially Connected. Talking to other people keeps us grounded and gives us an opportunity to relate to others. Social connection means talking to a person about the lighter things in life, e.g. 'Did you catch any fish last weekend?' 'How are you coming along on that project at work?' This is a separate contact from the accountability partners. I recommend one to two contacts daily.

Recreation. Time to wind down and take a break is vital. Hobbies or activities are a way of helping us cope with the stresses and pressures of life and renew our physical and mental well-being. Daily participation in recreation is crucial in developing the coping skills necessary to handle what life dishes out. I recommend thirty to ninety minutes daily.

Sexual Purity. Each person sets his own bottom line of what sexual behavior or thoughts are healthy and what sexual behavior or thoughts are out of bounds. This rating is how well you maintained your bottom line."

Additional Explanation of the Daily Rating Sheet

Developing healthy relationships is critical. The individual in recovery needs to have at least four solid relationships with other men: 1) a mentor, an elder who can teach him the ways of men; 2) a fellow struggler, someone else on the journey towards healing; 3) a friend who is secure in his gender identity, is supportive, and knows about his struggle; and 4) a friend who is secure in his gender identity, is supportive, and unaware of his struggle. With these and other men, he is accountable for his stated goals. They stand by and around him in order to lend support and love. By learning to be open and honest, deeper feelings, thoughts, and needs will emerge and healing will ensue.

He also needs to be a giver, not just a receiver. Through giving, he experiences his own gifts to the community. He has been endowed with many spiritual gifts from God. Learning about his gifts and sharing them with others brings more positive energy and feedback into his life.

Having fun and playing games is of equal importance to the other parts of his healing program. Piaget, one of the great child psychologists, stated that the developmental task of childhood is to play. When we lose the ability to play, we lose our childlike nature. Also, in this fast-paced, stressful world, it is critical to take time out and smell the roses, appreciate the roses, and play with the roses.

Maintaining sexual purity is important for several reasons: 1) integrity with one's belief system; 2) not taking on the energy of the other person; 3) not inheriting sexually transmitted diseases; 4) not burying uncomfortable feelings through sex; and 5) learning to take care of self in a positive way. Self-sex or sex with others is most often used as a coverup for unresolved feelings and thoughts and unmet needs for intimacy. He needs to learn to express himself honestly and openly with others and fulfill his affectional needs in healthy same-sex relationships.

Homosexual arousal: This category monitors fantasies and physical responsiveness to other men. Here he learns the correlation between sexual response and his internal state of being. This goes back to the HALT paradigm: Hungry, Angry, Lonely, and/or Tired. Also, he may be attracted to someone who has characteristics that he has disidentified with himself. Many times a man who experiences same-sex attractions is attracted to other men who have similar physical or personality characteristics. He cannot recognize his own beauty and self-worth; therefore, he idolizes another man in order to get back into his own body and soul. By practicing this list of healthy behaviors, he will begin to experience his own sense of well-being and self-worth, not needing another man to complete himself.

Now the individual looks at all this long list of activities and says, "Wow. No way. I'm already defeated before I begin. Too many things to change. Too many things to do. Too many things to think about. Help! I'll never accomplish all of these things!" Yes, there are a lot of things to do and create. And the best way to go about them is slowly and one at a time. Benjamin Franklin made a list of characteristics he wanted to incorporate into his character. He, too, was overwhelmed about the thought of accomplishing them all. So, he decided, I will prioritize and begin with the most important characteristic. I will work on inheriting that personality trait. And he did. And when he had accomplished the first goal, he moved on to the next. And so it is with this Daily Rating Sheet and healing. Begin with a few tasks and gain success, rather than trying to accomplish everything at once and failing miserably. Step by step, one by one, build a solid foundation, and your house will stand strong.

EMOTIONAL

• Building a good rapport

It is very important that the therapist, counselor, pastor, priest, rabbi, parent, mentor, or helper develop a close and supportive relationship with the individual in recovery. The homosexual condition represents unhealthy attachment or extreme emotional detachment from either one or both parents. A distant or aloof attitude by the helper will only exacerbate the already-existing Same-Sex Attachment Disorder. Therefore, one needs to be a good listener, paraphrase and mirror much of what he hears, and join with the individual to see life through his eyes. Attributes of a good helper include: compassion, patience, empathy, nonjudgmental attitude, encouraging, and quiet strength.

A man will best be served by a male therapist and a woman by a female therapist. An opposite-gender therapist will best facilitate Stage Four work (healing hetero-emotional wounds).

• Building a strong support network

Having given up old playgrounds, playmates, and playthings, it is very important to replace them with healthy, healing, loving, and supporting people, places, and things. The facilitator needs to assist the individual in creating a new holding environment. Various components of the support network listed in chapter 4 are helpful. This support system surrounds the individual and provides the love, understanding, and accountability that he needs in all stages of recovery. Eventually, he will internalize the different sources of love and support, developmentally inheriting that which he did not accomplish in childhood and adolescence.

When Bruce came for help, he had completely isolated himself in his struggle with homosexuality. We worked together for several months. Before continuing with his treatment, I insisted he investigate support groups in his area, as he lived several hours from my office. For weeks, he dragged his heels about doing this. Finally, I had to insist, "Unless you find a group and begin to participate, I am afraid our work is finished. I cannot in good conscience help you if you are unwilling to help yourself and let others help you." That sobered him up very quickly, and the next week he was in a group! It was one of the most rewarding experiences of his life, as he found other men who had suffered as he had. Some were far ahead, others far behind, in their recovery. The important thing was that Bruce was finally surrounding himself with fellow journeymen. He was no longer alone.

PHYSICAL

* Exercise, sports, proper diet, and healthy, same-sex social activities

A big part of the homosexual condition is a poor self-image. Developing a sense of physical well-being is very important in the process of recovery. Therefore, the individual needs to exercise regularly, eat healthfully, and get involved with same-sex group activities.

There may be a need for mentorship here, as he may have felt socially, athletically, and physically inferior to others during his school years. Some ex-gay ministries have developed sports teams, helping men heal past sports wounds and find the joy and fun in playing together.

As a child, George always felt unable to compete with the other guys. As an adult in his thirties, he felt athletically incompetent. He determined to overcome his fears and began to participate in neighborhood games. He asked a few guys if they would be willing to coach him privately. He explained that he felt athletically challenged as a kid. They were happy to help him. Today, George is one of the best players on his local team.

I recently counseled a fifty-year-old man who had carried a very heavy burden since he was twelve. He thought that he had no eye-hand coordination, could not throw a ball, and therefore was less than the other boys and less than a man. I paired him up with a friend of mine who was willing to play ball with him. Within a few days, a new man was born. He *could* throw a ball! He just needed some practice and a sympathetic man to show him the ropes.

Another gentleman I shared with said even though he learned to throw a ball with some confidence and skill, and even though his friends affirmed his abilities, deep down he still felt like a misfit. His mind knew he was capable, but his heart was confused. So, what he did was have his friends videotape the ballgame, and more specifically, focus on his playing. Seeing that he really was competent made all the difference. His heart then believed his mind.

Please prescribe a heavy dose of fun and play. This may be work for many who have lived much of their lives in suffering and pain. It is important in the healing process to balance both light and dark energies. Having fun and learning to play with others is as important as inner healing work.

SPIRITUAL

- Building self-worth

Clients use meditation tapes on a daily basis. Regular practice of meditation helps center the individual and brings greater awareness mentally, emotionally, physically, and spiritually. I have created several tapes that I prescribe: 1) Affirmations and Commitment; 2) Meditations for healing gender identity and developing inner awareness; 3) Inner-Child Healing; and 4) Memory Healing. Making and fulfilling goals helps him increase his self-esteem (see Resource Materials for tapes).

There are twelve major aspects in making goals:

1. Have a clear and definite **purpose**. What do you want to achieve?
2. Make a simple **plan**. Your plan needs to be measurable and specific.
3. Keep it **positive**. If you find yourself hearing others say, "You can't, you shouldn't, you won't," then remove these people from your life. You can. You will. You are destined to fulfill your purpose. If you hear negative voices within saying, "You can't, you won't, you shouldn't," and so on, listen to them, give them a voice, and embrace your doubts and fears. Do not suppress or repress your negative voices. Express them, embrace them, and then they will eventually give you the support you want and need.
4. See it in the **present**. Speak about your purpose and plan as though you have already accomplished it in the present. Imagine it, and you will create this reality.
5. Fill it with **passion**. See, say, and sense passionately what it is like to have fulfilled your purpose. Your inner soul, inner child, unconscious will only respond to passion and strong emotions. What is good about achieving this goal? What are the payoffs?
6. Know what you will give in return and leave behind for **posterity**. What are your talents and gifts that you will bequeath to future generations?
7. **Picture** it. Visualize, picture the fulfillment of your purpose and goal. Visualizing strengthens your will and reinforces your inner soul to support the goal.
8. **Practice** it. Say, see, and sense your purpose and goal every day. The two best times to do this are before getting out of bed in the morning and before going to bed in the evening. At these times, our unconscious is more open to autosuggestion. You may also

repeat and practice saying, seeing, and sensing your goal several times throughout the day. Write it down on a note card and put it on the steering wheel of your car, your desk at work, the refrigerator, or the mirror in your bathroom. Put it anyplace to remind you of your goal and purpose.

9. **Pray** for it. Invoke heaven's support for your purpose and plan. If you think you can, you will, and you will attract like spiritual forces to support your desire.

10. Enlist other **people** that you know and trust to support you in fulfilling your purpose and plan. Be accountable to them. Ask them to speak loving, affirming, and positive words to you—"I know you can. I believe in you. I love you. I trust you. You can. How is your plan working? Are you repeating your goal on a daily basis and making steps toward fulfilling it?"

11. **Praise**. Have an attitude of gratitude. Find the gift in the wound. Be grateful for each step gained.

12. Develop a simple **phrase** that captures the essence of your goal.

Here is one example from my life:

First: My **purpose** is to treat my wife more lovingly and stop criticizing her.

Second: My **plan** is to visualize her inner child twice a day and say two positive things about her, to her, twice a day for the next forty days.

Third: I will keep a **positive** attitude about her, no matter what happens or how many things she does that I do not like. I will surround myself with people who tell me good things about her and stay away from people who speak poorly of her.

Fourth: I will repeat my goal daily as though I have already accomplished it in the **present**.

Fifth: I will speak **passionately** about this goal daily.

Sixth: I will leave behind a new pattern for my children and lineage, as my father constantly criticized my mother, my brother, my sister, and myself. I will change this negative pattern for my lineage/**posterity**.

Seventh: I will see myself saying positive things to my wife, and I will see her as a little girl, **picturing** her wounds being healed and her unmet needs being fulfilled.

Eighth: I will **practice** saying my goal every morning and night and several times throughout the day.

Ninth: I will **pray** for heaven's support, to help me overcome my critical, judgmental nature and support me in becoming a more loving, supportive husband.

Tenth: I will enlist three **people** to call me a minimum of once a week to see how I am doing, affirm my small victories, and speak words of love and support.

Eleventh: I will give thanks and **praise** each day for the progress that I make in fulfilling my goal.

Twelfth: I will then develop a simple **phrase** that captures the intention and meaning of my goal. Here is my simple phrase: "By saying words of love to my wife, Jae Sook, twice a day for forty days, I transform myself, my wife, and my lineage."

This is an example of how to construct a goal. Use these twelve points, practice them on a consistent basis, and you will accomplish anything your heart desires. When making your simple sentence or phrase, be sure not to use any not's, can'ts, won'ts, don'ts, or never's. Do not use contractions or negative words. For example, do not say, "I will not say negative things to my wife." The unconscious only hears the verbs and nouns and omits the modifiers. The unconscious will hear, "I will say negative things to my wife." Therefore, leave out contractions and not's.

Often, I will make a tape for each client based upon his specific needs. The tape will consist of affirmations and encouragement of specific goals and behaviors. A good book on making affirmations is *Words That Heal* by Douglas Bloch. *Self-Sabotage* by Martha Baldwin lists other good books on this topic. It is also an excellent book about healing in general.

• Building value

I encourage each person to get involved with some kind of spiritual practice, whatever his faith may be. Studies have shown that those who are involved with spiritual practice heal quicker. Finding one's value in relationship to a loving God is more lasting and fulfilling than seeking brief sexual encounters. I also encourage those in recovery to seek a personal relationship with God as their loving parent. True value comes from *being*, not *doing*. He needs affirmation on a daily basis for just being loved as a son of God.

I immediately take the focus off of sexual identity—not being homosexual, bisexual, or heterosexual. Disassociate from the problem and associate with the solution. True identity is in being a child of God. This is where lasting value remains. Encourage spirituality and value building.

Principles in Napoleon Hill's classic, *Think and Grow Rich*, apply directly to the healing of homosexuality and other burdens of the heart. Just change the goal of "growing rich" to "going straight." Then you get, "Think and Go Straight!" This book is available on cassette from the publisher. I suggest the client listen to this wonderful, timeless treasure and others like it.

Therapeutic Tools and Techniques
Stage II: Grounding

Intellectual	Cognitive Therapy Communication Skills Problem-Solving Techniques
Emotional	Inner-Child (IC) Healing Three Stages of Healing IC Support Network
Physical	Exercise/Diet/Sports/Fun/Bioenergetics/ Breathwork/Therapeutic Massage
Spiritual	Building Self-Worth Experiencing Value from God Meditation/Prayer/Affirmations/Study/Spiritual Community

© Richard Cohen, M.A., January 1999

Stage Two: Grounding

1. Continuing with the support network
2. Continuing to build self-worth and experiencing value in relationship with God
3. Building skills: assertiveness training, communication skills, and problem-solving techniques
4. Inner-child healing: identifying thoughts, feelings, and needs

INTELLECTUAL

- Cognitive Therapy—Understanding faulty thinking

"The greatest revolution in our generation is the discovery that human beings, by changing the inner attitudes of their minds, can change the outer aspects of their lives."

—William James

Peter used to think he never fit in and was different from everyone else. One issue he had throughout his school years was sharing at the lunchroom table. Thus, as an adult he was ill-at-ease with fellow employees when they lunched together. He convinced himself that he alone suffered from this malady of feeling different and not fitting in. So, at a healing homosexuality seminar, we took a poll: How many feel like a geek at the lunchroom table? About 90 percent of those in the room raised their hands. Ninety percent! Peter was stunned. He learned that he was not alone and that many others shared his same fear of not belonging.

The person in recovery must understand how the mind works and the many tricks it plays on him. Therefore, I use a heavy dose of cognitive therapy. One of the best and simplest tools I have found is Dr. David Burns's workbook entitled *Ten Days to Self-Esteem* and its companion, *The Feeling Good Handbook*. There are ten clear and simple lessons to learn. I generally have the client do one lesson every two weeks, filling in the workbook assignments and doing the supplemental reading from the handbook. These are very good skills to eradicate cognitive distortions and faulty and self-destructive ways of thinking that lead to bad moods and depression.

I make sure he masters the art of the Daily Mood Log, a skill Burns teaches to slay self-sabotage and poor self-esteem. Dr. Richard Carlson's books, *Don't Sweat the Small Stuff and It's All Small Stuff*, continue where Burns ends. Other useful books are *The Search for Significance* by Robert S. McGee, and *Reinventing Your Life* by Dr. Jeffrey E. Young and Dr. Janet S. Klosko.

- Learning communication skills

Being responsible for one's thoughts, feelings, and needs is a very important lesson to learn. Reclaiming personal power and the ability to represent oneself in the world is essential to mental and emotional well-being. Therefore, I teach basic communication and assertiveness skills. In his

Feeling Good Handbook, Dr. Burns dedicates the last third of his book to communication skills. I have the client practice these skills, and I also give him several of my handouts.

From Dr. Harville Hendrix, I use a threefold technique to teach the art of **reflective listening**:

First: Mirror or paraphrase someone's communication.

"If I heard you correctly, you said. . . . " "Did I get it?" "Is there more?" "So, in summary, you said. . . . " "Is that the essence?"

Second: Validate his thoughts.

"You make sense to me because. . . . " "Is that the validation you need?"

Third: Empathize with his feelings.

"Given all that, I imagine you feel. . . . " "Are those your feelings?"[2]

During reflective listening, the listener does not have to agree with what the other person is sharing. The important thing is to hear and understand him. Then the speaker will experience being validated and understood. Most of the time, we do not need advice; we just need to be heard. During the reflective listening process, make sure *not* to interject one's thoughts or opinions. Wait for your turn after the speaker has completed his sharing. Reflective listening is learning to walk in the other person's shoes, seeing life through his eyes.

Next, I teach a skill for **negotiating needs**:

First: Present the facts—what someone said or did that caused him to have a strong reaction.

Second: Acknowledge feelings—he uses only feeling words (sad, mad, glad, afraid, etc.).

Third: Identify judgments and beliefs he has about what the other person said or did.

Fourth: State what needs, desires, or wishes he has of the other person.

Fifth: State what he is willing to give to make the relationship work.

Here is an example from a couple that I was recently counseling. The wife had a need to share with her husband. Many times, she would initiate conversations around 11:00 P.M., just as they got into bed. This irritated him because he felt very tired and had to rise before 5:00 A.M. to get to work the next day. This was his communication: "When you want to share with me late at night, I feel angry, hurt, upset, and frustrated. I think you are not considering how tired I am and that I have to get up early tomorrow morning. If you would like to share with me, I request that you do so before 9:00 P.M. I am willing to listen then and give you the time you need because you are important to me and I love you."

Do not make assumptions. Assumptions generally mislead. When I assume anything, I make an "ass" out of "u" and "me." Make a "reality check" if you think someone is upset with you. Here is an example of a reality check: "Were you angry with me when I saw you in the kitchen this morning?" A reality check is asking about a belief or judgment that you have about the other person. It helps objectify perceptions.

Do not expect others to know what you need. *Expectations kill.* We need to learn to express our needs, rather than expect others to know what we need (expecting them to mind-read). Infants and toddlers expect care because they are totally dependent upon the parent or caregiver for survival. As adults, we must learn to express that which we need rather than assume or expect others to know what we want, need, or desire.

Another communication skill is the **sandwich technique**:

First: State how he feels about the relationship. "I really care about you." "I really love you." "I value our relationship."

Second: State the difficulty that he has with the individual. State what outcome he would like to see. "Recently, you have been screaming at me a lot. That hurts me deeply. I feel unloved, unimportant, and rejected. I think you are under a lot of pressure, and I'm taking the blame for your frustrations. I need you to deal with your feelings more responsibly and not take them out on me. I am willing to help you in a positive way, but not be your punching bag."

Third: State again how he feels about the relationship. "I love you and I commit myself to our relationship."

In this way, he sandwiches the problem with how he really thinks and feels about the other person. It makes it easier for the other person to receive his sharing. He must be responsible in all communication, using "I" statements instead of "you" statements. He must take ownership for his thoughts, feelings, and needs without blaming the other person.

I always teach that it is not the situation or person that upsets him. It is his unresolved wounds of the past that are being restimulated in the present that cause him distress. Therefore, he must learn about his core issues, take care of himself properly, and communicate in responsible ways.

Of course, there are many other communication skills; these are but a few I use. The key is to learn responsible communication, sharing one's thoughts, feelings, and needs, rather than blaming and accusing others— "I" statements rather than "you" statements.

•   Teaching problem-solving techniques.

Some methods that I use are HALT, focusing, emotional map, and journaling.

HALT

This is a useful technique to help the person in recovery deal with addictive behaviors. If the adult-child feels like acting out, he can HALT, and take this inventory: Am I Hungry, Angry, Lonely, or Tired? If the person acted out already, he can identify what led him into the behavior.

> One day, Bryan's boss was in a bad mood. He reprimanded Bryan for handing in a report that he thought was incomplete. Bryan was also having a hard time at home. He was married with several children. His wife was calling out for attention, as she had many needs. Bryan felt like a candle burning at both ends.
>
> After leaving work, Bryan headed for an adult bookstore, found a man in a nearby booth, and had sex. Afterwards, he felt terrible and did not know why he had done such a thing. He had promised God, himself, and his wife that he would not do this again.

Now, let me explain the use of HALT as a diagnostic tool for a sexual addiction:

"H" is for Hungry.

When we do not eat properly (physically, emotionally, mentally, or spiritually), we lose control of our Self (Self = higher self, true self, real self). Lusting after another person is usually a message that the adult-child feels a sense of low self-worth, looking at someone else to fill his emptiness. This may come from feeling rejected or criticized, whether real or perceived, by a boss at work, a parent at home, a close friend, a spouse, or a partner. In the case of same-sex attractions, the adult-child envies in another what he feels lacking in himself. He hungers after another man to fill the pain or void.

Bryan felt rejected by his boss and pressured by his wife. The void may be filled with either healthy or unhealthy things. In Bryan's case, he chose the latter.

Another "H" is Happiness.

When he feels excited about something and tries to share that joy with someone else, and if the other person does not respond or rejects his sharing, he may feel rejected and immediately become depressed. Next, he might head for the bedroom or bathroom to masturbate, or go out the door to have sex. In this situation, masturbation is used as a means of emotional medication to numb the hurt, pain, and disappointment.

"A" is for Angry.

Does the adult-child have upset feelings toward someone or some situation that he has not expressed? Is he withholding frustration, anger, fear, or guilt? If he has not expressed those feelings appropriately, then sexual desires may emerge, almost magically, seeming to come from out of nowhere.

Bryan felt angry with his boss for criticizing his work. He felt frustrated and unable to meet all his wife's demands. He did not express or deal with these feelings. Instead, he repressed them and used sex as a means of escape, to numb his pain. Had Bryan taken care of those unexpressed feelings in healthy and appropriate ways, the sexual feelings would have dissipated.

"L" is for Lonely.

Is the adult-child meeting his legitimate needs for intimacy in appropriate, healthy, loving nonsexual relationships? Everyone has a need to love and be loved. *Isolation equals death.* It separates us from the many possibilities of giving and receiving love. Sexual desires will increase in proportion to the loneliness one experiences. Everyone needs touch. Touching is an important part of maintaining health. If a person does not fulfill basic needs, then sex becomes a substitute for intimacy. The individual must keep his love bucket filled. Otherwise, he will go on overdrive, dry up, and use all kinds of unhealthy substitutes, like sex, to fill the void.

Bryan overworked and undernourished himself. He was isolated from family, friends, and God. He was running on empty.

"T" is for Tired.

Tiredness and stress cause the adult-child to revert to old ways of taking care of his needs, such as acting out sexually. The adult-child must come to know himself, his assets, and his liabilities. He must learn to take care of himself healthfully. If not, then he cannot genuinely love others, for self-hatred works its way out. Living under too much stress may work for some but be disastrous for others. Keeping the balance is important. Sexual desires may seem to appear out of nowhere when someone is under pressure. Sex will not solve the problems. Change of lifestyle or present circumstances will. The adult-child is in charge of his life, no one else. He must transform his life from victim to victor.

Bryan needed to share with his boss and wife about his situation, communicating his needs in a positive and assertive manner. He needed to reduce his stress level and build some quiet time into his schedule.

Another "T" is Transference.

If the adult-child is spiritually and emotionally sensitive, he may pick up on someone else's vibrations, someone who is putting out a lot of sexual energy. He may feel sexually drawn to or repulsed by another person and have no idea why. It is important to help the adult-child develop healthy boundaries, learning to separate me from thee. He will need to learn how to discern what is his and what is theirs.

The HALT technique is a useful diagnostic tool to help the individual learn about his triggers or sore spots and proper self-care.

Focusing

This is a very simple technique created by Dr. Eugene Gendlin. You can read about it in his book entitled *Focusing*. This is a very effective tool to help the individual get in touch with his deeper feelings. Gendlin teaches a six-phase model:

1. Clear the space, put aside other cares and worries, and focus on the main issue.
2. Discover the felt sense within the body; identify where it is.
3. Give that felt sense a name or phrase, e.g., hurt, anger, pain, confusion.
4. Resonate the felt sense and the name to make sure they correlate; then be with that feeling for a minute.
5. Ask the felt sense several questions to find the deeper truth: "What is it about _____ that hurts so much?" or "What is it about _____ that is so uncomfortable?" The mind will come up with many rational responses to the question or questions, but the real truth will

come from deep within the body and soul, below the neck. Sometimes this takes quite a while to uncover. He will know when he has found his deepest truth when he experiences an "Ah hah" response from deep within his gut. After he discovers his truth, I have him ask, "What do you need?" Then I have him create a visualization for healing, or negotiate the fulfillment of specific needs with that part of himself. He must make good on all promises. Broken promises further wound the soul and destroy trust. He must become a good parent to his inner soul.

6. Thank the part of himself that spoke, honoring his truth. Be grateful.[3]

Kevin was sitting all alone in an office, waiting for an appointment. The receptionist told him to wait until the person he came to see had arrived. He waited and waited. Suddenly, he felt as if the walls were caving in on him. He ran out of the room, forgetting about the appointment altogether.

In the next session, we used focusing. I had him close his eyes and put all cares and worries aside. I then asked him to locate where in his body he felt the feeling he had experienced when the panic began. After discovering that place in his gut and groin, I asked him to give that feeling a name or phrase. He came up with "fear" and "dread." Then, I asked him to resonate the felt sense in his body and the feeling words to make sure they correlated. He did, and they did. After a minute of having him sit with those sensations, I asked him to talk to those feelings and ask them, "What is it about fear and dread that hurts so much or is so uncomfortable?" I instructed him that his head would give many logical answers, but the deeper truth was below his neck, lodged deep in his heart and soul. After sitting silent for many minutes, Kevin began to panic, shake, and cry intensely. He recalled being held down by a friend's father when he was six years old. The man had locked the door, and Kevin was too small to unlock the latch. The man then sexually abused him, performing every kind of sex act imaginable. After he had had his way with Kevin, the man threatened to hurt him if he ever told anyone about what happened. Kevin had buried this memory for well over twenty years.

After that, memory healing allowed his inner child to grieve the losses of innocence and childhood and then receive support. It was a remarkable beginning in unraveling the connections that had kept him locked into compulsive homosexual acting-out behaviors. It took many months of grieving and processing his thoughts and feelings. Today, Kevin has healed those memories and has no more need to act out sexually. Also, he learned how to create healthy boundaries in relationships with others.

Focusing is a very effective tool to get in touch with deeper thoughts, feelings, and needs. Not all focusing sessions are as potent as Kevin's was. However, it is a very useful technique to help people get in touch with their bodies and their feelings, especially if they tend to intellectualize.

Emotional Map

This is a skill developed by Dr. Barbara De Angelis. It is a very practical tool in expressing feelings and creating intimacy. There are six stages to the emotional map:

1. Anger
   This is the phase of blame and resentment. "I hate it when you. . . ." "It makes me so mad that you. . . . " "I'm fed up with you. . . . "

2. Hurt
   This is the phase of sadness and disappointment. "It hurts me that you. . . . " "I feel so sad when you. . . . " "I felt so disappointed when you. . . . "

3. Fear
   This is the phase of insecurity and wounds, when the individual recognizes his core issues that are being triggered by the event. "I am afraid that you. . . . " "It scares me when you. . . . " "It reminds me of. . . . "

4. Regret
   This is the phase of understanding and taking responsibility. Here the individual takes responsibility for projecting his fears and feelings onto the other. "I am sorry that I. . . . " "I did not mean to. . . . " "Please forgive me for. . . . " "I know sometimes I. . . . " "I understand that you feel. . . . "

5. Intention
   This is the phase of solutions and wishes. "I want to. . . . " "I promise to. . . . " "I hope that we can. . . . " "Let's try to. . . . "

6. Love

> This is the phase of forgiveness and appreciation. "I love you because. . . ." "Thank you for. . . ." "I forgive you for. . . ."[4]

This is another model for bringing healing intrapersonally and interpersonally. One can practice this alone or with another person who agrees to the process. Give equal time to each phase, not focusing solely on anger and hurt and then shortchanging the other stages. This can be written or spoken. You can read more about this method in Dr. John Gray's book, *What You Feel, You Can Heal.* He and Dr. Barbara DeAngelis developed this model together for the Los Angeles Personal Growth Center.

Journaling

This is an excellent method to assist the individual in identifying his thoughts, feelings, and experiences. It will also stand as a record of his healing journey. I encourage journaling on a regular basis as a means of meditation and self-reflection. Also, through regular journaling, he will come to understand what triggers unhealthy thinking and inappropriate behavior(s). Journaling is a helpful tool for relapse prevention.

EMOTIONAL

- Inner-child healing

Here he begins the work of healing his inner child(ren). It is important to introduce inner-child work in the later part of Stage Two to help the individual get in touch with his deeper feelings and needs. A more intellectually inclined individual, living from the left brain and out of touch with the right brain (body and emotional awareness), often does well to begin with inner-child work before using the Burns workbooks and other cognitive techniques.

The concept of the inner child is interchangeable with the unconscious. The term *inner child* represents the accumulated experiences a person had as a child. He can imagine himself as a toddler, an infant, a preschool child, and a child in elementary, junior high, high school, and perhaps college. During these stages of development, the child may have experienced many wonderful and painful things. *Feelings buried alive never die. Time does not heal all wounds.* Unless a person releases those feelings, they remain stuck in the body and soul.

"The Inner Child is a powerful presence. It dwells at the core of our being. Imagine a healthy, happy toddler. As you picture this child in your mind's eye, sense its aliveness. With great enthusiasm, it constantly explores the environment. It knows its feelings and expresses them openly. . . . As time goes on, the child runs head-on into the demands of the adult world. The voice of grown-ups, with their own needs and wants, begins to drown out the inner voice of feelings and instincts. In effect, parents and teachers say, 'Don't trust yourself, don't feel your feelings. Don't say this, don't express that. Do as we say, we know best.'

"With time, those very qualities that gave the child its aliveness—curiosity, spontaneity, ability to feel—are forced into hiding. . . . For survival's sake, the growing youngster sends its delightful child spirit underground and locks it away. That Inner Child never grows up and never goes away. It remains buried alive, waiting to be set free. . . . The Inner Child is constantly trying to get our attention, but many of us have forgotten how to listen."[5]

Every child needs to experience what I call the three T's of successful parenting: Time, Touch, and Talk.

Time: being with Mom and Dad, doing things together, sharing in activities. Touch: being held, embraced, hugged, stroked, caressed by Mom and Dad and other trusted family members. Talk: sharing with Mom and Dad, being listened to, letting them know who you are, and finding out who they are.[6]

From experiencing the three T's of successful parenting, a child will gain a sense of value, belonging, and competency. Value is an inner belief that I matter, that I am special, valuable, and unique. Belonging is an awareness of being wanted, accepted, cared for, enjoyed, and loved. Competency is a feeling that I can do any task, cope with any situation, and meet life without fear.[7] From relationships with Mom, Dad, family members, and influences from our faith, community, society, and culture, we gain a sense of our value, belonging, and competency, or lack thereof.

The path of growth from infancy to adulthood has various stages of development. There are specific tasks to accomplish during each stage (see the chart, Seven Stages of Development).

If basic needs for love, affection, appreciation, and instruction remain unmet, and our wounds remain unhealed, they will prevent us from actualizing our full potentials as adults. *Same-sex attractions are merely a smoke screen, a method by which the inner soul is desperately attempting to get the attention of the adult self.*

Seven Stages of Development

Stage	Time	Activity	Needs	Learns
1) Bonding	0–6/9 mos	cries	mirroring	Being Trust Hope
2) Exploring	6/9 mos– 18/24 mos	explores	protection	Doing Self-Motivation Will
3) Separation	18/24 mos– 3 yrs	rebels	acceptance/ limits	Thinking Independence Will
4) Socialization	3–5/6 yrs	questions	answers	Identity Power Purpose Cause-Effect
5) Latency	5/6– 12/13 yrs	doing arguing	rules reasons	Skills Structure Negotiation Competence
6) Adolescence	12/13– 18/21 yrs	all of the above in a more mature form		Identity Sexuality Separation Autonomy
7) Adulthood	18/21–	recycle through all stages in ways that support specific adult tasks		Independence Interdependence Fidelity

Source: Jon and Laurie Weiss, *Recovery from Codependency*

Using a model from transactional analysis, we have three major parts of our personality: the child, the parent, and the adult (see the chart, Structure of Our Inner Family). There are two sides of each subpersonality, or ego state.

• Inner Child

We have a healthy, authentic, genuine, or true inner child full of wonder, love, creativity, playfulness, magical thinking, and true spirituality. The

Structure of Our Inner Family

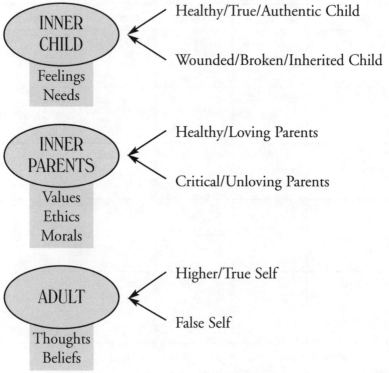

INNER CHILD

Feelings
Needs

Healthy/True/Authentic Child

Wounded/Broken/Inherited Child

INNER PARENTS

Values
Ethics
Morals

Healthy/Loving Parents

Critical/Unloving Parents

ADULT

Thoughts
Beliefs

Higher/True Self

False Self

© Richard Cohen, M.A., January 1999

shadow side is the wounded or broken inner child, who may experience either pain, heartaches, guilt, shame, loneliness, fear, despair, hopelessness, and/or misperceptions. The wounded inner child may be an accumulation of our unresolved heartaches, our parents' unresolved issues, and/or those inherited from previous generations.

• Parent

There is the healthy, loving, nurturing inner parent that affirms, appreciates, and accepts the inner child. The healthy parent uplifts, encourages, and praises the inner child. The shadow side, or dark side, is the critical, unloving inner parent who may be either judgmental, critical, cold, conditional, abusive, or neglectful of the inner child. The inner parental voices are an accumulation of introjections from parents, authority figures, religious figures, and cultural messages.

• Adult

There is the higher or true self, with understanding, problem-solving abilities, unconditional love, forgiveness, connectedness, and a strong sense of self-worth. The shadow side, or dark side, is the false self, the protective armor, character defenses, coping strategies that we develop to protect the wounded inner child. These are the masks we wear, the games we play, that shield us from further pain.

Each of these subpersonalities has distinctive roles:

> The inner child focuses on feelings and needs.
> The parent focuses on values, ethics, and morals.
> The adult focuses on thoughts and beliefs.

To change his life in the present, he needs to awaken, discover, recover, and heal the wounded child and children within. He needs to bring into consciousness that which has remained unconscious. He needs to quiet the voice of his inner critical parent, and develop a loving, encouraging, nurturing inner parent. Unless he brings into the light that which has been in the darkness, those parts of him will continuously sabotage all adult efforts to succeed and will create "dis-ease" in his present life. Therefore, he needs to heal the unresolved wounds of the past.

To begin this process of healing, he must first learn to listen to the voices of his inner family. Then he must distinguish who is speaking and learn to satisfy the needs of his inner child in healthy and appropriate ways. He may also need to discipline and set boundaries for his inner brat or his inner tyrant who wants his way, the way he wants it, when he wants it.

Martha Baldwin describes this character as the Saboteur. "Ignoring the Saboteur empowers it. Trying to get rid of it only teaches it to hide itself in more clever ways. The only route to ending self-sabotage is through facing and knowing the Saboteur intimately. Only then can you acknowledge its destructiveness, accept its presence, learn to contain its power, and say 'no' to its attempts to destroy your life. Only when you ignore and deny its existence can the Saboteur do its deadly work secretly and successfully."[8]

- Three stages of healing the inner child

I have divided the process of healing the inner child into three stages.

> ## Three Stages of Healing Your Inner Child
>
> ### 1. Self-Parenting
> - Listen to thoughts, feelings, and needs.
> - Be a good parent: time, touch, and talk.
> - Healing behaviors.
>
> ### 2. Spiritual Parenting
> - Prayer, meditation, study.
> - Experience value as son/daughter of God.
> - Healing of memories with spiritual mentors.
>
> ### 3. Mentoring
> - Heal homo-emotional and hetero-emotional wounds.
> - Mentoring relationships.
> - Developing same-sex friendships and activities.

© Richard Cohen, M.A., January 1999

Stage One (Inner-Child Healing): Self-Parenting

The three tasks in Stage One are:

1. Listen to thoughts, feelings, and needs
2. Be a good parent: time, touch, and talk
3. Healing behaviors

First, he must learn to listen to the voice of his inner child. Before he looks to others to take care of his needs, he must first become a good parent to himself. He needs to enhance and/or create a nurturing inner parent and quiet the critic. Most of us desperately want acceptance. Acceptance begins within, not from the world outside. First, he must learn to accept himself before looking to others for acceptance. Otherwise, he determines his well-being by how others think and feel about him, rather than how he thinks and feels about himself. World peace begins within, not outside.

To begin this work, I have all my clients use the workbook, *Recovery of Your Inner Child,* by Dr. Lucia Capacchione. In this workbook, she helps the individual identify different parts of the inner family—the vulnerable child, angry child, nurturing parent, protective parent, critical parent, wounded child, playful, creative, and spiritual children. It is a very good primer to begin inner-child recovery. The individual will need to do the drawing and writing exercises. It is important to complete all the assignments. It will be of tremendous benefit.

Other books that might be helpful are *Healing the Child Within,* by Dr. Charles L. Whitfield; *Self Parenting: The Complete Guide to Your Inner Conversations,* by John K. Pollard III; *The Inner Child Workbook,* by Cathryn L. Taylor; and *Recovery from Codependency: It's Never Too Late to Reclaim Your Childhood,* by Dr. Laurie Weiss and Dr. Jonathan B. Weiss.

> Russell struggled with homosexual thoughts, feelings, and desires for over thirty years. He went to several therapists in his life. Mostly, they helped him "manage" his desires, but never helped him identify where they came from and then heal those wounds. During his inner-child work of drawing and dialogue, he discovered an angry, frustrated child hiding behind a compliant, "nice boy" image. By accessing these feelings and allowing them to surface, his homosexual desires began to diminish immediately. He discovered that his homosexual behavior was masking an angry and hurt child within.

> Mark was over forty. He had tried just about every method to change. Nothing took away his voracious appetite for men. During his inner-child work, he discovered a horrific memory of being sexually abused when he was about four years old. Until he had created the time and space for his inner child to heal, this wound was not revealed. Through deep grieving and mentoring, he released the pain and replaced it with new experiences of healthy, masculine love. Mark is now free from homosexual desires, since he found the key to his treasure. Entering through the wound, he found his heart.

A brief note about *False Memory Syndrome.* (This is the condition where one remembers abuse that did not, in fact, occur. Thus, the memory is false.) I am very cautious not to suggest the presence of sexual abuse with any of my clients. In Mark's case, it came to the surface on its own accord. In my healing, the memories emerged without my therapist suggesting any possibility of abuse.

Second, spend time with his inner child, e.g., drawing, dialogue, meditation. John Pollard's book, *Self Parenting,* describes a simple and effective method to dialogue with the inner child. With the dominant hand, he allows the voice of the parent to speak. With the nondominant hand, he allows the voice of the child to speak. In this way, both voices communicate and share with each other. It may sound bizarre, but it is very effective. The reason to draw or write with the nondominant hand is that it bypasses the intellectual neurology and gets him in touch with his body and feelings. He may divide the paper down the middle. On one side, he lets the adult or parent voice speak and ask questions. On the other side, he allows the voice of the inner child to speak and respond.

Meditation is another tool to access the inner child. I have developed an audiotape called *Healing Your Inner Child*. I have my clients use this on a regular basis. There are many other wonderful tapes on healing the inner child. I suggest using inner-child meditations and other meditation/affirmation tapes at least once a day, and optimally, twice a day (upon rising and before bed). If that seems like too much, I have him begin meditating less frequently. He uses the tapes several times per week and then increases until he builds up to a daily routine.

Third, create healing activities with his inner child, i.e., bike rides, walks in the park, skating, and taking trips. Through dialogue, drawing, and meditation, his inner child will reveal what he needs. It is important to meet those needs in a timely and appropriate manner. He must never make promises that he cannot keep. Consistency is the key to successful parenting. He must keep his word. In this way, his inner child will begin to trust him, and then reveal increasingly deeper truths.

Again, he needs to keep a balance between light and dark energies—go into the well and play in the fields. Heal the wounds, and learn to enjoy life.

Stage Two (Inner-Child Healing): Spiritual Parenting

The three tasks of Stage Two are:

1. Prayer, meditation, and study
2. Experience value as a son or daughter of God
3. Healing of memories with spiritual mentors

First, through prayer, meditation, and study, the individual may get in touch with the wounds and needs of his inner child/children.

Second, he may use affirmations on a daily basis to recreate his inner child's sense of self-worth. I have my clients use affirmation audiotapes, either custom-made (ones that I have made or they have made for themselves) or those of other healers. The important thing is to continuously reprogram the mind, heart, and soul to believe in oneself as a precious child of God. "Autosuggestion is the agency of control through which an individual may voluntarily feed his subconscious mind on thoughts of a creative nature, or, by neglect, permit thoughts of a destructive nature to find their way into this rich garden of the mind. . . . *Repetition of affirmation of orders to your subconscious mind is the only known method of voluntary development of the emotion of faith.*"[9]

The third task is the use of memory healing. Through creative visualization, the individual will age-regress to painful memories and there imagine his inner child being mentored. A spiritual mentor may be a religious figure, an idealized parent, a trusted friend, a loved one, or one's own parent(s) in an idealized form. For this, I also developed a meditation tape called *Memory Healing*.

If the individual is ready to retrieve and release the past, this is a very effective tool for healing. Please note that if the memory is one of severe trauma, the individual must heal those wounds in the presence of another. There needs to be, as noted psychiatrist Alice Miller calls it, a "sympathetic witness," someone to be there through the pain and process of healing, and perhaps to hold and nurture the individual if necessary.

Memory healing may also be used to create wonderful and happy experiences. The spiritual mentor may engage his inner child in fun, learning, and nurturing activities, thus fulfilling his deepest unmet needs. The spiritual mentor may play ball, go fishing, take a walk, or hold the individual's inner child.

Stage Three (Inner-Child Healing): Mentoring

The three tasks of Stage Three are:

1. Healing homo-emotional and hetero-emotional wounds
2. Mentoring relationships
3. Developing same-sex friendships and activities

First, after the individual has gained a greater sense of self-worth, self-knowledge and self-parenting, he may reach out and have others assist in the process of healing homo-emotional and hetero-emotional wounds. The first and best choice is his own mom and dad. If the parent or parents are available and willing, I begin working with the entire family. I recommend the client invite his mom, dad, and siblings in for a marathon session. This generally lasts for many hours, depending upon how large the family is and how many unresolved issues remain between them. I use Dr. Martha Welch's model of Attachment/Holding Therapy, which you can read about in her book, *Holding Time*, and hear more about on her audiotape or videotape series. I will speak more about this process of holding in Stage Three of recovery. Here the parents and child begin to resolve their attachment strains. It is a very deep and rewarding process for all involved. Working directly with the parents will save the individual years of time in therapy.

Second, if the parents are deceased, unwilling, or unable to participate, I encourage the individual find mentors to assist in the process of healing. If he belongs to a church, synagogue, or spiritual organization, it is good to seek mentors from this supportive community. The point is to find mentors who act as the loving and supportive mom or dad that he never experienced. Successfully married people make the best mentors. You can read more about this in chapter 12 on mentoring. There I list the roles and responsibilities of both the mentor and the adult-child.

The individual will heal wounds and fulfill unmet needs in the context of such a loving, committed relationship. I envision the elders of our communities, whose children have grown up and left home, being wonderful mentors to these individuals who desperately need parenting. It is a win-win situation for all involved. The young receive blessing from the elders, and the elders receive their rightful position in our culture, being respected for their wisdom and love.

Third, it is very important to encourage the individual to build healthy same-sex friendships. This, too, provides opportunities for healing. Again, the types of friendships are: 1) fellow strugglers; 2) secure heterosexuals who know about his struggle and are supportive; and 3) secure heterosexuals who do not know about his struggle and are good role models and friends.

• Voice Dialogue

Voice dialogue is a tool that can be used to explore the unconscious and its relationship to our conscious self. Voice dialogue helps us understand and retrieve those lost parts of our character. Many subpersonalities live within each of us. Each one of these characters has an important task. Each one has its purpose. By accessing these subpersonalities, we gain greater understanding and peace. Then our higher self will stand in its rightful position as the CEO, learning to listen and validate each part of our character. It does not mean that we must act upon each voice; it simply means that we give a voice to each part.

You can read more about voice dialogue in *Embracing Our Selves*, by Drs. Hal and Sidra Stone, the creators of this technique. When someone is "stuck" and cannot progress in his healing work, this is a great vehicle to create movement, understanding, and breakthrough. I have found it quite effective with many who are more analytical and out of touch with their feelings.

Some of our subpersonalities include the protector, pusher, pleaser, rebel, loner, martyr, performer, showoff, caretaker, victim, complainer, creater, teaser, and vulnerable child. (See the diagram, Layers of our Personality, "False Self," in chapter 4.)

I was counseling Sam, who compulsively logged onto the Internet to view male pornography. He emotionally flagellated himself for these moments of weakness. Rather than continuing to beat himself up, I suggested that he explore the meaning behind his desire(s) to look at male nudes. We used voice dialogue, which was extremely revealing of his inner needs. Here are Sam's words about the session:

"He [Richard] had me explore my Internet viewing via feelings in my body. First, from the chest, came Strength. I took the posture of a posing bodybuilder. Strength didn't want me to look at the [Inter]net. He felt it was a waste of time because I have what I look at in them. His desire for me was to listen to him 100 percent of the time instead of 85 percent of the time.

"Second came Fear from the stomach. Fear wanted me to look at the Net. He feels power in forcing the naked men to do his will. He said it was like having a powerful animal in a cage in front of me with all the thrill of its power, yet completely safe. Fear wants me to look in order to make them do my will.

"Third came Power/Anger. I named him John. [Often, during a voice-dialogue session, I will ask the client if he would like to name the particular subpersonality.] He came from the groin, not the penis so much. John also wants me to look at the Net, to see that they have nothing more than me! John came into Sammy's life at age thirteen. [Sammy was Sam's nickname as a kid.] Sammy was afraid and hid him in the back closet. Sammy wanted to be Mommy's boy or girl, as long as I was hers. As long as John was there, he was a threat to that relationship. So, John hid. Sammy both feared John and squashed him, and then blamed John because Sammy didn't feel manly enough. He couldn't have it both ways. Either he would grow up to be a man or he wouldn't! Thank God, Mom eventually said that Billy was her favorite and broke the unspoken agreement, setting Sammy free. [Billy was Sam's younger brother.]

"Richard said I need to listen to all three of them. If I look at the Net, I should change seats and let each of them speak.

"Lord, thank you for an excellent session. I need to let all three of these guys live appropriately within me. I must let You set me free and strike a balance in all this."

As you can see, each of Sam's subpersonalities had a different reason for watching the naked men. By allowing each voice to speak his truth, Sam was able to be a good parent to his inner family. He shared at subsequent sessions that his desire to look at male nudes on the Internet had virtually disappeared, now that he understood what had been driving his desires.

Voice dialogue helps bring greater awareness to the healthy adult and parent selves so that he can make better choices in his life. Again, through accessing feelings in his body, he is able to get in touch with various sub-personalities. Focusing is a process of internal exploration. Voice dialogue is a process of internal exploration through externalizing those inner voices. Both are highly effective.

PHYSICAL

• Bioenergetics

I use *Bioenergetics*, as taught by Alexander Lowen, and *Core Energetics*, as taught by John Pierrakos. You can read about these techniques in their books of the same names. Both of these men worked with Wilhelm Reich and developed their own styles of body-centered therapy.

The main reason I like to use these methods is to help the individual get in touch with his power. I have found that the homosexually oriented individual has repressed or suppressed a tremendous amount of anger. Because I have found the emotion of anger so important in the healing process, I will devote chapter 8 to this subject.

Through bioenergetic and core energetic exercises, the individual may access anger, fear, pain, and other repressed emotions. With different bioenergetic exercises, twenty-year-old Christopher had a flashback of being sexually abused when he was seven. All those years, he blocked this memory from his conscious mind. Through bioenergetics, he was able to access that memory. The reason is this: There is a repository of unexpressed emotions locked deep in the musculature of the body. Old feelings and old thoughts that we buried long ago still exist in the cellular structure of our bodies. We can retrieve memories of early infancy, childhood, and adolescence through bioenergetic or core energetic exercises. Christopher hit pounding pillows with a tennis racquet and sometimes with his fists. During the session, the memories came flooding back, and the healing began.

I have constructed a special set of cushions for pounding. They stand almost waist-high. I cover them with a sheet and I give my clients exercise gloves to protect their hands. (Many got blisters before the use of gloves because they had pounded so hard, releasing years of pentup anger and pain.) Then I give them a tennis racquet to hit the pillows. I tell them to imagine the person who hurt them is standing on the opposite side of the pillows. Then I commission them to release their anger and pain. It is important to have them verbalize while they express their thoughts and feelings. (See photos on page 176.)

Proper breathing is important in order for this process to be effective. Deep belly breaths help support the release of pent-up emotions (diaphragmatic breathing). Sometimes they do not know what to say to the person, or they are afraid to speak their truth. I have them start by saying the person's name repeatedly until some thoughts or feelings emerge. For example, if it's a father issue, I have them say, "Dad," "Dad," "Dad," "Dad," over and over, using proper diaphragmatic breathing. The individual needs to speak the word or words that he used when addressing his father as a child, i.e., Dad, Father, Daddy, Padre, etc. It is important to have him speak in his native tongue, even if he is living in a foreign country and is fluent in that language. This is because we store past memories in the original language of childhood. I will further detail the use of bioenergetics in chapter 8.

A word of caution for those with chronic anger problems: The use of bioenergetics is contraindicated in this situation. He will need to learn alternative ways to get beneath the mask of anger and deal directly with his wounds and loss of self-worth.

• Breathwork

With deep breathing, the individual may access many past memories and remove emotional blocks. Deep breathing brings light into the dark areas of our psyche. I have found the technique of transformational breath to be extremely helpful and revealing. I have used this tool both in individual and group sessions. The group I led for the past six years enjoys this technique very much because it allows each one to enter into his own space and discover, in the safety of the group, hidden places that need healing.

A breath session generally lasts about an hour and could easily go for several hours. First, we establish a consistent pattern, breathing into the belly, inhaling and exhaling both through the mouth. The pattern of breathing is one beat in (one second) and two beats out (two seconds). This is done for about forty-five minutes. The natural body rhythm seems to determine how long the process will last. One might think that it is impossible to sustain deep breathing for that length of time. However, after the first 10 minutes or so, the body takes over and it becomes quite a natural process.

I have seen people make incredible breakthroughs by using this breathing technique. It is very important to find a qualified facilitator to lead others through such an experience. One must not try this on his own at first, as he may access areas that need professional assistance. (Rebirthing is a similar technique.)

• Exercise, Sports, Diet, and Fun

It is important to reclaim the body. Having a poor self-image is an integral part of the homosexual condition. Encouraging individuals to participate in sports and exercise is another important part of healing and growth. He may need male mentors to teach him athletic skills. She may need female mentors to assist her in reclaiming her femininity.

• Therapeutic Massage

Healthy touch is very important and necessary, not just for those healing out of homosexuality, but for every man, woman, and child. I know that through healthy touch we will improve our emotional, mental, physical, and spiritual well-being. Alcoholism, drug addiction, sexual abuse, sexual addictions, gambling, workaholism, shopaholism, sports addictions, and the like will end when we learn to touch in healthy and appropriate ways. I will talk more about this in chapter 10.

If the individual in recovery has experienced any sexual or physical abuse or severe neglect, then healthy massage therapy will accelerate the healing process. However, it is critical to find a massage therapist who is safe, has experience with survivors of abuse and neglect, and is secure in his heterosexual identity.

SPIRITUAL

Using affirmations, meditations, prayer, and study will enhance spiritual development. I encourage the participation in any spiritual community that is a safe place for the individual to experience God and the love of others.

He needs to learn to be content with what he has and who he is right now, rather than what he will get or who he will become in the future. Learning to be content and accept himself now is a very important lesson to learn and practice. He must develop an attitude of gratitude. There is a tendency of these SSAD men and women to feel discouraged and/or depressed. For this reason, each man and woman in recovery needs to practice speaking at least fifty or more "gratitudes" per day.

Therapeutic Tools and Techniques
Stage III: Healing Homo-Emotional Wounds

Intellectual	Understanding Root Causes of Homo-Emotional Wounds
Emotional	Grieving/Forgiving/Taking Responsibility Techniques: Memory Healing/Voice Dialogue/Role-Play/Psychodrama/Holding/Mentoring/Inner Child Support Network
Physical	Exercise/Diet/Sports/Fun/Bioenergetics/Breathwork/Therapeutic Massage
Spiritual	Building Self-Worth Experiencing Value from God Meditation/Prayer/Affirmations/Study/Spiritual Community

© Richard Cohen, M.A., January 1999

Stage Three: Healing Homo-Emotional Wounds

1. Continuing all tasks of Stage Two
2. Discovering the root causes of homo-emotional wounds
3. Beginning the process of grieving, forgiving, and taking responsibility
4. Developing healthy, healing same-sex relationships

In this phase, he begins the psychodynamic or emotional work of recovery.

INTELLECTUAL

It is very important for the individual to understand the basic root causes that created his same-sex attractions. First, a man must address the wounding he experienced with his father, brother(s), and any other close male figures that may have influenced his growth and development. The woman must address the wounding with her mother, sister(s), and any other close female figures that may have influenced her growth and development. It will also be necessary to address peer wounds, body-image wounds, [homo]sexual abuse, and other painful experiences from infancy through adolescence.

If there is still an unawareness about the root causes of homo-emotional wounds, the individual must read books on the etiology of same-sex attractions.

EMOTIONAL

I use a wide variety of methods for healing the heart: Voice Dialogue, Gestalt Therapy, Breathing, Role-Play, Psychodrama, Mentoring, Memory Healing, Inner-Child Healing, Attachment/Holding Therapy, Transactional Analysis, Family Constellations, Bioenergetics, and Core Energetics.

The important task is to feel it in order to heal it, grieving the wounds of the present and past. The quickest and most effective way to heal is to deal directly with the source whenever possible. For this, I strongly recommend working with the parents, no matter how old they and their adult-child may be. From eight to eighty, it is never too late to heal and grow. God has built into each one of us the ability to completely heal and recover at any time. Simply put, this is called the *process of grieving*. If you watch a child when he gets hurt, he will scream and cry and let you know how he feels. After releasing his pain, he wants comfort and a kiss, and then he is on his way to play. That is the long and short of it, how every person is meant to deal with pain.

The problem with adolescents and adult-children is that they have learned to shut down, close up, and numb out. They have learned many ways how not to feel and deal directly with their feelings, thoughts, and needs.

I will briefly describe a few of the methods I use.

* Attachment/Holding Therapy

In the process of recovery, it is essential to heal at the source of the pain. If the parents are living and willing, please encourage the healing to take place within the family system. Attachment/Holding Therapy, as taught by Dr. Welch, is a wonderful model to bring intimacy and attachment between parents and children. My wife, three children, and I have been using this in our family. It works wonders, helping to resolve longstanding conflicts, buried hurts from the past, and simple arguments in the present.

Through physical touch and holding, the child and parent are safe to express deeper feelings. Through touch, we create a safe container. (It is important to note that holding therapy is not advisable for unsafe families where there is violence, addictions, or abuse.)

I have done holding with my parents, and in a matter of hours we healed years of buried anger, hurt, pain, and misperceptions. I am constantly amazed how the individual who developed same-sex attractions has misperceived or misinterpreted many of his parents' actions and words. Therefore, in the process of healing the parent-child relationship, the adult-child will need to first discharge his anger and pain. After he does this, then the parent or caregiver may share his or her perspective of what occurred. The child is then open to receive the parents' love and truth.

> I worked with sixteen-year-old Jared for a short while before inviting his parents in for a holding session. Jared fantasized nightly about being held by men and having sexual relations with them. When his dad held him, he wanted to run away and went cold. Jared had so many stored-up "angries" toward his dad, and therefore was unable to receive his father's love. Jared's dad was a genuine, caring, and loving father. For many reasons, Jared had cut off emotionally from his dad. One main reason was this: When Jared was in elementary school, his dad worked very hard and traveled a lot for business. Jared missed his father so much, and so did his mom. In her frustration, when her husband was away, she would often lose her temper and get angry with Jared and his siblings.

A quick aside: One thing I have observed about most men I have counseled is that they have a more sensitive nature than other males. If there is a biological factor for those who experience same-sex attractions, it is with this sensitive nature. Consequently, they take things to heart more deeply than other kids and cannot let things go. Instead of coming out with the goods (their deeper thoughts, feelings, and needs), they keep it bottled up inside and then cut off, unbeknownst to the parents.

> So, Jared missed his father and feared his mother. Then an interesting phenomenon occurred. He unconsciously blamed his dad for not being there to protect him from his mother's outbursts. Jared secretly held onto his feelings of blame and hurt toward his dad. Throughout this time, his father continued to play an active role in his life by reading him stories at night and doing all kinds

of activities with him by day. The feelings of blame and anger were buried deep in Jared's unconscious.

When Jared entered puberty, he started to experiment sexually with other boys. Through the Internet, he accessed male pornography and thus began his active fantasy life. Having internally cut ties with his dad and not wanting to receive his hugs and kisses, Jared began masturbating several times a day.

Another important influence was that Jared's father forbade him to express his anger. When Jared's dad was a little boy, he, too, was not permitted to express his anger at home. Therefore, he passed on to Jared a part of his disowned character, the repressed angry boy (Exodus 34:7). Beneath the repression of Jared's anger were his hurt feelings. Underneath them were the warm feelings he had had for his dad. So, to access the love, first he had to discharge the anger and pain.

Through holding with his dad, the anger began to emerge. With Dad holding on tightly, Jared began to reconnect with all the reasons that he learned not to trust his father. "I needed you and you weren't there." "Where were you when Mom was screaming at us?" And on he went through his list of grievances. His father had absolutely no idea how hurt Jared was all those times he was away. He grieved about his son's aches and pains, and then apologized in tears. Jared's heart began to melt. After several sessions of Jared expressing his anger and pain, while being held by both Mom and Dad, he began to reattach to both his parents.

After that, quite naturally, his homosexual desires were assuaged as he came into his full identity as a son and young man, no longer disconnected from his deeper feelings and from his parents. For truly, the homosexual condition is simply a form of psychological and spiritual detachment from self and others.

Harvey Jackins, founder of Re-evaluation Counseling, explains so simply and clearly about this process of healing. First, we need to revisit the painful experience. Second, we need to discharge the emotional pain and unpleasant thoughts we experienced at that time. Third, we come to understand what really happened and then process that information into our conscious mind.[10]

Attachment/Holding Therapy with family members is the quickest route home. If this is not possible for whatever reason(s), then I use such methods as memory healing, role-play, bioenergetics, psychodrama, voice dialogue, and breathing to help the individual get back in touch with the wounds and release the pain.

Dr. Jane Myers Drew's book, *Where Were You When I Needed You Dad?* contains more than fifty exercises to help in the process of recovery. All the exercises contained in her book are useful in healing other relationships, e.g., mother, stepparent, sibling, and grandparent.

- ## Memory Healing

Memory healing is a process of going back to the painful event, reexperiencing the thoughts and feelings, discharging the pain, and creating a mentor to help reframe the event, this time with a positive outcome. The mentor may be a spiritual figure, a trusted parent, a loving friend, or the individual himself as an adult. I have a meditation tape that details the memory healing process. As mentioned previously, the individual must heal the deepest wounds in the presence of a sympathetic witness. What was created in an unhealthy relationship must be healed within the context of a healthy, loving relationship. Some books that I have found useful on memory healing are *The Broken Image*, by Leanne Payne; *Healing of Memories* and *Healing for Damaged Emotions*, by David Seamands; *The Gift of Inner Healing*, by Ruth Carter Stapleton (out of print but available at the library); and *Making Peace with Your Inner Child*, by Rita Bennett. (One may participate in Leanne Payne's Healing Prayer seminars to experience the healing of memories.)

- ## Role-Play

Through role-play, someone else plays the part of the person who created the pain or whom he perceived as creating the pain. The individual gets to share all of his thoughts and feelings, those kept hidden for so long. He can scream, cry, and release as necessary without physically hurting himself, the other person, or the furniture!

- ## Bioenergetics

If the rage is strong, he may need to do some bioenergetic work. Generally speaking, women bury their anger beneath their tears, and men bury their tears beneath their anger. However, a man detached from his gender identity may store anger much like a woman, under his tears.

This is a very liberating, healing, and safe way for people to release their anger and pain. For many, it is very frightening to express anger. Perhaps their parents forbade their anger. Perhaps a sibling or parent was the owner of anger, and in response the individual became the good little boy or girl.

• Psychodrama

In our support group, we may create a psychodrama, reenacting a past event that symbolizes the painful relationships and experiences. Different members of the group act out the parts of the parents, siblings, or whoever took part in the event. Then the client gets to reexperience his feelings and thoughts. He may have someone else play himself so that he might watch the drama unfold. Many times, this is very provoking. Another way to help access feelings and thoughts is by having the client play all the different roles: He plays his father, mother, siblings, and others, acting and speaking as he imagines they would. In this way, he gets to feel/think what the others might have experienced.

• Family Constellations

Bert Hellinger's work is instrumental in healing generational wounds that affect present-day situations. He has observed many unseen factors that have influenced the family system, e.g., former lover, war experience, aborted child, extramarital affair, theft, murder. By constructing a family constellation in a group situation, the individual in recovery may experience great insight and relief from these hidden influences that have impacted his life.

> Neil always felt as if he did not belong in his family. He thought he was adopted, even though he resembled his father and mother. In his family constellation, he set up his mother, father, two brothers, his father's first wife, his mother's dead former lover, and his father's war victims and buddies from World War II. His father had served in the army and had killed many people during the war. He had also lost many of his fellow soldiers. By seeing and participating in the constellation, Neil realized that he had taken on the energy of the dead soldiers and war victims. He thought his father loved them more than himself; therefore, he would become like them and willed himself to die. In this way, he would finally obtain his father's love. In the constellation, the father figure was instructed to tell Neil, "I want you to live. I love you now." When he spoke these words, Neil's heart opened to his father, and he grieved in his dad's arms. At last he realized that he did belong.

• Mentoring

Mentoring is an important method of restoring love, especially if the parents are deceased, unavailable, incapable, and/or unwilling to participate. Mentors are invaluable to help men heal the father wound and to help women heal the mother wound. The unmet needs and wounds of the past heal more quickly with the assistance of a same-sex role model. Through these mentoring relationships, same-sex attractions wane when the pain is felt and the wounds are healed. I experienced this, and so have the numerous men and women that I have counseled.

> Norm came to me ready to die. He had been having anonymous sex with men in parks and restrooms for over fifteen years. Having sought counseling from previous therapists, he was ready to call it quits. The pain was too much. Norm had already accomplished Stage One and Stage Two work in therapy. However, his previous therapists did not understand about Stage Three and Stage Four dynamics of recovery. They had used cognitive and behavioral approaches, but did not understand the deeper origins of his wounds and the need for emotional reprocessing. Through memory healing, I took Norm back to the events that created his homo-emotional wounds: painful memories with his dad and brother and sexual abuse by several men. A boy who has a deep father wound is very susceptible to sexual abuse, as this becomes a substitute for his father's love. The root of homosexual pursuit as a teen and adult is in the need for the lost or never-obtained father's love. The individual repeats behavior from previous conditioning, whereby sex becomes a substitute for love.

> Norm grieved years of tears as he reexperienced the memories of abuse. Since his father had passed away, I had a mentor hold him during this session. In those moments of grieving and receiving love, Norm's homosexual feelings were lifted and never returned. The sexual desires connect neurologically to the painful experiences of the past. Once he retrieved the memories and released the feelings, the sexual desires waned. They were unnecessary because his inner child was heard and healed.

Christian, whose story you read in the previous chapter, came to me at the point of almost divorcing his wife of twenty years. He had been to many therapists. They told him to accept his homosexuality as a God-given condition. He was ready to throw in the towel and leave his wife and kids. Through accessing the original wounds (anger and hurt toward Mom, missing an absent father, and sexual abuse by a neighbor), he was able to let go of the homosexual desires. He finally experienced freedom from the "aching that was in my gut" since he was a child. We used bioenergetics, memory healing, psychodrama, and mentoring. Now he and his wife are very close, and today he is a free man.

I believe in total healing, not just a Band-aid method or a spiritual starvation diet because the desires are "wrong." I know that the desires are connected to painful memories. *They are not gay, nor bad, but SSAD.* Once a person accesses and relieves those memories, the homosexual desires will naturally dissipate. He will experience true gender identity when the walls surrounding his heart are removed.

Once a person releases the emotions, three tasks are important to achieve: 1) emotional makeup work; 2) mental reprocessing; and 3) behavioral changes.

Emotionally, he may need more time with parents or mentors to receive the healthy touch and bonding that he missed. He will also need to do makeup work for developmental tasks yet unaccomplished. Therefore, being with same-sex friends and mentors will initiate him into the ways of men.

Mentally, the brain needs reprogramming. Healthy thinking, assertive behavior, and good communication skills replace years of faulty thinking, immature behavior, and poor communication.

He must unlearn bad habits. Dr. Harville Hendrix found that emotional breakthroughs were insufficient to create lasting change. An individual must also make behavioral changes. "Insight into childhood wounds is a critical element in therapy, but it is not enough. People also need to learn how to let go of counterproductive behaviors and replace them with more effective ones."[11] It takes months of vigilant effort to change a habit. Old behaviors, such as running away from problems and throwing temper tantrums, will not disappear overnight. Love and limits, learning proper boundaries, will be most important to fill in developmental gaps.

It's important to reiterate that emotional healing alone will not work. Mental and behavioral changes must also take place. This is another piece of the puzzle, reprogramming the mind and creating healthy habits. "Any significant long-term change requires long-term practice, whether that change has to do with learning to play the violin or learning to be a more open, loving person."[12] Here the work of Dr. Christopher Austin and others is very helpful. If parents are participating, they can coach and discipline their son or daughter in the renewal of the mind, body, and spirit. If the parents are not present, then the mentors, counselor, spiritual leader, and others may assist.

PHYSICAL

Maintain proper exercise, sports, diet, and fun. Therapeutic bodywork with a qualified therapist is also helpful.

SPIRITUAL

To rebuild the mind and develop self-worth, continuous use of affirmations is important. He is transformed with love and truth by listening to audiotapes with positive messages. He needs to meditate, pray, study, and use affirmations.

I will briefly mention the relationship between spirit influence and same-sex attractions. My core belief is that each man, woman, and child possesses both a physical body and spirit. Upon death, we shed the physical and live in spirit eternally.

I believe there may be a component of spirit influence in the homosexual condition. You may read a psychologist's appraisal of the situation in *The Unquiet Dead*, by Dr. Edith Fiore. She found that an opposite-sex spirit influenced each of her homosexual clients. Female spirits influenced male clients, driving them toward men, and male spirits influenced female clients, driving them toward women. Perhaps these spirits were connected in some way through the lineage, either direct ancestors or those who were hurt by their ancestors. These influencing spirits may be seeking revenge, retaliating for wounds inflicted upon them. "Yet he does not leave the guilty unpunished; he punishes the children and their children for the sin of the fathers to the third and fourth generation."[13] A good film that depicts how the "sins" or mistakes of the ancestors may later "curse" their future generations is an Italian movie called *Fiorile* (1993).

Others believe there are "spiritual strongholds" that drive individuals toward homosexuality. This knowledge does not make the course of restoration any easier. It does help to explain why some might suffer through no fault of their own. However, it is still up to each individual to undo the wrongs of his past.

A warning to those with a strong religious orientation: Spirit liberation or deliverance alone will not heal the homosexual struggler. Spirit influence is just one part of the condition. Well-intentioned people of faith have deeply harmed many men and women seeking healing from same-sex attractions. These men and women were "delivered" from spirit, yet their homosexual feelings and desires continued. Rightly so, since there was no healing of root causes or fulfillment of unmet needs. If there were no base in the individual's life for the spirit to influence, he would never have had homosexual feelings in the first place. Therefore, ridding an individual of spiritual influence may simply be an adjunct to the entire program of healing, if this is the desire of the individual in recovery. (See References to spirit liberation at the back of the book.)

Therapeutic Tools and Techniques
Stage IV: Healing Hetero-Emotional Wounds

Intellectual	Understanding Root Causes of Hetero-Emotional Wounds Learning About: Men/Women Differences Marital Relations
Emotional	Grieving/Forgiving/Taking Responsibility Techniques: Memory Healing/Voice Dialogue/Role-Play/ Psychodrama/Holding/Mentoring/Inner Child Support Network
Physical	Exercise/Diet/Sports/Fun/Behavioral Reeducation/Bioenergetics/Breathwork/ Therapeutic Massage
Spiritual	Building Self-Worth Experiencing Value from God Meditation/Prayer/Affirmations/Study/Spiritual Community

Stage Four: Healing Hetero-Emotional Wounds

1. Continuing all tasks of Stage Two
2. Discovering the root causes of hetero-emotional wounds
3. Continuing the process of grieving, forgiving, and taking responsibility
4. Developing healthy, healing opposite-sex relationships and learning to understand and appreciate the opposite sex

INTELLECTUAL

Here the individual needs to explore any possible wounding with the opposite-sex parent or significant people of the opposite sex. Many men may have had a close binding, unhealthy attachment with their mothers. Many women may have had a close binding, unhealthy attachment with their fathers. There may also have been physical, emotional, mental, or [hetero] sexual abuse that needs healing.

It is very important for the individual to understand the basic causes that created a fear of intimacy with the opposite sex. Unless the individual addresses these issues, he will unconsciously project the unresolved wounds and unmet needs onto his future spouse or any other close opposite-sex friend or coworker.

Another task in this final stage of recovery is to learn about and appreciate the opposite sex. Some books I recommend about male/female differences and marital relations are: *You Just Don't Understand*, by Deborah Tannen; *Men Are from Mars, Women Are from Venus*, by John Gray; *Getting the Love You Want*, by Harville Hendrix; *Hot Monogamy*, by Patricia Love; *Dancing in the Dark*, by Doug and Naomi Moseley; *Why Marriages Succeed or Fail*, by John Gottman; *Saving Your Marriage Before It Starts*, by Les and Leslie Parrott; *Light His Fire* and *Light Her Fire*, by Ellen Kreidman; and *Making Love Work*, by Barbara De Angelis.

EMOTIONAL

Basically, we follow the same protocol as in Stage Three, using Voice Dialogue, Gestalt Therapy, Breathwork, Role-Play, Psychodrama, Family Constellation, Mentoring, Memory Healing, Inner-Child Healing, Attachment/Holding Therapy, Transactional Analysis, and Bioenergetics.

The important point, again, is to feel it in order to heal it. The individual must release the emotional toxicity of the hetero-emotional wounding. For some in recovery, the hetero-emotional issues may not be as meaningful or potent as the homo-emotional issues. However, for others, the hetero-emotional wounds and needs may be more profound.

Whenever possible, the most effective way to heal is to deal directly with the source. If it is an issue with Mom, Dad, sibling, or relative, I recommend working with that person. To prepare for those sessions, I have the individual do many of the exercises from Dr. Jane Myers Drew's book, *Where Were You When I Needed You Dad?* Again, all fifty exercises are applicable to any close relationship.

Dr. Drew has created an 8-stage model of recovery:

1. Increasing your awareness of the person's impact on your life
2. Mourning and letting go of your pain
3. Reappraising your parent or significant person
4. Healing the child within
5. Becoming your own good parent
6. Finding the wisdom in the wound
7. Reconnecting with your parent or significant person
8. Building satisfying relationships.[14]

These are good exercises to use in preparation for meeting and healing with the individual or individuals with whom the wounding occurred. Please be advised: First, the individual needs to do much processing before reconciling with his parents. If done prematurely, it may become a blaming session. This will be disastrous for all involved. Processing and preparation are key to successful reconciliation. The adult-child needs to take full ownership of his thoughts and feelings. Preparation may take anywhere from several months to several years.

Attachment/Holding Therapy with the opposite-sex parent is the most direct way to heal. If he or she is unavailable for any reason, then I strongly suggest the participation of other opposite-sex mentors. A happily married couple is the best mentor for the adult-child. First, it is important to create a healthy, nonsexual bonding experience, rather than jumping right into dating and more intimate experiences with the opposite sex. Our culture is grossly oversexed, and most men have not been able to separate sex, love, and intimacy. Most women are hungering for physical intimacy from their husbands. Most men think sex is intimacy and have not understood the difference between the two.

PHYSICAL

Employ the same exercises and techniques of Stage Three. In addition, he may need behavioral reeducation. Men with a Same-Sex Attachment Disorder may have a more feminine manner, and women may have a more masculine manner. Men need to inherit masculine behaviors, women more feminine behaviors.

Video therapy is very helpful during this stage, allowing him to see his behaviors. Through behavioral reeducation, a man may inherit what he missed in the early stages of child development—being and acting like a man, rather than being and acting like his mother or sister. If a video camera is not accessible, then I use a mirror. In this way, the individual is able to see his behavior and how he might change it.

I do not focus on behavioral reeducation until this final stage of recovery, because there are too many important changes that need to take place before this.

SPIRITUAL

Continue as in Stage Three. Finally, once an individual experiences and restores a secure sense of masculine or feminine identity, then he or she is ready to move on and give back to others.

Conclusion

He needs to heal his mind, heart, body, and spirit. He needs to create true intimacy with himself, God, others, and creation.

> One night, after our support group, I was cleaning up and spilled a five-tier candleholder on the carpet. There were red, green, and white stains everywhere. I asked Jessica, my daughter, how to get the wax out of the beige carpet. She showed me how to put blank paper over the wax and apply a hot iron, thereby reheating the wax and allowing it to be absorbed into the paper. I sat there for almost one hour, amazed at how the different color waxes were lifted out of the carpet and onto the many pieces of paper.
>
> As I sat there, I asked God, "Why is this happening? I feel so exhausted from the group, from counseling all week, writing my book, being a husband and father. I am wiped out. What is there to learn here?" Very clearly, I heard, "I am the iron. You are the paper.

The carpet is your clients, and the wax is all their pain, wounds, and hurts coming to the surface and leaving their bodies. I am the heat, which brings forth the healing. You are merely an instrument by which I help relieve them of their suffering and pain."

Helping men and women heal out of homosexuality and any burden of the heart is no simple task. It takes time, guts, and persistence. It is definitely the path of greatest endeavor, rather than the path of least resistance, that leads to a rich and full life.

CHAPTER SEVEN

Mark

I grew up in what you call a "nice family"—father, mother, older brother, and me. Things looked so perfect. We were actually the envy of the town because of my father's work. We traveled to different parts of the world when we were kids. We lived in an East European country that had been under communism for decades. Without knowing it, that also affected our family in ways that I would only understand years later.

I didn't know what was going on with me. I was too young to remember being different or feeling different. As far as I could remember, I felt unusual towards men, a feeling that unsettled me, that confused me. I vaguely remembered the first time I felt that way. It was in a locker room, and the only picture that stuck in my mind was that of a naked man standing in front of me. Since then, that feeling stayed with me. It was a mixture of fear, excitement, pain, need, and confusion. I felt that feeling around my brother, around my father, and around any other man I was with. I felt that in my dreams, in my alone times, always longing for, and at the same time, fearing closeness with men.

At an early age, I started to pleasure myself, and that felt good. Perhaps it was the only thing that felt good in my life. Later, I showed my brother, and we did it together. It felt good for a moment, only to feel worse afterwards. It was a way to numb the pain. It became like an addiction later in my teenage years. Without realizing it, over the years it completely took over my life, controlling my every feeling and sense of who I was. I based my self-worth on whether or not my brother showed interest in me, and later, on whether or not the other men around wanted me.

I became an invisible kid. Nobody ever knew what was in my mind, and my parents could never see what I was going through or understand my struggle. By the time I turned thirteen years old, the only thing I had in mind was to have a man perform anal sex on me. Nothing else had value. Nothing else was interesting. I could not study. I could not have friends. Luckily, the environment prohibited homosexual relations, and the fear of going to jail or having my father lose his job kept me from acting out. So, I played it safe and only had sex with my brother. Looking back at it from where I am now, I don't know how I managed to survive, how I could live with so much confusion and pain. Nevertheless, at the time all of this was happening, I considered myself lucky.

My father is a good man who came from a broken family. His father ran away and left him and his sister with their mother. He mostly focused on providing for the family and not so much on meeting our emotional needs. By the time I realized how much I needed him, there was no relationship whatsoever between us. That need, that longing for a strong male presence in my life to guide me and love me, became a sexual desire over the years.

When I reached my twenties, because of the fall of the communist regime and the "freedom" that people were experiencing, I decided to go for it. I got involved in a couple of homosexual relationships. It was like a roller-coaster ride. All that emotion that I had been stuffing for years got loose, and all those fantasies took form. Like popping open a warm can of soda, everywhere was a mess. I was a mess. I realized that this was not what I wanted, that world that I had imagined was not real, and the love that I was looking for was not there.

I tried also the "right" way, getting involved with a girl, thinking that such activity would straighten me out. It didn't work that way either.

It took me a while to realize that I was very unhappy, that my life was a mess, and that I wanted things to change. I remember taking time to meditate. I found myself trying to make sense of who I was and where I wanted to go from there. The homosexual feelings were still there, the temptation was there, the pain and confusion were there, and on top of that, the knowledge experienced in my skin was there too. I had nobody to talk to about my struggle, nobody to share my pain with. I turned even to God to search for help, a thing that I was not used to doing.

Locally, I sought help talking with different people, from therapists to counselors, without getting any clear answer. I could see them trying to help me. Some of them felt the pain I was going through, but didn't know how to help. Most of all, I was getting more and more frustrated. I talked with my parents about it, too, but they were completely ignorant of this matter. I determined myself that if there was anything, anywhere in the world to be found out about this issue, I would find it. That's when, through some friends of mine and through a miracle, I first heard about healing in general and, in particular, healing homosexuality through Richard's healing foundation. My friends ordered his videotape and I watched it. It was a tape about the healing process, and it made so much sense that I said to myself that this is it. It took me a little more than two years from that date on to manage to come to the U.S. and work with Richard.

Once I got here, I heard all the explanations, I got the tools, and I saw where I had to go and how to get there. Believe it or not, that was just the beginning. Just knowing and understanding the facts brought a great relief. However, the work was just starting. Building self-worth and acquiring communication skills was the first battle. Then mentoring and reparative therapy was the next step. We met twice a week. The first weekly session involved a lot of head work. We did my family history. We dialogued a lot, and that helped me understand how to communicate my thoughts and feelings, how to assert myself, and how to be a more functional and social person. Those things helped me to better understand my thinking patterns and how to take charge over my life and the events that I experience.

The second weekly session centered more on emotions and expressing feelings like fear, pain, and anger. It was about being and letting myself be loved and accepted, feeling worthy and feeling good about myself, experiencing healthy love through time, touch, and talk. That was something new. For the first time, somebody was taking an interest in me without wanting me sexually. I was just supposed to receive love and enjoy it. That was a battle. I learned to trust, set boundaries, and let myself experience love.

Two years passed, meeting regularly and doing my homework. Meanwhile, I started to make friends, mostly in the support group that Richard formed. That helped me to practice the skills I learned. It became much easier to deal with feelings and find out where they were coming from. I was feeling relieved a lot. However, the struggle with the homosexual feelings was still there. I knew and I felt that there was still a wall around my heart, which was surrounding me, preventing me from receiving the love that I needed to heal the innermost wound. My soul still felt wounded deep inside, and still there was that pain.

After searching for some time, I felt strong enough to try a more focused and intense approach by attending a weekend seminar organized by a group of men. The weekend went, step by step, deeper and deeper to the wounded parts of each of the participants. Having so many other men around me dealing with deep issues and seeing them sorting out feelings, letting go and healing wounds, and having the support of a dedicated staff, gave me the courage to take a risk. I plunged into that part of me where the wound was, the core of my being. It was hell. Everything that I had learned in the past two years with Richard came together and brought fruit in those fifteen minutes. It was the right place and the right time— perfect timing. I sank into the fear and then made my way to the wall. I saw in front of me, and surprisingly, that all the work I had done over the past two years had chipped away, little by little, pieces of the wall. Now, with a single blow, it crumbled.

I saw that little boy in the locker room, helpless and scared to death. There was nobody there to protect him and to save him from the threat in front of him, the naked man. I relived the panic, the fear, and the rage I felt then. I grieved for that innocent child and his pain. I let go of that horrible experience, and when I came back into the room, surrounded by all those men with tears in their eyes, I felt for the first time free. I felt reborn. I didn't feel that pain in my chest anymore.

It took me months to ground that experience in my life and to really believe that it happened. My homosexual feelings disappeared the moment the healing of my wounds began. The days and weeks after, I felt more and more the change, and the feeling of peace and happiness settled into my life. Once that happened, everything else in my life fell into place. It's been more than two years since that weekend experience, and I became the person I wanted to be. I got married, and I am looking forward to meeting the challenges of parenthood. I am happy with myself. I don't regret a second of what I did and what I went through in my healing process. I have people in my life that I feel close to. I love and I am deeply loved. Life is good.

Comment

Mark and his wife now have two children.

CHAPTER EIGHT

Anger: Accessing Personal Power

"Anger exists to protect us from predators. It is an automatic response triggered whenever we feel threatened. . . . But more often, anger is a reaction to psychological hurt or threat of hurt. . . . Anger is almost always a reaction to a temporarily painful or diminished sense of self."[1]　　　　　　　—Steven Stosny, Ph.D.

A Poison Tree

I was angry with my friend:
I told my wrath, my wrath did end.
I was angry with my foe:
I told it not, my wrath did grow.
And I watered it in fears,
Night & morning with my tears:
And I sunned it with smiles,
And with soft deceitful wiles.
And it grew both day and night,
Till it bore an apple bright.
And my foe beheld it shine,
And he knew that it was mine.
And into my garden stole,
When the night had veiled the pole;
In the morning glad I see,
My foe outstretched beneath the tree.
　　　　　　　　—William Blake, 1794

Why Anger?

The main function of physiological anger is to protect us from danger, thus the fight-or-flight response. Anger is a means of defense. The main function of psychological anger is to protect us from further hurt and pain.

There is a repository of unexpressed anger in many individuals who experience same-sex attractions. Because psychological anger is a secondary emotion to mask hurt and pain, these people are out of touch with their core issues/wounds. Therefore, I have found it necessary to help them access the energy of anger to recover their lost selves.

"We have impaired our ability to express our positive feelings by impairing our ability to express the negative ones. When one set of emotions is blocked, the other set is inhibited. In order to keep the lid on the bad feelings, people tend to keep the lid on the good."[2] The bad news is that when we lose the ability to express our negative feelings, we also lose touch with the positive ones. The good news is that when we learn to express our negative feelings in positive ways, we will then experience the good feelings trapped below.

"Anger is a survival emotion, a warning signal that needs are not being met. . . . If we don't allow our children to show their anger, then they learn *not* to listen to their warning system (of self-protection) and they lose their true self."[3] The "good little boy" syndrome created a demasculinized male. The pleaser, the nice guy, the sweet one—all of these roles have betrayed his essential masculine nature. He operates from the more feminine side of his character. Between the ages of one and a half to three, he failed to separate and individuate from his mother and bond with his father. He may also have lost his ability to say "no." The overly sweet girl or woman has lost touch with her more masculine, aggressive nature. She, too, holds an imbalance in her emotional ecology.

We have a saying in our support group—"Nice Sucks." Literally, it does. It sucks on the approval of others. When one is nice, sweet, and good for the sake of winning the approval of another, he is sucking the life energy from the other person. It is a form of idol worship. Feeling unlovable and feeling a lack of self-worth, he then lives for the acknowledgment of others. If people approve of him, then his life has meaning. If they withhold their approval, then he must again modify his actions to gain acceptance. Another term for this is *emotional dependency* or *codependent behavior*.

I am not putting down being "nice" or kind altogether. If these emotions are genuine, and if one is aware of who he is and is not seeking the approval of others, then it may be a genuine attribute. However, my experience with men, women. and adolescents coming out of homosexuality, and many others who were abused, neglected, or abandoned, is that they did not successfully individuate from the (perceived) perpetrator(s). Therefore, in their adult lives, they continue to capitulate to the needs of others without an awareness of their own feelings, thoughts, and needs. And, if they are aware of their feelings, thoughts, and needs, oftentimes they do not express them for fear of losing what little love they perceive they are receiving. Therefore, they say "yes," when they feel and or think "no."

When the child repressed hurtful feelings, thoughts, and desires, he lost himSelf (Self = true self). As a result, Mr. Nice Guy was born and Mr. Hurt was disowned. Therefore, I have found the use of anger work to be a necessary part of the healing process. Here, one can retrieve lost thoughts, feelings, and needs that he buried alive. Bioenergetic and core energetic methods are excellent tools to help "pop the cork." When someone is stuck in his head, I will oftentimes lead him over to the pounding pillows and have him begin to breathe, hit, speak, and scream (see photos).

Again, proper diaphragmatic breathing is important in the process of recovering lost feelings. I have him breathe into his belly as he inhales. I have him pound the pillows with the racquet as he exhales, while saying the name of the person about whom he has unresolved feelings. It is important that he keeps his jaw open and relaxed as he exhales and speaks the person's name, or speak whatever he needs to say.

"Dad, dad, dad, dad, dad," he repeats over and over again until he gets in touch with his deeper feelings. Once he taps into that reservoir of repressed or unexpressed emotions, I instruct him to let them out and let them go. With continued deep breathing, he releases the years of pent-up feelings: "Where were you when I needed you?" "Why didn't you hold me?" "Why didn't you teach me how to be a man?" "I needed you and you weren't there." He goes on, allowing the voice of his inner child to speak.

This takes time. Getting angry is scary for some people. Perhaps one's parents never gave him permission to express such feelings at home. Perhaps he feels it is unacceptable to show anger toward his mom or dad, that this will make him a bad person. Perhaps he grew up in an angry environment and the expression of anger triggers unresolved traumatic feelings.

The person who is out of touch with his anger needs gentle coaching to express this emotion. I demonstrate how it works, showing my willingness to express anger and help him express his. We hold the racquet together (I stand behind him), hitting and screaming simultaneously. Modeling that it

Hold the tennis racket over your head; take a deep diaphragmatic breath; place your feet shoulder width apart; and imagine your dad standing on the other side of the pillows.

Your jaw needs to be relaxed and wide open as you speak "Dad" on the same, sustained breath.

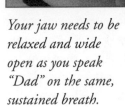

Photos by Ken Weber

Hit the pillow at the end of the breath. Repeat the process over and over, without delay, until deeper feelings/ thoughts emerge.

is acceptable to express powerful feelings is very important. Many people never learned how to express the feeling of anger in healthy ways, or the family of origin rejected the expression of this feeling. The person who thinks that anger is unacceptable needs to understand that this is a natural, God-given emotion. We do the pounding (bioenergetic work) together, until he feels comfortable enough to express it on his own.

The person who grew up in a hostile environment may be afraid of his anger or losing control. The child within feels that if he lets go and lets out his pain, he will die. This is a natural response to feeling intense hurt and pain. I reassure the adult-child that when he does express his anger and pain, he will not die, and I will be there with and for him. When a person lets out the anger and eventually taps into the hurt and pain, he eventually experiences a deep sense of relief. It happens every time, because this is the natural process of healing that God has built into each one of us. Our children demonstrate for us every day this healing process. When they get an "ouchy," they scream and/or cry. After they let the pain out, they need our comfort and love. Then they feel much better and can understand what happened and use the information to avoid a dangerous situation in the future.

I have observed that many religious people think that to be truly devout, they must always be "good." This becomes confused with the natural expression of the full range of our emotional vocabulary. Both the Old and New Testaments in the Bible address anger. They do not forbid this emotion. They speak of ways to express it in a healthy and appropriate manner: "The old tradition says that if a man loves God he can become holy in twenty years; but if he hates God, he can do the same work in two years."[4]

By accessing repressed anger, we gain entry into the soul. If one is unaware of the shadows (hidden wounds) in his life, all he needs to do is observe the people that he dislikes or that easily upset him. There he will find his wound(s). *Again, it is not the event or individual that upsets us; it is our unresolved pain being resurrected.* We generally avoid our wound and pain by blaming others. However, when we open up to the pain and grieve the losses, healing will naturally occur. When we release the feelings, we need to replace them with healthy love. That is why healing touch is an important and integral part of recovery.

"The Iron John story proposes that the golden ball [golden child] lies within the magnetic field of the Wild Man, which is a very hard concept for us to grasp. We have to accept the possibility that the true radiant energy in the male does not hide in, reside in, or wait for us in the feminine realm, nor in the macho/John Wayne realm, but in the magnetic field of the deep masculine."[5]

After grieving the wounds, understanding occurs, and one can integrate the lessons he has learned. Through such a process as this, he will naturally attach (or reattach) to his own sense of gender identity, no longer invested in the coverup. Again, at its deepest level, this is a Same-Sex Attachment Disorder. Once the wounds are removed, natural feelings of connectedness will emerge.

Note: People who have anger problems will need to learn skills of self-regulation. There are many books and techniques on anger management. The anger work I am referring to in this chapter is for those who have placed this part of their personalities in the closet.

CHAPTER NINE

Joseph

I was born in Europe. I grew up and lived there for more than twenty years. Thinking back always brings to mind the image of not having a particularly happy childhood. I was a very sensitive child, and so the confrontation with reality was much more difficult for me than it was for others. I can't tell exactly when I started to feel attractions towards boys. However, several years ago, I found out that my uncle sexually abused me. I spent much time with him when I was three to five years old. When I first retrieved these memories, I felt terrified to remember the actual events that happened. What were more painful and intense were the feelings connected with the abuse, all the feelings that were stored up in my body and mind for so many years. I virtually reexperienced the feelings I had as a boy. Believe it or not, I am very happy to have had this memory, to know about it, because it is one factor that led to my homosexual desires.

My mother was at home with my brother and me. When I was a toddler, she did not give me the opportunity to break away from her and find my way. I was educated to be the good boy! My father worked a lot and was almost never home, so there was no one who could have balanced out my mother's role. My brother was born when I was nine years old. From the time of his birth, I was very jealous because I felt that he was the main focus of the family.

Growing up as a teenager was a good time because I had lots of friends in school, but at home I was still unhappy. What happened was that my friends became my family. With some of my male friends from school, I had sexual encounters. Mutual masturbation and oral sex were the things we did together, and I started to like it. At around the same time, I found pornographic magazines of my dad's, and masturbation became more and more like a friend in my lonely life at home.

I never understood why I felt attractions towards boys and men. I felt it was one of the biggest burdens in my life because I also liked being with women, and I definitely wanted to have a family. After finishing high school, my life became even more confused. A good friend of mine went into the gay lifestyle as I was standing right next to him. I didn't know if I should do the same.

At the same time, I was in love with a girl that somehow protected me. I still felt confused, and a trip to the U.S. helped me to clear the picture of confusion. During my visit, I stayed with a gay couple for some time. Through that, I realized that the gay lifestyle was absolutely not right for me. Being clearer about it really helped, but I still felt attractions towards men. In a way, it was harder for me now because I knew for sure that I did not want to go into the gay lifestyle.

At that time, I started to act out. I had sex with men in public parks and bathrooms. Even though it did not happen so often, it still gave me the feeling that I could meet my need for intimacy with men. It did not take too long until I realized how terrible the whole thing was. I tried to stay away from acting out as often as I could. I was partially successful because I relied more and more on masturbation to calm down my need for male intimacy while using gay pornography.

At this time, I was studying at a university. I met a friend and she helped me a lot. Through her, I heard about a therapist who specialized in helping people with exactly the same problem that I had. I could finally meet him on one of his seminar tours through Europe. For the first time in my life, I talked to someone about my problems and desires. Richard was very understanding and helpful. He explained to me the root causes of the condition. He told me that there was the possibility of healing. At that point, I had hope again. God, who helped me to get through all those years, gave me a wonderful gift.

My plan was to go to America and to get into therapy. A year after I first met Richard in Europe, I came to the U.S. There I went into therapy with a colleague of his. It was great because, for the first time, I could really share my story, and I found a lot of understanding and help. I felt understood and not alone for the first time in my life.

After a couple of months in the States, I had to return to Europe to finish school. I also started to prepare to come back for a longer time to get more therapy and also to get in a support group. Back at home, I had wonderful friends who totally supported me and especially a close friend of mine who knew my story, and he literally was there for me whenever I needed him. He held me and we did sports together, had fun together, and worked together on different projects on campus.

At the time, I also met my wife-to-be, and I told her from the very beginning about my homosexual attractions. She said, "We will master it together." She accompanied me back to the States. I got into therapy with Richard and joined his support group. I also found a healing partner, which helped a lot. It was sometimes tough, but I learned more and more about myself. I found my inner child, which helped incredibly to heal the wounds of the past.

Today, I feel I have come a long way. Quite infrequently, I experience attractions towards men. I learned it is just an indication that there is something wrong, something I'm not caring for properly. When I do address the issue, those attractions go away instantly. I feel very good, and I see that I grow closer to my wife every day.

I am grateful to God to have had this opportunity to heal. I am grateful to those who pioneered this way of transitioning.

Comments

I worked with Joseph for two years. He made tremendous progress in that time. One of the most important parts of his therapy was learning about his inner child. Joseph not only had problems with compulsive masturbation and anonymous sexual behavior, he also had an eating disorder. Food and sex were his way of medicating his pain. Food and sex were love.

When he did the Capacchione workbook, he discovered a whole new world. Because of his devotion to his healing work, the voice within began to disclose more and more about his past and present situation. Joseph became a good parent to his inner family. The more he listened, the more he learned. Because of this and his healing relationships with other men, the homosexual desires naturally disappeared.

Joseph also had to learn a marvelous new word, which had not been a part of his vocabulary in either English or his native tongue. That word was "no." As he stated, he grew up being a "good boy" for his mommy and others. In his recovery work, we did a lot of bioenergetics to reawaken his masculine energy. When he finally got the hang of it, Joseph cut loose, and oceans of rage and pain were released. The support group was of tremendous benefit to him. Also, he was a gift to the group, as he readily shared himself with others. In this way, he mentored the newcomers.

Toward the end of our work together, Joseph invited his entire family over to America for a marathon holding session. It lasted a day, and it was simply magnificent. He was able to hold with his mom and tell her how much pain he experienced by her overprotective nature. They wept together. She apologized, not realizing that what she had done had hurt her son so deeply.

He held with his father, crying the tears of a child who so longed for his father's affection and attention. He told his dad how much he missed him when he was out working and in the pubs at night with his friends. "Why didn't you ever take me with you to work?" They, too, wept. His father apologized, and finally Joseph felt his strong daddy's arms around him. Now, their relationship is deepening with each visit. Joseph has requested that his mother back off for now so he and his dad can bond.

Another amazing event took place during the family holding session. Joseph was able to apologize to his younger brother for the abusive way that he had treated him because of the intense jealousy he felt toward him. His brother let out his pain, screaming about what he had gone through. They held each other, grieving together and reconnected in heart. Finally, his younger brother shared with Mom and Dad how their fighting hurt him. The entire family held each other, all crying, releasing years of unexpressed pain.

It was a new beginning for this family. Today, Joseph is more and more in love with his wife. Their sex life is great, his same-sex desires are gone, and they are expecting their first child.

CHAPTER TEN

Touch: The Need for Bonding and Attachment

"The impersonality of life in the Western world has become such that we have pro-duced a race of untouchables. We have become strangers to each other, not only avoiding but even warding off all forms of 'unnecessary' physical contact, faceless figures in a crowded landscape, lonely and afraid of intimacy. To the extent that this is so, we are all diminished. Because of our untouchableness, we have failed to cre-ate a society in which people touch each other in more senses than the physical. With our inauthentic selves, and wearing other people's image of what we should be, it is not surprising that we remain unsure of who we really are. We wear the inauthen-tic selves that have been imposed upon us as uncomfortably as an ill-fitting gar-ment, ruefully, at times, and unknowing, wondering how we got this way. As Willy Loman says in Death of a Salesman, *'I still feel kind of temporary.'"*[1]

—Ashley Montagu

The Healing Power of Touch

Understanding the significance of touch is a foundation for understand-ing mentoring. Touch is the greatest healing power in the world. The topic of touch is very uncomfortable for most people. As a therapist, husband, and father, I practice and encourage healthy touch.

Touch is a necessary component in the process of healing. As a therapist of mine used to say, "First, pull the weeds, and then plant the seeds." First, we take out the bad stuff, and then replace it with the good stuff. The "bad stuff" is the homo-emotional and hetero-emotional wounds. The "good stuff" may easily consist of healthy, healing touch. Men and women who experience same-sex attractions are often touch-deprived, at least touch-deprived in healthy ways. This is a developmental disorder due to a lack of attachment with the same-sex and/or opposite-sex parent.

The individuals coming out of homosexuality may need a significant investment of time, touch, and talk. Please realize again that the essence of same-sex attractions is *lack of attachment*:

- Detachment from parents (especially same-sex parent)
- Detachment from one's gender
- Detachment from one's body
- Detachment from others
- Detachment from one's soul

We cannot underestimate the healing power of touch. It must be administered with great compassion, sensitivity, and understanding. Proper timing is everything. Giving touch without having the individual learn about himself may be as destructive as withholding any form of touch. Therefore, as mentioned earlier, first, the individual coming out of homosexuality must go through the process of behavioral changes and cognitive reparation. Next, he must learn about his inner world through inner-child work or other means to understand his feelings, thoughts, and needs. As he becomes centered and stable, having mentors assist in his healing program will greatly accelerate recovery.

Administering Touch

Touch must be administered in an appropriate manner, at the right time, and by the right person(s). Otherwise, it can reinforce unhealthy patterns and/or abuse. The one to give healthy touch must be secure in his own sense of gender identity. The best ones to offer healthy touch are happily married men and women.

If the parents are unavailable or unwilling to assist, I suggest my clients find mentors who are willing to provide healthy touch. This has been an extremely frustrating and difficult task for many. They long to receive that which was unobtained in early childhood and adolescence. "God is the love of our mother's kiss, and the warm, strong hug of our daddy's arms."[2] However, what they find are men and women scared to hold or touch them. (I will be more explicit about the technique of holding in chapter 12.)

"I asked him to hold me and he freaked out." "Why do you think my pastor or elders in the church will not support me in this way of recovery?" "I have asked many people, but they all said 'no.'" I have heard these comments and questions time after time by my clients. Most people feel frightened to hold or touch the individual in recovery. I know this is because of the big four letter word, *fear*. "When it comes to fears, we often fear most the things we do not understand. If your understanding of homosexuality is limited, you may be reluctant to get involved counseling homosexuals or you may be fearful of relating to them."[3] Fear is a primary emotion, created to protect us from that which we do not understand. Education and understanding will ultimately assuage irrational fears.

I recently read Dr. Paul Brand's book, *The Gift of Pain*, about his life's work with lepers. There are striking parallels between leprosy and same-sex attractions. Leprosy is a nerve disorder whereby the individual has no feeling sensations in the extremities of his body. It represents a severe detachment from feelings in the hands, feet, and/or facial muscles. After helping lepers heal this nerve disorder and reeducating them to live without sensations in their extremities, Dr. Brand sent them back into their communities to live healthy and productive lives. Upon their return, the family and community members expressed fear of relating to them, afraid they would "catch" leprosy. Dr. Brand explains that this is not a contagious disease.

What Dr. Brand and his colleagues realized next was that they had to educate the family members and community about the true nature of leprosy. Once they had done this, fears began to vanish. "Fear and superstition had melted away as they understood the nature of the disease. They listened to the new patients' stories, unrevolted, unafraid. They used the magic of human touch."[4] No longer afraid of "catching" the condition, family members, friends, and those in their communities began to hold and touch them. The healing power of touch restores both giver and receiver.

People's reactions to leprosy and homosexuality have been quite similar. What we do not understand, we fear in order to self-protect. When we understand that which we fear, walls come down and we learn to embrace. We may also fear in others what we are repressing or suppressing in ourselves. Most men in our culture harbor father wounds, not having experienced sufficient bonding/attachment with their dads. I believe that if a man experienced a salient, loving, and supportive father, it would be natural for him to reach out and embrace other men. Men in this and other cultures are both touch-deprived and emotionally repressed.

"From early childhood, boys learn to suppress their emotions while girls learn to express and manage the complete range of feelings. . . . A man is more likely to equate being emotional with weakness and vulnerability because he has been raised to do rather than to voice what he feels."[5] (A friend of mine made it clear to me that this may also be true for many girls. They, too, had to repress their feelings while living in a dysfunctional environment.)

Same-Sex Deficit

Ashely Montagu states, " . . . In short, one learns to love not by instruction but by being loved."[6] In the book *Recovery from Co-Dependency*, Drs. Laurie and Jon Weiss write, "Adult-children who didn't bond successfully often spend their lives searching for unconditional love, and find Co-Dependent relationships instead."[7]

If a man has not sufficiently bonded with his dad, then he himself has a same-sex deficit. In most men, this is not visibly apparent or manifested by same-sex attractions. However, many cultures accept that men do not share their feelings and are activity-centered, oversexed, and poor communicators. I believe that most men are oversexed because they are undernourished and out of touch with their deeper feelings. Men are often stimulated sexually, bypassing feelings in their mid-section—gut, stomach, chest, and heart—making an immediate connection between the head and genitals. Lusting after women is as unhealthy as homosexual lust. Both represent a defensive detachment—one with the same-sex parent (SSAD), the other with the opposite-sex parent (OSAD).

One place where it is culturally acceptable for men to touch is after winning a sports event. When we see a baseball game and the team wins, then men openly embrace and hug one another, sharing in their victory. However, we generally condemn that same display of open affection between men off the field. If men publicly show such affection for one another, they are immediately suspect for being homosexually-oriented.

This confusion over sex, love, and intimacy entraps us into addictions and disorders. When we deprive body, soul, and spirit of healthy touch on a regular basis—and I mean daily—we become sick mentally, emotionally, physically, and spiritually. For an overview of our indelible need for touch, I suggest reading Ashley Montagu's book *Touching: The Human Signifi-*

cance of the Skin. Also, *Holding Time,* by Dr. Martha Welch, is another example about the healing powers of healthy touch (her audio and video tapes are excellent in explaining how holding works and the powerful benefits it brings to relationships).

Setting healthy boundaries is absolutely necessary when it comes to touch. Some people have boundaries that are too permeable, allowing others to touch them in inappropriate ways. Others have walls around their hearts and do not allow anyone to get near or touch them. Whether the struggle is homosexual or not, lack of healthy touch keeps us prisoners in our bodies and emotionally stunted in our souls. "Those who have been failed in such stimulation [healthy touch] remain, as it were, imprisoned within their skin, and then act as if the skin were a barrier that shuts them in, and being touched becomes for them an assault upon their integrity."[8]

It is noteworthy that several of the sexually addicted men with whom I worked did not want touch or hugs at all. Hugging meant intimacy, and intimacy would stimulate pain. The body does not lie. Therefore, intimacy for many equals pain. Deep within the musculature of the body are the hidden wounds. Anonymous sexual encounters are a "safe" way to receive physical gratification without getting emotionally intimate. Of course, it is a short-lived gratification leading to addictions.

I have observed that the more distant the person is from his core wounds, the more extreme his attitude is about giving and receiving healthy touch. On one end of the spectrum, there is an abhorrence to being touched or giving touch to others. On the other end of the spectrum, there is an insatiable need to touch and be touched. I have learned that both symptoms represent an extreme form of detachment from core wounds and unmet needs.

"It is a striking fact that by the time the human child has attained its third birthday it has virtually achieved full adult brain size. The average brain volume of the human three-year-old is 960 cubic centimeters, while the brain volume of the human adult, attained at the age of twenty years, is 1,200 cubic centimeters. . . . In other words, at the end of three years of age the human child has achieved 90 percent of its brain growth. . . . Almost two-thirds of the total growth of the brain is achieved by the end of the first year."[9]

That is why most psychologists say that our personalities are basically formed by the time we are three years of age. If a person does not receive sufficient touch and holding by that age, then a deep sense of deprivation and detachment will ensue. When a person receives inappropriate touch, he will also detach and emotionally withdraw. Alternatively, in adolescence and adulthood, he might seek sexual relationships to fulfill unmet needs for healthy bonding/attachment.

Mentoring the SSAD Individual

I commission anyone who wants to help those in recovery to become a mentor, and to see those with a Same-Sex Attachment Disorder as children. Even though they inhabit adult bodies, they are developmentally little children. Of course, this does not apply only to those with a Same-Sex Attachment Disorder. My judgment is that this applies to most of the population. The primary difference is that others are able to hide their unmet needs in more socially acceptable ways or use more socially acceptable addictions. The result, however, is a very numb and unhealthy society.

Without the loving, supportive, and nurturing touch of many men and women, I would not be here today. I received wounding by a man's inappropriate touch, and I needed to receive healing by a man's appropriate touch. I would not have broken through the walls of pain if Phillip, Peter, and Russell had not held me while I grieved the many losses of my past. These brave men were willing to hold me through the tremendous amounts of pain that I needed to grieve. Without their bravery and courage, I would not have made it through the dark nights of my life.

Holding works. The best mentors are parents if they are open, willing, capable, and available to participate. I primarily recommend Mom and Dad as the bearers of healthy and loving touch. If they are unwilling, incapable, or unavailable, then men and women of God need to stand in the gap. I believe that if the congregation of a particular church, synagogue, or mosque would get together and jointly minister to the needs of those suffering from this SSAD condition, healing would occur much more quickly and beautifully. This would truly be an act of putting one's faith into practice.

Here are the words of Pete, who mentored one man I counseled:

I first met Rob at the door of my house and greeted him with a strong embrace. He was very friendly, but I could sense that he was uncomfortable not knowing if I accepted him or was one more judgmental, heterosexual male.

Soon, Rob realized I loved him just as he was and wanted to help him find his male identity. That night, over supper, we frankly discussed his past and where he was in his recovery. The bond and friendship between us grew.

The following evening, Rob returned to my house and we continued our discussion. We then began a session of holding. I cradled Rob in my arms, as a father would a son, and encouraged him to talk about himself and his past. At first, we were both a bit uncomfortable, but within a few minutes we were past this barrier and real feelings and emotions began to flow. There were tears and deep regret expressed over his stolen childhood. I assured Rob of God's love and my healthy male love for him. I encouraged him to continue to discuss what was on his heart. It was a time of honesty and growth for both of us, myself as the "parent" and Rob as the "child."

A few evenings later, Rob and I (a couple of middle-agers) played catch in my backyard. He had told me earlier that the lack of sports prowess had left painful scars on his soul. When we first began playing catch, Rob was stiff and uncomfortable. As we threw the ball back and forth several hundred times, he began to relax and really enjoy the experience. His throwing motion became smoother and smoother and, as I encouraged and coached him, the smile on his face grew broader and broader. What a pleasure to see him budding before my eyes! I asked God several times during the time we were playing catch to help and support Rob. He did! This experience was a true milestone for Rob, and it was a thrill for me to see him grow.

My vision is to have all the elders in our country mentor the youth. In this plastic, material culture, our grandfathers and grandmothers have been put aside for younger, more improved models of "performance." This is the betrayal of our survival. In the hearts and minds of our elders lie the wisdom and treasures of a lifetime. When we call upon them to assist us in our journey, we connect our present to our past and future.

"Skin is the human body's largest organ. It accounts for 18 percent of our body weight and covers about 19 square feet. . . . After massage, office workers completed a math test more quickly and with fewer errors. . . . PET scans of severely touch-deprived infants show that critical sections of their brains are barely active, stalling entire areas of development. . . . 'America is suffering from an epidemic of skin hunger,' says Dr. Tiffany Field, director of Miami's Touch Research Institute (TRI). . . . TRI set up a study in which volunteers over age 60 were given three weeks of massage and then were trained to massage toddlers at the preschool. Giving massages proved even more beneficial than getting them. The elders exhibited less depression, lower stress hormones, and less loneliness."[10]

If you have any interest in mentoring, please call, fax, e-mail, and/or write to me. I wish to connect those who have a heart for mentoring with those who are in desperate need of being mentored. I am now offering training for these mentoring relationships. Through these activities, we will create a national and international network of mentors. It is a win-win situation when our grandmothers and grandfathers mentor our youth. It gives life to both. When the mentee heals, he may then become a mentor for others. The investment of the many men and women who loved me to health has paid off manifold, as I have been able to share that love with others.

CHAPTER ELEVEN

Bonnie

Hope has been vital to me. In spite of the trauma and wounds in my life, I have always had hope, and so I would like to share my story to give my "account for the hope that is in me" (I Peter 3:15).

The word "lesbian" is only a seven-letter word. I read it for the first time in Ann Landers's newspaper column where I obtained much of my sex education. I saw Ann's words about women who loved each other, who had sex together. Did this word describe me? I began to consider that possibility, together with the stigma and moral judgment surrounding this identity.

Lesbian. I didn't adopt the title until age fifteen, but I am not certain how old I was when I first realized I was uncomfortable as a girl. With one brother five years older than I and the other only fourteen months my senior, my conception was more than likely a mistake. Tagged along with them, I became a "tomboy."

My mother attended a world-renowned university and had a career in a respected field. She didn't enter the work force until I began school. I became very close to her, very attached. My father was mechanically gifted, but he never seemed as intelligent as she did. With a German upbringing, he seldom showed signs of affection and love. He was a strict disciplinarian who punished first and asked questions later. Whenever he spent time at home, he was always busy with household repairs or other self-interests. He seemed to care for my mother, and as long as she was happy, so was he.

My world changed when I was three. I experienced traumas that I would repress for thirty years. My mother's father died three days after my third birthday. I barely remember it or him. In her grief, my mother withdrew from me. I became very lonely. Most of my memories from that time were nearly nonexistent.

Fortunately, I was exposed to a religious spirit as I grew up. Our entire family attended church regularly, participating in many church activities such as choirs, Vacation Bible School, and youth groups. In retrospect, I was embracing a Christian attitude in order to please my parents and appease a God whom I viewed as a formidable judge. However, I now realize this religious training provided me with knowledge of God which He was able to use as a springboard as He coaxed me into a personal relationship with Him.

As puberty approached, I was attracted to males on some level, while at the same time I felt an inordinate interest in my girlfriends. There was one to whom I felt unusually attracted, which worried me. It seemed abnormal, so I never told her how I felt; I was too afraid. Wanting to be with her all the time, I desired affection from her. One night we slept together, as normal teenage friends do. I took advantage of the situation when I gently touched her breasts as she slept. It was electrifying, but left me with feelings of guilt.

As I entered high school, I still experienced an attraction toward boys, but I did not feel desirable to them. That only increased my lesbian feelings. My first love was for a girl who was younger than I, who was lonely and rejected by her peers. Although I never overtly sexualized my feelings toward her, I spent inordinate amounts of time with her and enjoyed the closeness and subtle touching. While sleeping at her house, I intensely wanted to be sexual with her. She and her family moved away before those feelings were acted upon.

My secret love and sexual feelings were mistakenly revealed to my parents in a letter, which had been written to my friend after she moved. As a result, they took me to see a psychologist who concluded it was a normal developmental stage and said I would outgrow the attraction.

Emptiness was growing inside me, which brought feelings of confusion, anger, fear, loneliness, and sorrow. I needed love and intimacy from a woman. My determination to meet that need increased. During my junior year in high school, I met a girl my age who was starved for friendship. I sensed that she would not reject me. She seemed a desperate soul, someone who would do anything to get love. She did not resist my advances. I did not love her in the beginning, but as we continued to share our lives and bodies, we became dependent on each other. When I left for college, I had every intention of moving in with her after graduation.

Throughout the relationship, we were never free of guilt. She was active in her church, as I was in mine. We knew the Scriptures, but we wanted God to bless our love. I thought, if only I were a man, then it would be okay. Our sexual intimacy was less satisfying as the relationship continued. We met regularly, but had to keep the nature of our friendship a secret. I often slept with her in her parents' home, but many times we met in the youth room in her church. We had sex in God's house, committing such blatant sin! I could not stand myself, yet I felt helpless, unable to stop.

We went to see my pastor, and we met with him for several weeks. He never told us it was sin and he never condemned us, but he could see our distress. He encouraged us to break off our relationship. To him, it was obvious how unhealthy our behavior was, but we were so enmeshed, needy, and addicted that we felt it was impossible to change.

A distance of 250 miles separated my lover and me when college started. I tried repeatedly to end the relationship, but could not. Although it was immoral and socially unacceptable, I wasn't ready to give her up. I was miserable and contemplated suicide.

Members of a religious group on campus, Inter-Varsity Christian Fellowship, befriended me. They saw my knowledge of religion and my hungry heart. They confronted me, picking up on my lack of commitment, and challenged me to accept Jesus, not just as my Savior, but as Lord of my life. They questioned "why I was unwilling to take that step of faith."

With anger and hurt, I explained that I was a lesbian. Knowing how God felt about homosexual behavior, I would not make a commitment I could not keep. They did not condemn or judge me as I had anticipated. What I had not foreseen was their faith in God and compassion. One of them suggested that I truly tell God how I felt.

In a Roman Catholic church in January 1973, I challenged God to do *something* with my screwed-up life. I did not know what I wanted or what to do. I could not change my identity or my feelings. I felt unacceptable to Him. If He did not act, I was going to end my life. I knelt at the altar, and when I got up, something had changed. I felt peaceful.

My lover and I finally did stop seeing each other when our parents intervened. I did not love her enough to defy them, nor was I willing to sacrifice my education. I wasn't prepared at that point to commit to a lesbian lifestyle. It was a painful time, but the relationship had to die. Since that time, I have had very few lesbian encounters.

Unfortunately, my feelings of emptiness did not go away. I still wanted intimacy with women yet feared it because of the sexual feelings that it stirred. My roommate was a Christian, and I had a terrible struggle with my feelings for her. I expressed some of them and she was very kind and loving. She did not reject me, nor did she give in to my pressuring her to have sex; however, those desires did not go away. I chose obedience to God because I knew what He expected.

I continued to grow in faith, and my relationship with the Lord got stronger, but I was not willing to completely give up my lesbianism. It went on in my fantasies about women. Since I was not acting out, I felt less guilty. I was beginning to accept God's forgiveness and to perceive Him as loving.

In my senior year, I met the man who is now my husband. We felt that God brought us together, but I did not tell him of my struggle or my past. We married, and homosexuality was behind me—or so I thought.

Our marriage was good. My husband and I were active in our church and shared nightly devotionals. Although I had not acted out sexually, the lesbian thoughts never went away. I fantasized from time to time, but I never intended to commit adultery, to hurt my husband, and to be disobedient to God. My husband was faithful. He treated me well. There were no reasons for my looking for another relationship.

After sixteen years, I met a woman at work and felt tremendously attracted to her. I thought I was falling in love with her. I went to her home and asked how she felt about me. We both cried, and she told me she was not in love with me. She was sorry for any signals that I may have misinterpreted. It was humiliating. It hurt very deeply. I had risked so much for her, and she rejected me. I was so depressed, I cried daily. I could not keep these problems from my husband any longer. I needed help.

Graciously, he did not leave or respond in anger. Fortunately, since my coworker and I did not become sexual, it was easier for him to forgive. I continued to work in the same office with her, and it was very difficult to get over what happened. I went to see my pastor, knowing that in essence, I had a spiritual problem. Why was I willing to turn my back on God? After all these years of striving for obedience to Him and choosing to be faithful to my husband, what had gone awry? I wondered if I would ever feel at peace. He referred me to a counselor.

After six months in counseling, I reached a point of stability. My therapist told me I could stop our sessions, but I needed answers about my lesbianism. Why had it developed? I knew that I did not choose the feelings, nor did I think they were inborn. I continued therapy and talked about my childhood.

BONNIE

I did some writing, and one week I shared some things about my mother. When he asked who else the writing described, I thought he meant me. I saw myself as much like her, but he said the name of the coworker to whom I had been so attracted. Then I understood. I had not seen it before. Indeed, she was much like my mother, only more attractive and affectionate. I had never perceived the connection between my relationship with my mother and my lesbianism. I had assumed it was related to my distant father and how I never felt appreciated by him.

I also wrote of an experience that occurred between my mother and me when I was about eight years old. I expressed it without much feeling, noting only that it was "weird." Minimizing it, I denied how damaging it was. My counselor asked me how I would feel if she had done the same thing to my brother. I had to admit that my own mother had sexually abused me. I wanted to die. Nothing could have been worse.

I worked with two other therapists over the next four years and was once hospitalized in a mental-health unit. More memories surfaced when my mother sold her home, the house where I grew up. I began to understand that I had been used by her and was reenacting that abuse with other women. Seeking to be in control instead of being used, I wanted to please and satisfy. I sought the perfect woman who would love me, like my mother had before the abuse began.

My struggle was not the result of problems in my marriage. My husband had not pushed me away or failed to love me. My temptation to be unfaithful was not due to any hurts inflicted by him. It was about pain that was deep inside me long before we ever met.

When I was in college and accepted Christ as Lord, I changed my conduct. I remained faithful to Him, but there was no healing. I was stuck in a place of pain. I had to ask difficult questions and trust God to help me live with the answers.

Tears still come easily as I mourn my losses. For so many years, I felt there was something terribly wrong with me. Why didn't my mother love me as I wanted to be loved? I learned that it was her problem. She was wounded and unable to love me as I needed. She made horrible decisions and used me to fulfill her needs. There was nothing that I had done which caused her to treat me as she did.

I shared my history with a few women whom I felt I could trust. I continued meeting with my minister and receiving my husband's encouragement. I joined a support group for child-abuse survivors, which built my self-esteem. It was helpful to know there were others who understood my emotions. I learned about EXODUS International, the support group for persons who are seeking help for changing their same-sex attractions. Hearing a former lesbian's testimony was very freeing, and it gave me hope. Unfortunately, there were no local support groups in my area that dealt with homosexuality from the perspective of change.

I was trying to satisfy legitimate needs for nurturance from women, and that was not sinful. Trusting God to meet those needs in healthy ways, I could be healed. More willing to accept my human frailty, I then understood that much of my identity was based on lies and misperceptions. I asked God to make me willing (to be willing) to forsake my longing for a lesbian relationship, and prayed that He replace it with a true desire to love Him and to depend on Him to fill the hole in my heart.

I read books like Elizabeth Moberly's *Homosexuality: A New Christian Ethic*, and Joe Dallas's *Desires in Conflict*. Both brought enormous insight about the way I thought and behaved. I learned about defensive detachments and the reparative drive. God did not condemn me for having feelings that I did not choose. He asked for my obedience that I would not act out, while seeking healthy ways to meet my needs. He wanted me to trust Him.

I faced my past and stood in the presence of God. Throughout my recovery, I was praying, reading Scripture, attending worship, and steadfastly seeking His will and guidance. I started accepting myself as a unique child of God. My depression lifted, and I wanted to tell others what God had done. By sharing my testimony, I could offer hope to other strugglers. There could be healing and change; we do not have to remain in homosexuality.

Yet I could not be truly affectionate with women. I was ill-at-ease and inhibited in my ability to love them. I just accepted that I could never get too close. When I wanted to help my women friends by giving a comforting touch, I would respond, but it was always with some coolness. I also longed for a motherly woman to truly nurture me, but was resigned to the fact that it could never be. That kind of relationship presented too many conflicting feelings.

In the winter of 1998, I began sharing with a woman whose son is living a homosexual lifestyle. We had become friends a year before that. She heard me speak of my losses and need. She opened her heart and told me she felt God wanted her to help me to heal if I was willing. She understood my need for nonerotic, deep affection and love. It seemed too good to be true. God knew my longing, and He touched my heart. I am learning to love, as He wants me to love, without fear or pretense.

It was very painful sharing my story with her. I learned that I had to expose my sexual thoughts to her, even if they were about her. As shameful as that is, they need to be revealed and brought into the light so that I do not get stuck in them. It is excruciating when I have let her into the deep, dark places of my soul. She has been God's agent. I feel God's love pouring through her into me. When she embraces me, I feel as though God is embracing us both. We pray together. We keep the relationship open, honest, and free of manipulation.

The struggle to resist sexual temptation is not nearly as arduous as permitting her to love me! When she asks if I want to be held, I have four options: 1) I can run away in fear; 2) I can regress into sexual fantasy; 3) I can tell her no, I don't want to be held (but that would probably be a lie); or 4) I can accept the genuine, nonsexual love she offers. Usually, it is an effort to respond in the healthiest way.

Recently, I heard the Holy Spirit tell me to stop initiating physical contact with her. I had to allow her to minister to me, and to do so without reciprocating. It was extremely difficult to allow her to comfort me with touch, to *feel it* and to *let it in*. I am finding that as God gives me the courage to press on, I can find a peace that is more satisfying than any sexual encounter. God knew my need, my true longings, and He answered in ways beyond my imagination. He has provided a spiritual mother who is replenishing many of the things stolen during my childhood. In many respects, she loves me more than my own mother was capable of doing.

Mentoring has been a vital part of my journey. It has come at the end of the process. I had to be at a place of obedience where I was consistently choosing not to act out my sexual thoughts and where my heart was attuned to God. I need to listen to His direction and be willing to obey. I feel as though He is putting His "finishing touches" on me. It is enabling me to love others, to be affectionate with women, to minister to them with healing touches without fear, without reservation. My faith is maturing, and my heart is more open to God. My marriage has improved. I am less demanding of my husband and more receptive and open to him. I am more comfortable with my identity. There is still work to be done, but hope lives in me as I am recreated in God's image.

Comment

Bonnie received help from other therapists before contacting me. She attended a presentation I gave on the healing of homosexuality. During the talk, I shared about the mentoring model to restore love. Since then, I have been supervising her in this mentoring relationship.

CHAPTER TWELVE

Mentoring: Restoring Love

"A boy cannot change into a man without the active intervention of the older men."[1]

—Rituals of Manhood

Why Mentoring?

Anyone who did not experience successful attachment, love, and intimacy with either Father and/or Mother seeks to heal these needs in other relationships or activities. Mentoring is a means whereby one may restore the parent-child relationship, but may also be employed to heal other relationships, i.e., with siblings, relatives, and friends.

"Many of the here-and-now conflicts people have with their spouses, lovers, ex-lovers, bosses, partners or children are in part emotional reenactments of suppressed feelings stored from incidents that happened when they were children. The same unresolved conflicts they had with their parents always seem to 'mysteriously' reappear in their adult relationships."[2]

Intimacy is at the core of our being. The central core principle of the universe is the parent-child relationship, and the place where we learn to be intimate with others and ourselves is the family. Unless one experiences this core love between parent and child, developmental tasks will remain unfulfilled and growth arrested. Deep restoration of the parent-child relationship is essential for successful growth and maturation in love.

Mentoring is an attachment model whereby two people participate in a relationship mirroring the parent-child paradigm. One acts as the parent, called the mentor, and the other acts as the child, called the "adult-child." Parents are in the position of God to their children. Father is Mr. God, and Mother is Mrs. God. Because parents are like "gods" to their child, the child will always self-blame even when the parents are at fault. If a parent gets drunk and screams at the child, if a parent dies, if there is divorce in the family, if a parent is negligent and does not spend time with the child, if a parent is overly critical and verbally abusive, the child will blame himself for these events. He will say internally, "If only I had been a better son, this wouldn't have happened. It's all my fault." Of course, he buries these messages deep in the unconscious because he has had to adopt a variety of defense mechanisms to survive and cope with the pain.

To restore past wounds, healing needs to take place between the adult-child and the internalized parent. For this model to be effective, first, the adult-child must become aware of his inner child. He must begin a program of self-parenting. Otherwise, the adult-child will become excessively dependent, or codependent, on the mentor. This is very dangerous, because the mentor will never be able to satisfy all the needs of the adult-child.

Before establishing this mentoring relationship, be sure the adult-child is well underway with a program of self-parenting his inner child. Furthermore, I recommend the adult-child have at least three mentors. If the adult-child is working on healing his father wound, there should be at least three men in the father's position. If there is only one mentor, he will easily become exhausted. Also, when one of the mentors is unavailable to meet the adult-child's needs, generally at least one of the other two will be available. Pastors, rabbis, and other clergy, please have three families in your congregation mentor each overcomer.

Another caution: Make sure that all partners or spouses of the participants, both adult-child and mentors, are fully aware of this mentoring relationship. Without the spouses' support and understanding, do not participate in such a mentoring relationship. It is important for all involved to be accountable for their actions. If the adult-child is in therapy, it is important to keep the therapist informed about all healing activities. If the adult-child is not in therapy, there needs to be some system of accountability, with a pastor, minister, rabbi, or spiritual mentor. Do not try to manage things alone. Inevitably, there will be many questions along the way. Get help and support. Isolation = Death.

If the adult-child was sexually abused or participated in sexual relationships with the same or opposite sex, he may experience sexual feelings and desires for the mentor. Restoration works in reverse to the way in which the original wounding occurred. Therefore, to reach the deeper feelings of anger, hurt, betrayal, frustration, and pain, the adult-child may first experience sexual desires for the mentor. In some instances, the adult-child may even try to seduce the mentor. Do not be alarmed. This is a very good sign! The inner child is merely testing the mentor, unconsciously saying, "Can I trust you *not* to take advantage of me, or will you use me like all the other men/women in my life?" Therefore, it is critical for the mentor to be grounded in his gender identity and sexuality.

The mentor will need to assure the adult-child that he would never sexualize him, that his love is pure and he only wants the adult-child to heal and feel genuine love. In this way, the adult-child will finally feel free to uncover the feelings he has buried alive. Only new love, learning to trust others, grieving, and making new choices will restore his heart and his wounded child(ren) within.

In my course of mentoring, I tested each one of the men who mentored me. My inner child thought that since I suffered sexual abuse at a young age and acted out in homosexual relationships, I had to offer sex to receive affection. Therefore, when I became close to my mentors, sexual feelings emerged, and I propositioned each one of them. I asked them if they wanted to be serviced by me. My inner boy needed to know if they were safe or not. If I had received an affirmative response from any one of them, I would have been out the door. However, to their credit, each of them reassured me that they only desired to see me heal and give me the pure love of God. What a relief it was to hear those words, and each time I heard them, it broke my heart open a little more. To establish trust in a relationship, we need to share our "truth" with the other person and not be judged. In this atmosphere, we will eventually experience the love we so desperately need to feel.

This mentoring model is useful to heal both homo-emotional and hetero-emotional relationships. Men can mentor men and women, and women can mentor women and men.

Again, the best mentors are the parents of the adult-child. It will save much time if Mom and Dad are available, capable, and willing to go through this reprocessing with their son/daughter. If the parents are

unavailable, incapable, or unwilling, it is important that they not participate in this process, as it would further wound the adult-child.

Regardless of the mentor, the adult-child will move through three developmental stages: dependence, independence, and interdependence.
First, the adult-child will be dependent on the mentor, making up for lost
time to fulfill unmet needs. After healing his wounds and internalizing the
mentor's love, he will gain a sense of independence. Finally, he will learn
interdependence, when he can stand on his own feet and when he needs
help from others.

A particular difficulty for men is sharing their feelings, being emotionally intimate. Women are generally more able to express their feelings and
establish eye contact. Men are more activity-centered, not emotionally
centered. Men learn very early in life that it is socially unacceptable to express their feelings. Another reason is the physiology of the male. They are
prone to cut off because of their physiology. Emotional arousal is more
punishing on the male system due to their hormones; consequently, they
learn to cut off and shut down from an early age.[3]

A man dealing with same-sex attractions may be more in touch with
his emotional side. This presents a particular challenge for male mentors.
It may be easier for the mentor to involve the adult-child in bonding rituals, such as sports, hiking, and fishing. However, it may be extremely difficult for him to share his feelings, accept the feelings of the adult-child,
and give the gift of healthy touch. This will be a challenge for both parties.
The adult-child may have to coach the mentor about his specific needs for
intimacy and touch. The mentor needs to realize that beyond the adult
body lies the heart of a wounded child who never experienced, or experienced insufficiently, his father's love. The male mentor will hold the adult-
child the same way and ways in which he would hold his own son.

Some have asked me about skin touch with their mentors, such as taking off shirts. Healthy, nonerotic relationships are modeled after family
relationships: father/son, mother/daughter, brother/brother, sister/sister,
uncle/nephew, aunt/niece, grandfather/grandson, grandmother/grand-
daughter (all healthy same-sex family relationships). Just ask yourself,
"Would my actions fit within the boundaries of any of these relationships?"
If the answer is no, do *not* do it. If the answer is yes, proceed. Also, the
mentor and adult-child can think: "What is age-appropriate behavior?
What developmental stage is the adult-child moving through at this time?"

There needs to be a system of accountability, both for the mentor and
the adult-child. A spouse, pastor, rabbi, or counselor are good choices for

either party involved in the mentoring relationship. I suggest the mentors and therapist/spiritual advisor meet regularly (biweekly or monthly at the least) to share, support one another, ask questions, and monitor growth.

I have seen this relationship be a blessing not only for the adult-child but for the mentor as well. Through giving, we receive blessing, and by sharing in another person's healing, we ourselves learn and grow. This relationship will teach the mentor many things about himself. It will help stretch his abilities to understand another person's pain and how to be a more compassionate man.

> *Cautions: The therapist or counselor should not be the mentor. The therapist may help train mentors; however, it is ill-advised for him to stand in as the mentor.*
>
> *Several of the men I have worked with have tried to mentor each other. It cannot work for the simple reason that homosexual relationships do not work—you cannot give what you have not experienced or received. Two minuses do not equal a plus. They will eventually create a bigger minus!* Nemo Dat Quod Non Habet.

Roles and Responsibilities of the Mentor

The mentor, representing the father or mother, must maintain his or her position at all times. It is never appropriate for the mentor to cross the parent-child boundary. Let me give an example.

I saw an episode of the TV series, *Picket Fences*. A beautiful model had come to town to film a TV commercial. During her stay, it became abundantly clear to the sheriff that her manager-husband was physically and mentally abusing her. The sheriff expressed his concern for her and suggested she leave this unhealthy relationship. He took a very parental attitude toward her. She immediately started coming on to him. Her inner child was desperately looking for Daddy's love, which is how she ended up in such an abusive relationship, obviously mirroring her experience with her father.

What she wanted was for the sheriff to maintain his proper position as a true father, embracing her with unconditional love. Her inner child was longing for a daddy who would love her for who she was, not for what she did or how she looked. What she got was a broken man's love, as he responded to her sexual advances and they passionately kissed. Realizing that he had crossed the line, a married man himself, he pulled back and apologized.

What he neglected to see was that a broken adult-child stood before him, crying out for healthy Daddy's love. Instead of maintaining his proper position, instead of seeing a broken little girl in an adult body, he crossed the line and destroyed the relationship.

It is imperative for the mentor to always keep his proper position. Because of neglect and physical, emotional, or sexual abuse, it may be necessary for the adult-child to test the mentor on numerous occasions, to see if his love is genuine or fake. Only then will he feel safe enough to let down his guard. For when he attempted to be close to his father, or masculine role model, he experienced or perceived some deep rejection, and then he detached. In the process of reattachment, the pain will emerge when the individual experiences intimacy. Therefore, he may reject the mentor before letting go and opening up.

Dr. Patricia Love states, "When you long for something, it becomes a source of pain. Therefore, getting what you want is painful. We're not prepared for that. If I long to be touched and I hunger to be touched, I will actually resist your touching me.

"For years, I longed to be touched. I knew I was touched-deprived. From an early age, I didn't get enough touching . . . so I came into adulthood with this need for touching, this longing for touch. But there was also a resistance to touch because getting what you want is painful. You have to have the maturity to live through the pain, that bittersweet experience of getting what you want.

"Touching is so elementary to our existence. If you don't get touched when you are an infant, you die. It's not an option. You have to have tactile stimulation to survive. As an adult, you don't need it to survive, but you need it to thrive. It is such an important element to be touched that when you get touched, you often get in touch with the grief experience of not having it. That's the way it is with anything you've longed for."[4]

Four areas need to be addressed in the process of mentoring: 1) Break down the walls of detachment; 2) Develop healthy patterns in relationships (socialization); 3) Re-educate neurology with healthy touch and activities; and 4) Connect with God, self, and healthy parenting.

To keep the relationship centered, it is necessary to establish the roles and responsibilities of the mentor:

- Offering unconditional love

The mentor will need to offer nurturance, support, encouragement, and affection without any feelings or thoughts of sexual involvement. It is important that the adult-child experience parental love without the fear of sex entering into the relationship. If the mentor begins to experience sexual feelings toward the adult-child, he must center himself and refocus his attention to give pure love to the adult-child. He may bring the energy up from his genital area into his heart, maintaining his position as the father. Later, if he still feels bad, he may share his confused feelings with either his spouse or another accountability partner. The mentor should *never* share his sexual feelings (if he should have any) with the adult-child. This would violate the parent-child relationship, parentifying the child. He must show the adult-child the same love he would give to his own son or daughter. Even though the adult-child is older, his inner child still longs for the love yet unobtained from his original parent. (Note: It is natural for us to feel stimulation when we are intimate with either someone of the same or opposite sex.)

The mentor needs to be Mr. KYMS—Keep Your Mouth Shut. Do not be quick to "fix" the adult-child or offer advice. Listening is sometimes the greatest gift we can give to another. Some of the positive qualities of the mentor will be compassion, empathy, a nonjudgmental attitude, and encouragement.

- Affirmation, approval, and education

Affirmation is the act of nurturing the human spirit, loving the child unconditionally. Affirmations infuse the child with a sense of value, belonging, and competency. To create this sense of value, the mentor may hold, touch, hug, kiss, love, play with, and invite the child into his world. To create the sense of belonging, the mentor may accept the adult-child's offers for help, ask for his help, ask for his opinions, express appreciation for his efforts, share responsibilities, and offer him help. To create the sense of competency, the mentor may teach skills, encourage self-reliance, provide opportunities for learning, avoid too much criticism, accept mistakes, and show interest in his knowledge.[5]

Approval has to do with the child's behavior. Sometimes the adult-child's behavior may displease the mentor. It is important to teach the adult-child social skills, what is and is not acceptable. The adult-child may act inappropriately because he did not learn basic life skills about how to express thoughts, feelings, and needs in healthy, positive ways. He may also need coaching in how to regulate his feelings and modify his behavior. Many who experience the SSAD condition need help in learning self-discipline.

It is critical for the mentor to always affirm the adult-child's feelings;

however, he may not always approve of the adult-child's behavior. The mentor must be sure to make a clear distinction between approval and affirmation. This may be a new experience for the adult-child—not to have love withdrawn when he makes a mistake. The mentor needs to teach the adult-child that he always loves him, even when disapproving of his behavior. "I don't like it when you . . . ," and "I love you no matter what."

Help shy ones come out of themselves, and help extroverts go within. *Positive Discipline* by Dr. Jane Nelsen, *The Heart of Parenting* by Dr. John Gottman, and *Parenting with Love and Logic* by Foster Cline and Jim Fay are useful guidelines on how to lovingly discipline and educate your adult-child.

- Setting boundaries

The adult-child may want the mentor's attention twenty-four hours a day, seven days a week! His needs may be great, so it is very important for both the mentor and the adult-child to set clear boundaries and guidelines from the onset of the relationship. Get together and discuss what is and is not acceptable for both parties. A good book to help in this area is *Boundaries*, by Dr. Henry Cloud and Dr. John Townsend.

They will need to negotiate times to meet throughout the week. They might want to make a commitment to get together on certain days for a specific period of time. For example, they may decide to meet on Wednesday evenings from 7:00 P.M. to 10:00 P.M. and Sundays from 2:00 P.M. to 5:00 P.M.

They may negotiate times to speak on the telephone. The mentor must let the adult-child know what are the proper times to call. For example, the mentor might say, "You can call me between the hours of 6:00 A.M. and midnight. Please don't call after 12 or before 6 in the morning." Also, the mentor needs to make clear boundaries about the adult-child calling him at work.

The mentor must inform the adult-child what he can and cannot give. The mentor must keep his word and *not* make promises that he cannot or will not fulfill. He must not say one thing and be or do another. This will exacerbate the defensive detachments (emotional blocks toward the original parent). It is very important to set clear boundaries and never make unrealistic promises. Keep commitments.

- Activities

There are a number of things the mentor might do with his adult-child, as he would with his own son. Some examples are listening, holding, taking walks, playing sports, going to a game, seeing a movie, teaching a skill, and going camping or fishing. The mentor provides for the adult-child what he missed in early childhood and adolescence.

Holding/Touch

As parents, we hold our children from the moment they are born. We nestle them close to our bosom, allowing them to feel our heart, to feel protected and secure. This same holding position is useful in the mentoring relationship (see the photos on this page and the next). While holding, the mentor must maintain a vertical position while the adult-child maintains a horizontal position. This way, the adult-child will feel safe and experience pure love. Think of keeping a 90-degree angle: The mentor position is vertical, connected to God, and the adult-child position is horizontal, receiving God's love.

In this holding position, the adult-child places his arms underneath the arms of the mentor, completely around the mentor's back. This clearly establishes the parent-child relationship. If one of the adult-child's arms is above and around the shoulder of the mentor, it creates more of a mutual relationship.

Photo by Peter Holden

The mentor, in the parental position, holds the adult-child as s/he would his or his own son/daughter. S/he may speak loving words of affirmation, "You are strong, powerful, and whole. I love you and accept you just as you are."

Photo by Peter Holden

Here is an exercise you might try. While the mentor holds the adult-child, he says, "Allow yourself to experience the warm and safe touch of your father/mother (whichever is the appropriate gender). Please close your eyes and imagine you are being held by the father/mother you always wanted and needed. You can also imagine a spiritual mentor is holding you (Jesus, Mary, Moses, or any other spiritual mentor), pouring God's pure love into your heart." To create a more conducive atmosphere, you may also play beautiful music in the background. Simply hold your adult-child as you would your own son or daughter.

Touch is essential for proper physical, emotional, mental, and spiritual growth. "Above all else, it seems to me that it is our role as human beings always to join learning to loving-kindness. Learning to learn, learning to love, and to be kind are so closely interconnected and so profoundly interwoven, especially with the sense of touch, it would greatly help toward our rehumanization if we would pay closer attention to the need we all have for tactual experience."[6]

In his book, *Touching: The Human Significance of the Skin*, Montagu quotes study after study, describing the damaging effects on animals and humans as a result of touch deprivation or inappropriate touch. Skin is the largest organ in the body. Without proper care and maintenance, the child will not grow into a healthy, mature, loving adult. Montagu demonstrates that proper touch enhances all bodily systems. Scientists have observed in both human and animal studies that handling in the early days after birth results in significantly greater weight gain, more activity, less fearfulness, greater ability to withstand stress, and greater resistance to physiological damage.[7] Touch enhances all bodily systems, including the respiratory, circulatory, digestive, eliminative, nervous, endocrine, and immune systems. Inadequate stimulation creates numerous disorders like respiratory problems, weakened immune systems, fearfulness, and psychological problems.

Numerous studies show that infants die without touch during their first few years of life. "During the nineteenth century more than half the infants [in orphanages] in their first year of life regularly died from a disease called marasmus, a Greek word meaning 'wasting away.' As late as the second decade of the twentieth century, the death rate for infants under one year of age in various foundling institutions throughout the United States was nearly 100 percent."[8] It was found that these children were placed in cribs and not touched except for changing. Without tender loving care, not only will the child not grow, but even die, perhaps not physically, but psychologically and spiritually. "To be tender, loving, and caring, human beings must be tenderly loved and cared for in their earliest years, from the moment they are born."[9] It is essential for the mentor to provide healthy touch experiences for the adult-child, always separating love, intimacy, and sex.

A warning for both the mentor and adult-child about the holding technique: *Do not become hooked on holding.* This technique can be addictive for the adult-child, preventing him from experiencing his pain. *First the crap, and then the lap!* Pull the weeds, then plant the seeds of intimacy and love. When an individual is being held, endorphins are released, immediately creating a pleasurable sensation. This also strengthens his immune system. However, because it feels so good, he may suppress the unpleasant feelings. Therefore, the adult-child should first be encouraged to express his feelings and be held afterwards. Remember, first the crap, and then the lap.

On the other hand, there are those who are quite out of touch with their feelings. For them, I look at holding as priming water. To get water from a well, you must first put in some water. This is the priming water. Even after you put the priming water in the well, you still need to pump for quite a while. The same may hold true for those who are emotionally dry. It may take some time, much holding, and a lot of patience before you strike a feeling!

Bonnie, whose story you read about in the previous chapter, shares more about her mentoring experience:

> About eight years ago, I became attracted to a coworker, and although I did not feel that my marriage was bad, there was something inside that screamed for her attention. After she rejected my sexual interest, I was very depressed, almost suicidal, and went into therapy. In counseling, I learned about the roots of my lesbianism and gained more of a sense of identity. I was able to take responsibility for what was mine and try not to blame myself for those things that were not my fault. I recovered memories of early childhood sexual abuse perpetrated by my own mother. It was devastating. It still hurts a great deal, and it still complicates my life. My same-sex attractions have diminished greatly, and I can give myself a break when I do resort to fantasy and old patterns, but I know there is more healing for me. I want to get over my fear of emotional closeness with other women. I denied myself any kind of affection from them because of that fear. It was either don't touch, or have an orgasm—not much in between. I loved being hugged, yet felt terror at the same time. Ambivalence is an ongoing issue.
>
> My mentor has been working with me, trying to help me since 1998. I knew her for about a year before that, and I almost could not believe that she was serious about this. For me, it is work. I sometimes feel sexual, confusion, fear, ambivalence, discouragement, frustration, yet hopeful, and sometimes even loved. When she hugs me, I can feel her in my arms, but I don't often feel her arms around me. I covet her hugs, it feels really good, and it's beginning to feel safe, yet I feel uncertain. I have not wavered. I do not want a lesbian experience with her, at least not for the most part. Yet there are times when being sexual with her is a strong temptation, even though it is not what she wants. I feel frustrated in not being able to express my love for her in a sexual way. It is almost as though I don't know other ways to convey love to her. It seems kind of crazy to me. I believe God is working in this relationship to bring healing into my life, and already I am seeing benefits, as I am able to hug other women who need it without feeling shamed inside.

Through this mentoring relationship, Bonnie is learning intimacy without sexuality. This is a very difficult process for anyone who has been sexually abused or experienced much sexual activity in adolescence and/or adulthood. However, it works if one keeps working through the feelings. I know, because I have been there myself and come through the other side.

• Perceiving the adult-child in a variety of ways

Of course, the mentor will love the adult-child for who he is, and the mentor may also see this relationship symbolically. For example, if the mentor has ever abused or neglected someone, such as a son, daughter, brother, sister, or friend, he can imagine that he is holding that person and restoring his past failed relationship. The mentor might also imagine that he is holding his own inner child and giving him that which he never received by reparenting himself.

If any of this seems far-fetched, in truth it is not. In each one of our backgrounds—and I mean past generations—we have offended multitudes of people. Therefore, it is our privilege and blessing to be able to give back and restore the countless number of mistakes and abuses our ancestors performed.

The mentor should not try to "fix" the adult-child when he is in pain. The best gift the mentor can give is just "being there" and learning to be a good listener. Most of us do not want advice when we are in pain. We just need a safe space and a sympathetic witness to be there as we ride through the gamut of our emotions. Be empathic and compassionate sans judgment.

Everyone has an ability to self-heal. This mechanism works best when in the presence of another human being. This makes it safe for the adult-child to go through the necessary stages of grieving core pain. "Core pain" is the original wounding that took place in utero, infancy, childhood, or adolescence.

• Repenting as the abusive or neglectful parent

At times, the technique of role-play is useful. The mentor apologizes as the abusive or neglectful parent, saying, "I am sorry I didn't take care of you. I'm sorry I left you. Would you please forgive me? I didn't mean to hurt you."

This is a powerful tool to assist the adult-child in reexperiencing the repressed pain and begin the essential process of grieving. The mentor then takes the position of the repentant parent/perpetrator, giving the adult-child the love he never received. Do not fake it if you cannot make it real. The adult-child will know if you are insincere.

- Communication

It is important for the mentor to show affection and concern for the adult-child. For example, if the mentor knows that the adult-child is in pain or just went through a painful experience, he might give the adult-child a call. Please speak to the adult-child with verbal affirmations: "I love you." "You are a bright, handsome man." "You are powerful and strong." "I believe in you." The adult-child needs infusions of positive messages, replacing the negative circuitry, developing a positive self-image. The mentor must be sensitive to the particular needs of the adult-child. If the adult-child comes to the mentor in crisis or has strong sexual desires and wants to act out, the mentor might coach him using the HALT technique (see chapter 6).

- Prayer

The mentor may pray for the adult-child, that he can experience his inherent value, break down the barriers that prevent growth, and blossom into full maturity. The mentor may pray for guidance as to what the adult-child needs. He may also pray for the adult-child to uncover the root causes of his problems and for God's love to heal his broken heart. He may also ask for the right kind of love to give the adult-child.

Roles and Responsibilities of the Adult-Child

As stated earlier, if the adult-child has experienced any abuse, neglect, or trauma in early childhood or adolescence and has not successfully resolved these feelings, healing and reconciliation are imperative for successful functioning as an adult. The issues of sex, love, and intimacy infused with guilt, shame, and fear are at the core of human difficulties. Within the context of mentoring, these issues will necessarily emerge. Passive-aggressive, love-hate, and enmeshment-abandonment issues and behaviors will become a daily diet for the parent-child rebonding process. Healing self-doubt, self-blame, and low self-worth will also occur.

The following are some of the roles and responsibilities of the person in the adult-child's position:

- Expressing needs

As much as possible, the adult-child must learn to express his thoughts, feelings, and needs to the mentor. He must not repress or suppress. He must express! Perhaps during infancy, childhood, or adolescence, the adult-child experienced shame for expressing himself. Therefore, it is extremely difficult for him to feel safety in sharing his feelings, thoughts, and needs in present relationships. The adult-child must learn to take risks, be honest, and express himself freely. He deserves love.

- Falling in love

The adult-child may fall in love with the mentor. This is normal and healthy. If the adult-child experienced sexualization by the original parent or another perpetrator and/or had many sexual experiences in adolescence or adulthood, then sexual feelings and desires will naturally emerge for the mentor. He should simply share these feelings and thoughts. Be straight and be clear.

"One prominent Christian therapist has stated that he has not had a male homosexual with whom he has worked 'fall in love' with him without becoming free of his homosexual struggle. It takes courage to trust your own values and self-control in order to offer a loving noneroticized relationship."[10] After the adult-child works through infatuation and sexual feelings, then the core pain will emerge.

- Breaking through the defense detachments

As a result of the original wounds, the individual constructed walls of protection around his heart to keep the perpetrator from getting in. The adult-child defends himself against attachment with people of the same sex when the source of wounding was the same-sex parent or a significant person of the same sex. The adult-child defends himself against attachment with people of the opposite sex if the source of wounding was the opposite-sex parent or significant person of the opposite sex.

He constructed defensive shields for survival and protection. However, those defensive structures are no longer necessary in present-day relationships. Without reexperiencing the original pain and grieving through the repressed emotions, the walls will never come down. Therefore, the deepest phase of mentoring will occur when the adult-child feels safe enough to let go and simply grieve in the presence of the mentor. Tears cried in bed alone late at night will never heal the pain that led to mistrust, guilt, shame, fear, blame, and low self-worth. Core pain will be healed in the context of loving, nonerotic relationships of trust. Through the mentoring relationship, the defensive barriers will crumble and bonding will occur.

- Forgiveness

Forgiveness is like a period at the beginning and end of a very long sentence. First, it is a decision of the mind, a choice to let go of blame and resentment. Second, it is the result of the heart, naturally emerging after the process of grieving. Grieving may not take only one or two sessions. It may take days, months, or years. Forgiveness will occur in stages. As the individual sheds layers of pain surrounding his heart, he will experience forgiveness in each stage of grieving (like peeling away layers of an onion). There is a big distance between forgiving in the mind, because it is the right thing to do, and forgiving in the heart, because now the adult-child feels and experiences freedom from pain.

Forgiveness does not necessarily mean the painful feelings go away. One can still feel the effects of the painful experience and forgive at the same time. Forgiveness is lifting away the veil of blame and shame. This comes about by assigning proper responsibility to each individual involved in the original experience or wounding. It also comes about naturally after intense grieving has taken place. What I experienced in my mentoring relations while working through the emotional incest of my mother and sexual abuse of my uncle was that self-blame lay at the bottom of my pain. I believed that my uncle loved me, then sexually abused me. After working through the pain of his violating my boundaries and my love, I discovered that I blamed myself, and I blamed God for not protecting me. Who is God to a child? God is our parents, the visible manifestation of the invisible Creator. So, standing behind God were my parents who did not protect me.

Memory healing or healing of memories is very helpful in relieving deep wounds. Profound and life-changing experiences may occur for the adult-child if the mentor participates in this activity. I have witnessed this many times.

Forgiveness is a gift, given to the other, to self, and in some instances, to God. Again, when we do not forgive, we give energy to our pain and project that pain onto other people who remind us of the perpetrator(s).

- Learning new social skills

Emotional and mental growth were arrested when the adult-child experienced neglect, abuse, or abandonment. An adult-child now lives in a physically mature body, but the mind and heart remain frozen. Therefore, the adult-child will have to learn new skills in relationships, i.e., when it's appropriate to ask for things; how to ask for things; how to give; how to receive; how to communicate in a positive, assertive manner; how to take individual responsibility for his needs and well-being.

Through the mentoring relationship, the adult-child will learn these skills. It may happen in very painful and difficult ways, as the adult-child may act out, making strong demands upon the mentor, or the adult-child may withdraw, afraid to ask for what he needs. The mentor must lovingly and firmly teach the adult-child how to express himself appropriately. Proper socialization is an integral part of the mentoring process.

• Experiencing value

Value comes from the invisible and visible God: inheriting a sense of belonging, self-worth, and competency. Through bonding with the mentor, the adult-child will begin to experience a sense of liberation and freedom and begin to come into his value as a son of God. It is very important for the adult-child to internalize value, as he internalizes the mentor's love, who represents Mr. God, his role model of masculinity.

• Journaling

It is very helpful to keep a journal, writing down the many changes, experiences, feelings, and thoughts that take place on a daily basis. The adult-child may share these things with the mentor. It will also serve as a source of personal reflection—where he has been, what he has been through, and where he is going. It may also serve to illuminate what are the triggers that stimulate inappropriate behaviors and distorted thinking.

Finally, after going through the various stages of mentoring, the adult-child is ready to enter into a relationship of mutuality.

Conclusion

Dr. John Gottman writes:

Although our study of infants is not yet complete, such observations strengthen my belief that parental conflict can begin to take its toll in infancy—a time when the very pathways of a child's autonomic nervous system are developing. Whatever happens to that child emotionally during those first few months may have a significant and lifelong effect on a child's vagal tone—that is, the child's ability to regulate her nervous system. Whether an infant's cries are answered, whether she is frequently soothed or irritated by the sensations around her, whether the people who feed her, bathe her, and play with her are calm and engaging or anxious and depressed—all of this may make a difference in a baby's long-term ability to respond to stimuli, to calm herself, and recover from stress.[11]

Several mentors were overwhelmed when they read the text in this chapter. Relax. The men and women who experience unwanted same-sex attraction simply need your loving presence in their lives. They need to know that they are accepted and loved for who they are. The guidelines I have detailed are merely suggestions to help you find your way in this wonderful, healing relationship.

Do not back away when things get rough. And they will. Work through your differences. Conflict is the price we pay for intimacy. Each man and woman with same-sex attraction did not experience successful bonding either with parents and/or peers. Therefore, there will be an underlying paradox in the relationship: Fear of intimacy and a tremendous need for love. These two polarities will be a constant part of relating until the defenses begin to melt away. Be persistent and consistent.

For the men and women who wish to enroll mentors into their healing journey, your responsibility will be to educate them about the nature of same-sex attraction. Most people do not understand the meaning of homosexual desires. Their gut reaction is fear of the unknown. Realize that you have to mentor your mentors in understanding the meaning behind same-sex attractions. This is part of your growth into manhood and womanhood.

You may also need to obtain not just one, but several mentors. Some will help you on your spiritual journey. Some will help you with finances and business. Some are more tactile and open to healthy, healing touch. Each mentor will possess different qualities and abilities. Do not limit yourself to one person. Spread it out, the more the better. And, when requesting someone to be your mentor, expect rejection. Generally, you will receive one, "Yes," to about nine, "No." Keep going until you find the one.

For mentors and strugglers alike, there is a need for appropriate displays of physical affection. Again, same-sex attraction represents detachment from one's core gender identity. Experiencing healthy touch in adult relationships is paramount to growth into manhood and womanhood. For the mentors, realize that these are still immature kids in adult bodies. They possess a child's need for bonding and secure attachment. For the struggler, express your needs in healthy ways, and find mentors who are able to offer the gift of healthy touch. As Ashley Montagu said, "Where touching begins, there love and humanity also begin."[12]

CHAPTER THIRTEEN

Slade

From the beginning, it seems I knew that I didn't fit in. I felt unwanted and ashamed. An incident in the third grade sums up my perception. I was standing in the classroom with the other leftover children, those who had not been chosen for one side or the other. I remember the humiliation at not having been selected, evidence that I was not wanted. I waited, holding my breath and my stomach muscles tight, wanting to disappear. I could not let anyone know the fear and shame I felt. I waited for the teacher to step in and assign me to one of the teams. I knew that no one wanted me if I could not perform, and I could say nothing. This became a lifelong fear of expressing myself.

I always felt I was different from other children, especially the boys. I compared myself to them and always felt inferior. Compounding this was my sense that I was a disappointment to my father. By the time I was five years old, I felt that I was not the boy he wanted. I did not feel close to him and knew that I could do nothing to please him. Did he notice the distance between us? Did he know that I dreaded being alone with him? I had the feeling that I had to constantly prove my worthiness to him, and it was futile.

He wanted me to play sports. I never felt comfortable to play them. I played not to make mistakes, not to be in the wrong place to catch the ball or to drop it. I hated not knowing how to stand and hold a bat or how to throw a ball or shoot a basket. I feared being ridiculed. I felt that I should know how to do these things. After all, I was a boy, wasn't I? I decided that

I could not meet my father's, and thus other men's, standards. He wanted me to be tough. I was overly sensitive. I hated that my feelings were easily hurt, and I didn't want anyone to know it. My perception that I was a failure at sports served to further distance me from my father and other boys. To avoid further emotional hurt from my father, I detached from him (and thus from masculinity) and continued to feel comfortable in my mother's world. I felt close to my mother. I was sensitive to her hurt feelings and felt strongly connected to and protective of her. Although I do feel that my parents loved me as their son, on some level they did not love the individual that I was.

My feelings of not belonging and of being different continued through elementary school. I was painfully shy, yet desperately wanted friends and affirmation. I had no idea how to go about getting them. While no one picked on me or made fun of me, I experienced a great deal of hurt and isolation. I shared this pain with no one. I was the oldest of two brothers and a sister with whom I was close, but not even to them did I share my fear and hurt. I felt completely alone. I perceived that the only way I could get some of the approval I desperately needed was to be good, polite, and studious. I would be no trouble. I became good. I was so good that I thought that was all I was. I received some scraps of attention by pleasing adults with good grades, polite behavior, silence, and shy smiles.

I tried to discern what adults wanted from me in terms of goodness, and then I would be it. This never worked with other children. As I grew older, the only way of connecting with them was to listen to their stories. I listened, but never shared mine. So much of me went hungry for Father's love and approval, Mother's affirmation, and peer acceptance. So many unmet legitimate needs. I continued the pattern of wanting others to call my individuality out, and, short of that, to tell me how and who to be. I felt that something must be dreadfully wrong with me. Why couldn't anyone see that something was wrong?

By the time I got through junior high school, I was a good student, caused no trouble, brought no attention to myself, listened to others, prayed to God, and obeyed my parents. I was colorless, odorless, sexless, voiceless, and angerless. I was seen as that nice, polite little fellow who smiled all the time. "But," I would scream to myself, "I am so much more. Can't you see it?" I was lonely and had no friends. I was also short in stature, which I hated. I perceived my shortness in height to be a reflection of my shortness as a male.

During my early teens, I felt horrified to notice that I experienced sexual feelings toward other males. I was ashamed, confused, and depressed. "Why was I not strongly attracted to girls?" From where did this same-sex attraction come? I clenched my fists and prayed to God to take these feelings from me. I felt dirty and unworthy. I prayed for forgiveness. I had done nothing to acquire these feelings. I wanted no part of them. I did not want to be like that. I wanted to be normal. I had spent years already feeling different and separated, and now I was "queer." Now I had something else that I could not share with anyone.

Something was dreadfully wrong with me. I continued to feel uncomfortable with my father. He seemed to always be testing me, and I knew that I would fail no matter what the test was. I remember interpreting his various lectures and making them into a devastating threat. "Slade, if you procrastinate, if you are sensitive and not logical, if you make too many mistakes or try to become an artist, you will not grow to be a man." Inside my head, I raged against his threat. How did I know what it was to be or feel like a man? Who was to teach me? My father? He had not done so. Was I just simply to know because I was a male? Clearly, he was right. I was a failure, a reject to the core of my being. I would not grow into manhood as my father defined it. What would I then grow to be? How would I get there? Still, I needed his approval and attention. Still, I needed to meet his standards, even if at the expense of my individuality.

In my last years of high school, I wanted very badly to have male friendships. Other guys had something I knew I lacked, some secret to being a man that was not available to me. I wanted to be one of the guys and had no idea how to go about it. I got through high school without a sexual experience. I was good. Correct, normal sexual desire would come in time, I told myself. Because of the same-sex attraction, I felt full of shame. I was bad, unworthy, unlovable. I did not date until my senior prom, and for my date I had no sexual feelings. My persona as a nice guy who smiled, never talked, but was a great listener continued. I could be the shoulder to cry on. I had classmates, but no friends. I was liked in high school, but not known. I did not know how to connect with others and was afraid they would reject me if I attempted to do so.

In the last year of high school, I was given a small sum of money towards college tuition for being an "all-around good guy." I felt pleased but embarrassed. As they called my name, I stood to go to the stage and receive my award. As I stepped across my father, he said, "Don't smile." As I walked to the stage, I felt confused. What did he mean? Why did he say not to smile? Was my smile ugly? Could I not be happy about something that

I had achieved? Even this he stepped on, I thought. (Many years later, I would realize that much of my perception was misperception, that my father was not so cruel and uncaring as I had imagined. I would come to understand that I had contributed to much of my own pain and struggling.)

In college, I made no friends and had no social life. I remained unable to come out of myself. I lived at home and worked part-time. I felt that people found me likable, but did not know me. The few girls that I talked with during those four years seemed more than willing to turn me into a brother. Because I was afraid that I would not respond sexually, I could not be assertive and manly. I continued to struggle with guilty sexual feelings and fantasies about men.

Then, after I had taken my first full-time job after college, I met the first person that seemed to take an interest in me. He asked me about myself, he shared himself with me, and he encouraged me in conversation. The conversations, the shared books and music, the talk and meeting of women, the discussions of philosophy and of higher consciousness, and the travel were so stimulating and engulfing. I thought I had found acceptance. Wonderfully and frighteningly, there was the sexual attraction. It was the first time in my life that I had responded to another human being so powerfully. I felt sought after, and I felt known. It scared the hell out of me. He was straight. In my perception, he was all the man that I was not. He was everything that I wanted to be. Very quickly, I found myself wondering what it was like to be him, to feel his feelings, to feel his experiences, his life. In comparison, my life seemed invalid. I wanted to be him. We traveled together, and I fantasized about him. I used to wonder what I had done to meet someone so full of life, so free from other people's expectations and definitions. Because I did not want him to be aware of my sexual attraction, I had to continue my life's act of feeling one way on the inside and acting differently on the outside.

During this period of my mid-twenties, I met a number of women to whom I felt suddenly attracted. It was a wonderful time. I liked women, but I was still afraid of my sexual response to them. But I needed to know who I was as a man. When I approached sex, I found that unless I had a strong sexual attraction to the woman, 50 percent of the time I would not be able to achieve or maintain an erection.

Later, to my joy, I fell in love with two women. With one in particular, I experienced the same strong sexual attraction I had experienced with my friend. With her, I felt, finally, what it must be to feel like a man with a woman. She touched some sense of myself that I hadn't known was there—

some masculinity that I had feared wasn't in me. She was romantic. She would apply lipstick in the basement of our office building and let me kiss it off. I really wasn't just a good boy. She was strongly sexual, and I loved it. I felt strong, decisive, loving, vulnerable. I felt known. I felt that this woman loved me. I could not believe it. Because of my sexual desire for her, I thought that I loved her. I begged her to marry me, feeling that God had sent her to me to save my sanity. When we made love, I was ready. There were no doubts, no fears. I saw another side of myself. It was wonderful. I thought we would surely marry. However, she would always gently turn me down. Only later did I understand her own emotional problems.

I wanted very much to marry and have children. I thought that marriage would rid me of the unwanted sexual desires and grant me the approval I still needed from others. At the age of twenty-eight, I married a woman whom I did not love. We had a sexual relationship before our marriage, and I thought that she loved me and that I would grow to love her. My same-sex attractions were diminished, but still there. I never shared with her about my struggle.

I did not realize then that I had chosen a woman who combined the negative characteristics of both my father and mother. Just as with my perceptions of my father, she was demanding and critical. She triggered my "you are a failure" fears and manipulated me with behaviors that I read as "you have wounded me" and "you have an obligation to please me." She combined these with my mother's very demanding "poor me" and "you are responsible for me and must take care of me and my feelings and be on my side" manipulations.

My wife was a very angry woman and often flew into rages. I had never liked conflict and was unsure how to handle anger in anyone. I would do anything to stop the discomfort I felt when my wife became enraged. Our life was full of dishonesty. Consequently, my intention with my wife was to continue to "mind-read" to ascertain her moods and desires and then to meet them when I could.

My wife was demanding and critical and triggered my feelings of being a failure, and at the same time, relied on me to meet her emotional needs. I aided her in abdicating her responsibility to take care of herself. I owed her. After all, she had married me. I sought to meet the demands so there would be no conflict. I felt I was responsible for her unhappiness. We were codependent, and I enabled her to be an invalid. Into this mess we brought a beautiful three-month-old baby girl whom we adopted in 1980. My daughter became the love of my life, but she, too, was damaged through the marriage. In 1992, I separated from my wife and sought and got full custody of our then twelve-year-old daughter. This was the beginning of living my own life.

Because I felt so deeply inferior to others and inadequate to meet life's situations and because of my hatred of my homosexual feelings, I had spent my life in darkness, shame, and fear of rejection. I hid myself, and I blocked myself from experiencing my pain. In isolation and loneliness, I sought answers to my struggle, but I did not know where to begin.

In 1995, the course of my life changed. I met Richard and the International Healing Foundation. He helped me to recover my life and guided my journey to wholeness. I had always thought that if I didn't have this condition of homosexuality, I would be truly good and my life would fall into place. He helped me to understand that the condition was just the tip of the iceberg. He explained that this condition was only a symptom of much deeper wounding to my soul. I didn't know it then, but at our first meeting, the ice around my heart began to melt and my healing began. Years of unshed tears and unexpressed feelings awaited release. I understood that my life did have validity and that I could come out of this struggle and live a real life.

My therapy with Richard began with reading David Burns's book *Ten Days to Self-Esteem*. Although I love to read, I hated this book. There was homework, which triggered my lifelong pattern of procrastination, and structured daily logs to monitor my emotions. Richard instructed me to stop defining myself as either homosexual or heterosexual. Suddenly, I had the possibility of freedom from an oppressive thinking pattern that had so often led me to feel dejected. He explained that I was a beloved son of God and that I deserved to be loved merely because I existed. I did not have to earn love. I had always experienced shame when criticized. I learned that my thoughts—not actual events—created my moods. My feelings resulted more from the way I thought about things rather than from what actually happened. I came to see that only I could make me feel depressed, worried, or angry.

I learned to stop reasoning emotionally. My thoughts had always been, "I feel like a failure, so I must be a failure." I stopped labeling myself. Instead of calling myself stupid or a reject, I would say, "I made a mistake." I stopped dwelling on the negatives in my life and stopped criticizing myself with "should" or "have to" statements. I stopped identifying with my feelings. I had always experienced my physical shortness as another indication of my inferiority as a man. In my thinking, my shortness in height verified my shortness as a male. One day, after much work, it came to me that my physical shortness did not make me a failure as a man. The two were not connected. My self-worth grew.

Through therapy, I became conscious of the constant and harmful judging and evaluating that I did as I compared myself to other men. I stopped putting myself down. I stopped seeing myself through the eyes of others. I began to understand that I was a unique and valuable human being worthy of love, even when I had made a mistake and even though I was short.

As my therapy progressed, I experienced with Richard a profound sense of acceptance. For the first time in my life, I experienced unconditional love. Love without judgment. I experienced the love of a father for his son. All that this man asked of me was that I become myself, that I show up in life, that I be authentic. He explained that all of me was welcome, that it was safe to bring all that I was into the room. Someone cared about me, with all my fears and perceived inadequacies, as well as my strengths. I experienced acceptance. I felt loved for myself, not for what I did or knew or how I looked or didn't look. He cared about me just for myself.

I moved on to inner-child work. I learned that there was a stunted child in me who needed acknowledgment and unconditional love. I gave my inner son the love and affirmation that I felt I had never received. I welcomed him into my conscious life. I honored him for being there with me. I asked for his forgiveness, for my being unaware of him, for ignoring him, and for trying to kill him. One day, I suddenly realized that in telling my inner child that I loved him, I was actually loving myself. This was a revelation for me. I am worthy and valuable just by being. I learned to show up in life.

I also learned about voice dialogue. I became aware that I have many subpersonalities, or voices, operating in me. These voices are often in conflict with each other. Voice dialogue allowed me to objectify the voices, recognize them, and understand and work with them.

Homosexuality is not about sex. Rather, it is ultimately about rejection of and detachment from self, from others, and from one's gender identity. I came to see that my sexual fantasy about another man might have nothing to do with him. The fantasy was in my head, and the other person might be nothing like the fantasy. I felt the truth in understanding that the desire for homosexual union was to acquire some characteristic of masculinity that I perceived in another man but felt lacking in myself. The desires indicated that I was not living in the present moment. Therefore, I experienced a dramatic decrease in my sexual fantasies about other men.

During this time, I joined the support group. We used role-play, emotional processing, and nonerotic touch. I met strong, sensitive men struggling, like me. It took a while, but I learned to be myself with them. I came to love them very much.

A major goal in my recovery was to access my masculine energies. Richard strongly suggested that I join a men's organization with which he was familiar. The purpose of the organization was to initiate men into the sacred masculine. In the summer of 1997, I went through the group's weekend experience. I became a "New Warrior." During the weekly meetings in the following year, I perceived in myself something I had always feared wasn't there. I now realized that I was a man. My fear-ridden ten-year-old good little boy had died. Suddenly, I was seen as, and experienced myself as, a man among men.

Today, I see the gold in my wounds. I had brought into adulthood behaviors that were inappropriate. As one author put it, "I discovered that I had taken on identities that incorrectly or inadequately expressed my essential being." I found that I could be powerful and vulnerable. I could risk being wrong, risk making a mistake, risk loving and being loved. I could say no. I discovered I am a man with strengths and weaknesses. I am king and beggar. I am awakening the gift of life. My awakening began when a man asked only that I become myself, that I show up in life.

PART III:

Compassion

CHAPTER FOURTEEN

Guidance for Family and Friends

I have counseled and taught thousands of men, women, and adolescents dealing with the SSAD condition. I have also worked with many parents, friends, and relatives whose loved ones are experiencing same-sex attractions. It is not an easy subject to broach or understand. Therefore, I would like to offer several suggestions about how to love someone who is either SSAD or living in a SSAD lifestyle.

When a child tells his parents about his same-sex attractions, alarms go off in the hearts and minds of Mom and Dad: "Why us? Why you? Is it our fault? My God, is this really happening? Don't you know you could die from such behavior? This is against all of our religious beliefs."

As parents, we must first be quiet and listen so our children will speak (bite your tongue if necessary). Later, we can deal with our thoughts, feelings, and needs. It took a lot of guts and courage for your child to disclose. Do not back away. He needs you now more than ever. Remember to separate the behavior from the being. Having same-sex attractions is an indicator that wounds never healed and basic needs went unmet. The good news is that wounds can heal and needs can be met.

Do not try to "fix" your child or "preach" about the truth. First, listen and find out how he feels and what he thinks. This is *not* about you; it is about him. More than likely, he has been struggling for years before disclosing this information to you. Even though your gut may say back away, resist this self-protective urge and embrace your child. This, too, shall pass!

If you are a friend, consider it a special gift of honor and trust if he shares about his struggles with same-sex attractions. As with Mom and Dad, keep your mouth shut and listen. Perhaps he practiced for days, months, or years before sharing this part of his life with you. Be warm, embracing, and nonjudgmental. Ask questions sincerely in order to understand his heart and desire. If you are not sure what to ask, breathe, relax, and say how you feel, i.e., shocked, surprised, concerned.

Remember that a same-sex attraction is always a symptom of unresolved childhood trauma and unmet homo-emotional love needs. As parents and friends, we can help initiate healing by being there for him and filling in the gap.

Here are several suggestions for parents, spouses, and friends:

Guidance for Parents

1, Lift your child to God. Pray. Do not play God. A wise prayer would be that he does not find what he is looking for in the SSAD lifestyle. Pray for healing of his wounds and the fulfillment of his unmet needs in healthy relationships.

2. Do not blame yourself, each other, or anyone else. Take responsibility for the mistakes you have made and seek God's forgiveness. Then, forgive yourself as you are forgiven. It is very important that you forgive yourself. Walking around with this (toxic) guilt will only weigh you down and keep you from making changes in your life.

3. Next, ask your child to forgive you. If he is not ready to forgive, that is his responsibility, not yours. Do not live through your child. Realize that if you did make a mistake, it was a mistake. Once you apologize for your mistakes, then take responsibility by loving yourself and loving your child.

4. Learn to heal yourself. There is only one person you can ever change, and that is yourself. The changes you make in your life greatly affect your child, no matter what his age.

5. Investigate your child's wounds. What are the multiple causes of his same-sex attractions? Educate yourself about his past, and reappraise the situation. Ask questions and listen without judgment (Mr. and Mrs. KYMS: Keep Your Mouth Shut).

6. Investigate your child's unmet needs. (Why is he doing what he is doing?) What is the other side providing? Acceptance, affection, affirmation, and a safe place.
7. Help heal wounds and fulfill unmet needs. Create a loving environment of acceptance, affection, and affirmation, and a safe place to be. Separate being from *behavior*. You do not need to approve of your child's behavior; however, it is imperative to always love the being. As this is a Same-Sex Attachment Disorder, it is very important for the same-sex parent to become more involved with his or her child. Embrace your son or daughter. Build a closer connection. Listen to and find out more about your child's life. Remember, no matter how old he or she is, everyone needs Time, Touch, and Talk. The opposite-sex parent needs to support from behind, becoming a bridge for the same-sex parent and child to bond and attach.
8. Love unconditionally in the truth. Never compromise your values or morals, and at the same time continue to love, listen, embrace, and when necessary, set limits.

A good book for parents is *On Eagles' Wings: Family Manual* by Wendell and Nancy Anderson (1997). You can order it through Regeneration Books (See Resources at the back of the book for more information). This is a Christian program, but it can be adapted for Jewish families and those of other faiths.

Guidance for Spouses

1. Understand that you cannot solve or fulfill your spouse's unmet homo-emotional needs. Only God, your partner, and someone of the same sex can do that.
2. Work on your own issues. "Why was I drawn to a man or woman with a homo-emotional wound?" "What is in it for me?"
3. Get support from family, friends, spiritual community, and/or counselor. Isolation equals death.
4. Your husband or wife cannot give you what he or she does not have. You cannot get water from a dry well. Have patience. Give as much love as you can. Take care of yourself in healthy ways.
5. Pray. Do not try to change your spouse. He must want that for himself. Give him up to God.

Guidance for Friends

1. Pray. Lift him up to God. Ask for guidance on how to best love him.
2. Listen. Be a good friend. Let him know you are interested in his life. We all want to be accepted for who we are.
3. Love and embrace your friend, especially if he is of the same gender. Don't back away; move towards. Provide for him healthy, fraternal friendship and love.
4. Share the truth in love. Let him know that you do not believe that he was born this way and that he did not choose to have these feelings. And therefore, what was learned can be unlearned. Let him know that you are ready to be there with him through the good and bad times.
5. Never give up. Anyone who has same-sex attractions has experienced much pain and trauma. He may display a wide range of emotions, one moment desperately needing you, and the next moment rejecting you and never wanting to see you again. Hang in there. Love is patient and enduring.
6. Be consistent. Most homosexual relationships do not last. You, as a trusted and dear friend, may be the pillar that he needs to help him ultimately heal the deepest wounds that have led him into this condition. And through your presence and love, you just may be the one to see him come out of this.

Why Are So Many Men and Women Afraid of Homosexuals?

We fear that which we do not understand. For as it has been said, the meaning of fear is False Evidence Appearing Real. As long as we allow fear to rule us, we fuel hatred and division. It is through education that we come to learn about ourselves and each other.

1. Fear is a physiological response, one of self-protection when we feel threatened and do not *understand* the other. The fear response is a built-in defense to *protect* us from the threat of danger. This physiological response occurs in the limbic system, or the old brain, connected to the child within. Therefore, in the case of homosexuality, there is a lack of understanding that comes from the new brain (the cerebral cortex), the rational or more adult part of the mind. Most people have not understood the meaning of homosexuality as a same-sex attachment disorder. We fear that which we do not understand.
2. Underneath psychological fear is guilt and shame. If I harbor any guilt and shame about what I have done in the past, then it is con-

venient to condemn another. In this way, I do not have to deal with my own guilt and shame or take responsibility for my past/present actions. Homosexuals then become my scapegoat, as a defensive detachment from my wounds and mistakes.

3. Homosexuals have been social outcasts, and associating with "them" means we might risk *rejection* by others. If I am already insecure about some aspect(s) of my life, this may pose a further threat to my "value" or sense of emotional equilibrium.

4. We hate in another what we hate or deny in ourselves. Many people have same-sex parent wounds and are not homosexually inclined. However, some may have had homosexual experiences while growing up, and because of the social stigmas attached to this condition, the individual harbors guilt and shame. Therefore, he must condemn the homosexual, out of self-protection, out of this hidden sense of guilt, shame, and fear.

Responses to Commonly Asked Questions

Many parents ask, "What should I do when my son wants to invite his boyfriend home for the holidays or a visit? Is this OK to do? Am I giving him the wrong message if I say yes? Will he think that I approve of his homosexual behavior?" I have prayed and meditated on this issue for years. My conclusion is definitely allow your son to bring his boyfriend home to visit. Why?

- Your son's boyfriend is someone else's son, and perhaps he has been rejected altogether by his family. This is your chance to show him God's love.

- You are embracing your son, not his behavior. In accordance with your own religious or spiritual convictions, you might say, "Dear, you are both welcome to come and stay. However, we do not believe in sexual relations outside of marriage. Therefore you can stay in one room, and your boyfriend can sleep in another." You can only say this if you maintain the same protocol for another child who might want to bring home an opposite-sex friend. You must be congruent; otherwise you lose all credibility and your child will disrespect you.

- All great faiths speak about the power of love as the greatest medicine to heal all pain. Only love and truth will ultimately win any battle. By rejecting your child, you are only adding salt to his wounds. It is best for him to be close to you, and you to him. Remember, this is a same-sex attachment disorder. He needs attachment and bonding from Mr. and Mrs. God, first, last, and in between.

- This is your blessing, a chance to repair old wounds and make up for lost time. The same-sex parent especially needs to be present, involved, and embracing (physically, emotionally, mentally, and spiritually). A son needs his daddy's love, and a daughter needs her mommy's love.

- Finally, one part of the homosexual condition is rebellion. By embracing your child and his lover, you are short-circuiting his need to rebel. This will eventually have a positive effect upon him and his relationship with you. Tender loving care will reap bountiful results.

So what if your child misunderstands your intention and thinks you are accepting his lifestyle? That is his judgment. Keep loving in the truth. Never give up. Never stop trying. Those who endure to the end will be saved and win the race.

What if your child, friend, or relative invites you to attend a "commitment ceremony"? Should you attend? My response is *no*. The reason is basically the same as the one regarding special legislation for homosexuals. Your attendance or vote implies social acceptance, and homosexual behavior should *never* be accepted.

What about giving your child literature to read? If he is open to the possibility of another perspective, great—go for it. If he is dead set against it, do not even think about it. Why? Remember, implicit in this condition is oppositional behavior. If you push one direction, he will go another direction just to upset you. My suggestion is to ask him for his literature. Show your willingness to understand him and his belief system. Once you do this consistently over a period of time, then you have a foundation to ask him to read some of *your* materials. Do not read his books or articles with the intention of biding time so you can proselytize him. Read to understand, get closer to, and love your child. We all want to be understood and respected. You do not have to agree. Just listen and learn. Do unto others. . . .

Conclusion

My final word is this: Do not try to "change" your child, sibling, parent, spouse, relative, friend, coworker, neighbor, fellow student, boss, minister, rabbi, or adversary. He or she is not, was not, nor ever will be a homosexual man or woman. Homosexuality is always a symptom. It represents unresolved trauma and gender disidentification. The individual who experiences same-sex attractions is wounded and in need of healing. The best medicine to heal all pain is love. He needs secure attachment with men. She needs secure attachment with women. When secure attachment is achieved, same-sex desires will naturally wane. Therefore, men, please reach out to gender-disidentified men. And women, please reach out to gender-disidentified women. This is a war of love. Give your best and let God do the rest.

Note

Since the publication of *Coming Out Straight*, I wrote a new book for family and friends who have loved ones dealing with same-sex attraction. The book is entitled *Gay Children, Straight Parents: A Plan for Family Healing*. It offers a comprehensive approach to helping either gay-identified individuals and/or those who wish to change.

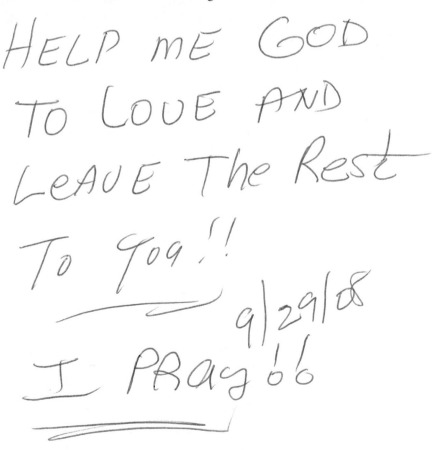

HELP ME GOD
TO LOVE AND
LEAVE The Rest
To You !!
9/29/08
I PRay 66

CHAPTER FIFTEEN

A Final Thought

A great service the Gay Rights Movement has done is to bring the issue of homosexuality out of the closet and into the light. Many people in religious and social institutions, and medical and psychiatric professions have failed these men and women. Not only did they ridicule without offering hope for healing, they exacerbated the wounds of detachment through socialized prejudice and discrimination. Instead of apologizing on bended knees, they have succumbed to acceptance in the name of tolerance. I find this cheap religion and superficial science.

Yet, behind closed doors, most people are disgusted by homosexuality. "People seem to strongly favor anti-discrimination measures and other civil-rights protections for gays and lesbians, while at the same time they view homosexuality negatively—a sort of distasteful tolerance. A national survey conducted last August and published in *The Washington Post* found that 57 percent of Americans questioned consider homosexuality unacceptable; when asked about gay sex, 72 percent called it unacceptable."[1] The solution is neither blind acceptance nor indiscriminate tolerance. The answer is understanding and love.

While I was finishing this book, I stayed at a church rectory, living in a flat surrounded by several unoccupied rooms. There was a shared bathroom. Obviously, no one had used it for a long time. Since I live in a household of three kids, my wife, a housemate, and myself, taking a quiet and relaxed bath is not an easy accomplishment. I looked forward to a peaceful soak in the tub while finishing the book.

My first view of the bathtub shocked me. It had a buildup of soot from over fifty years! The tub must have been white at one time, but now all I could see was caked-on soot and dirt. Determined to take my peaceful bath, I bought a good scouring pad, a can of Ajax and went to work.

The first day, I scrubbed for an hour and a half. It was summer. Sweat pouring off my entire body added to the dirt coming off the walls of this long-neglected tub. There was white! It was still there, lying beneath all the dirt. I could hear it speaking, "Thank you, thank you. Set me free."

After an hour and a half, there it stood. A beautiful white bathtub returning to its glory day. It smiled. I smiled back. I washed away years of caked-on soot. It was ready. I poured in the warm water and lay in that glorious, clean, and happy tub. We were one!

The following day, I focused on the walls and the glass sliding doors. They, too, wore a coat of dirt, grime, and crud. It took another hour or so to scrub off years of misuse. The walls and glass doors shined. They, too, were happy and set free. I took another relaxing bath. We were one!

The final day, I cleaned the outside of the tub. There, too, brown soot and dirty floors were an unwelcome greeting to my newly resurrected bathtub. Scrubbing away more years of dirt, we all sang for joy. There is life after misuse, abuse, and neglect. My final soak in the tub was a celebration of life!

Accepting homosexuality as natural and normal is like glorifying pain and brokenness. Perhaps in this tainted world, it is the path of least resistance, much like the story of *The Emperor's New Clothes*. Everyone knew the emperor had no clothes on, but it was politically correct to pretend as if he did. It took a child to stand up and say, "'But he isn't wearing anything at all!' When the emperor heard the child, he knew he had been fooled. The next day the Emperor issued a proclamation: 'I ask only that you do as the child did and always try to tell the truth.'"

And so it is today, politically correct to accept homosexuality as an alternate lifestyle. Yet, if we embrace someone's homosexuality as normal and natural, his potential for wholeness will remain dormant beneath the wounds, beneath the years of caked-on soot. Accepting homosexuality is normalizing detachment, both intrapersonally and interpersonally.

Let us stand up and say, "It's not gay, nor bad, but SSAD." Let us open our hearts, for the homosexually oriented men and women can heal. What was learned can be unlearned. Let us embrace these beautiful, sensitive souls. Let us love them into life. Let us help them heal by scrubbing away years of misuse, abuse, and neglect. For when one heals, we all heal a little more.

Notes

Chapter One—My Story: Coming Out Straight
 1. Robert Bly, *Iron John: A Book About Men* (New York: Vintage Books, 1990), 42.
 2. Leanne Payne, *The Healing of the Homosexual* (Westchester, IL: Crossway Books, 1984), 31.

Chapter Two—Definitions and Causes of Same-Sex Attractions
 1. Shirley E. Cox, David Matheson, Doris Dant, *Workbook for Men* (Salt Lake City, UT: Evergreen International, Inc., 1998), vi.
 2. Simon LeVay, "A Difference in Hypothalamic Structure Between Heterosexual and Homosexual Men," *Science* 253 (August 1991): 1036.
 3. Quoted in Marlin Maddoux, *Answers to the Gay Deception* (Dallas, TX: International Christian Media, 1994), 24.
 4. David Nimmons, "Sex and the Brain," *Discover* Vol. 15, no. 3 (March 1994), 64–71.
 5. David Gelman et al., "Born or Bred?" *Newsweek* (24 February 1992), 46.
 6. Quoted in Marlin Maddoux, *Answers to the Gay Deception* (Dallas, TX: International Christian Media, 1994), 26.
 7. Gelman et al., 46
 8. Ibid.
 9. John Horgan, "Gay Genes, Revisited," *Scientific America* (November 1995), 26.
 10. George Rice et al., "Male Homosexuality: Absence of Linkage to Microsatellite Markers on the X Chromosome in a Canadian Study" (paper presented at the 21st annual meeting of Sex Research, Provincetown, Mass., 1995); Quoted in E. Marshall, "NIH Gay Gene Study Questioned," *Science* 268 (1995), 1841. Combined Dispatches, "New Study Challenges Theory of 'Gay Gene' in Homosexuals," *Washington Times* (23 April 1999), A3; C. Chamberlain, "Where Did the Gay Gene Go?" Internet, www.ABCNEWS.com, April 23, 1999.
 11. J. Madeleine Nash, "The Personality Genes," *Time* Vol. 151, no. 16 (April 27, 1998): 60–61.
 12. John Horgan, "Gay Genes, Revisted," *Scientific America* (November 1995): 26.
 13. William Byne and Bruce Parsons, "Human Sexual Orientation: The Biologic Theories Reappraised," *Archives of General Psychiatry* Vol. 50, no. 3 (March 1993): 228–239.
 14. S. Marc Breedlove, Ph.D., "Sex on the Brain," *Nature* 389 (October 23, 1997): 801.
 15. Richard C. Friedman and Jennifer Downey, "Neurobiology and Sexual Orientation: Current Relationships," *Journal of Neuropsychiatry* Vol. 5, no. 2 (Spring 1993): 131–153.
 16. Ruth Hubbard and Elijah Wald, *Exploding the Gene Myth* (Boston, MA: Beacon Press, 1993), 6, 94, 98.
 17. John Leland and Mark Miller, "Can Gays 'Convert?'" *Newsweek* (17 August 1998): 49.
 18. John Money, "Sin, Sickness, or Status? Homosexual Gender Identity and Psychoneuroendocrinology," *American Psychologist* 42, no. 4 (1987): 384.

19. Jeffrey Satinover, *Homosexuality and the Politics of Truth* (Grand Rapids, MI: Baker Books, 1996), 77.
20. William Masters, Virginia Johnson, Robert Kolodny, *Human Sexuality*, 2nd Edition (Boston, MA: Little Brown, 1985), 411.
21. Quoted from Joseph Nicolosi, *Reparative Therapy of Male Homosexuality* (Northvale, NJ: Jason Aronson Inc., 1991), 18–19.
22. National Association for Research and Therapy of Homosexuality, Press Release 5, 1997.
23. Elizabeth Moberly, *Psychogenesis: The Early Development of Gender Identity* (London: Routledge and Kegan Paul, 1983), 67; E. Moberly, *Homosexuality: A New Christian Ethic* (Greenwood, SC: James Clark & Co., 1983), 9.
24. Joseph Nicolosi, *Reparative Therapy of Male Homosexuality* (Northvale, NJ: Jason Aronson Inc., 1991), 32–35.
25. Harville Hendrix, *Getting the Love You Want: A Couples' Study Guide* (New York: Harper Perennial, 1988), 26.
26. Elizabeth Moberly, *Homosexuality: A New Christian Ethic* (Greenwood, SC: James Clark & Co., 1983), 9.
27. Ibid.
28. Nicolosi, *Reparative Therapy*, 21.
29. E. Kaplan, "Homosexuality: A Search for the Ego-Ideal," *Archives of General Psychiatry* 16 (1967): 355–358.
30. Nicolosi, *Reparative Therapy*, 94–95.
31. Nicolosi, *Reparative Therapy*, 77–78.; Irving Bieber et al., *Homosexuality: A Psychoanalytic Study of Male Homosexuals* (New York: Vintage Books, 1962), 44–46; Gerard van den Aardweg, *Homosexuality and Hope: A Psychologist Talks About Treatment and Change* (Ann Arbor, MI: Servant Books, 1985), 64; Robert Kronemeyer, *Overcoming Homosexuality* (New York: Macmillan Publishing, 1980), 60–61.
32. Nicolosi, *Reparative Therapy*, 82.
33. Robert Kronemeyer, *Overcoming Homosexuality* (New York: Macmillan Publishing, 1980), 71.
34. Michael Saia, *Counseling the Homosexual* (Minneapolis, MN: Bethany House Publishers, 1988), 57–58.
35. Martha Welch, *Holding Time: Intensive One-Day Seminar*, 1996; M. Welch, *Introduction to Welch Method Attachment Therapy*, 1999.
36. James Bray and Donald Williamson, "Assessment of Intergenerational Family Relationships," in *Family of Origin Therapy* (Rockville, MD: Aspen Publishers, 1987), 31.
37. S. Allen Willcoxon, "Perspectives of Intergenerational Concepts," in *Family of Origin Therapy* (Rockville, MD: Aspen Publishers, 1987), 4.
38. Exodus 34:6–7, *New Oxford Annotated Bible*, Revised Standard Version (New York: Oxford University Press, 1973), 113.
39. John Pierrakos, speech presented at "Love, Eros, and Sex" seminar, Seven Oaks Conference Center, Madison, VA, December 7, 1996.
40. Bernard Nathanson, *The Genetic Auschwitz*, presented at the Human Life International Conference, Houston, TX, April 19, 1998.
41. Earl Wilson, *Counseling and Homosexuality* (Waco, TX: Word Books, 1988), 67.
42. Interview with Dr. Dean Byrd, April 13, 1999, Rockville, MD.
43. Irving Bieber et al., *Homosexuality: A Psychoanalytic Study of Male Homosexuals* (New York: Vintage Books, 1962), 44–46.
44. Charles Socarides, *Homosexuality: Psychoanalytic Therapy* (Northvale, NJ: Jason Aronson, Inc., 1989), 63–67.
45. Nicolosi, *Reparative Therapy*, 80.
46. Gerard van den Aardweg, *Homosexuality and Hope* (Ann Arbor, MI: Servant Books, 1985), 64.

47. Quoted in J. Nicolosi, *Reparative Therapy*, 77.

48. M. Siegelman, "Parental Background of Male Homosexuals and Heterosexuals," *Archives of Sexual Behavior* 3 (1974): 3–17.

49. G. A. Westwood, *A Minority Report on the Life of the Male Homosexual in Great Britain* (London: Longmans, Green, 1960). Quoted in J. Nicolosi, *Reparative Therapy*, 77.

50. M. Schoefield, *Sociological Aspects of Homosexuality: A Comparative Study of Three Types of Homosexuals* (London: Longmans, Green, 1965). Quoted in J. Nicolosi, *Reparative Therapy*, 77.

51. N. Thompson et al., "Parent-Child Relationships and Sexual Identity in Male and Female Homosexuals and Heterosexuals," *Journal of Consulting and Clinical Psychiatry* 41 (1973), 120–127.

52. Kronemeyer, *Overcoming Homosexuality*, 60–61.

53. Bly, 24.

54. Socarides, 63–67.

55. Kenneth J. Zucker and Susan J. Bradley, *Gender Identity Disorder and Psychosexual Problems in Children and Adolescents* (New York: Guilford Press, 1995), 254, 264.

56. Socarides, 18–25.

57. Moberly, *Psychogenesis*, 39; Nicolosi, *Reparative Therapy*, 43–45.

58. John Bowlby, *Separation, Anxiety, and Anger* (London: Hogarth Press, 1973).

59. Moberly, *Homosexuality*, 6–7.

60. Martha Welch, *Holding Time: Intensive One-Day Seminar* (audiocassettes, 1996).

61. Moberly, *Homosexuality*, 19. Nicolosi, *Reparative Therapy*, 113–114.

62. David Seamands, *Healing for Damaged Emotions* (Wheaton, IL: Victor Books, 1981), 69.

63. Nicolosi, *Reparative Therapy*, 26.

64. Moberly, *Homosexuality*, 21–22.

65. Saia, *Counseling the Homosexual*, 51–55.

66. Nicolosi, *Reparative Therapy*, 84.

67. Dean Byrd, *Understanding and Treating Homosexuality*, seminar LDS Church presented at Therapeutic Seminar, Washington, D.C., March 13, 1998.(Taken form combined research studies.)

68. Patrick Dimock, "Adult Males Sexually Abused As Children," *Journal of Interpersonal Violence* 3, no. 2 (June 1988): 203–221.

69. Michael Lew, *Victims No Longer* (New York: Nevraumont Publishing, 1988), 78.

70. David Finkelhor, *Child Sexual Abuse: New Theory and Research* (New York: Free Press, 1984), 195.

71. Robert Johnson and Diane Shrier, "Sexual Victimization of Boys," *Journal of Adolescent Health Care* 6, no. 5 (September 1985): 372–376.

72. Wendy Maltz and Beverly Holman, *Incest and Sexuality: A Guide to Understanding Healing* (Lexington, MA: Lexington Books, 1987), 72.

73. Wendy Maltz, *The Sexual Healing Journey: A Guide for Survivors of Sexual Abuse* (New York: Harper Perennial, 1991), 127.

74. John Gottman, *The Heart of Parenting* (New York: Simon and Schuster, 1997), 166.

75. Gerard van den Aardweg, *The Battle for Normality: A Guide for Self-Therapy for Homosexuality* (San Francisco: Ignatius Press, 1997), 41, 48.

76. Gottman, 171.

77. W. Gadpaille, "Cross-Species and Cross-Cultural Contributions to Understanding Homosexual Activity," *Archives of General Psychiatry* 37 (1980): 349–356.

78. Marshall Kirk and Erastes Pill, "The Overhauling of Straight America," *Guide Magazine* (October–November 1987), 9.

79. Alan Bell and Martin Weinberg, *Homosexualities: A Study of Diversity Among Men and Women* (New York: Simon and Schuster, 1978), 308–312.

80. Enrique Rueda, *The Homosexual Network: Private and Public Policy* (Old Greenwich, CT: Devin Adair, 1982), 53.

81. Dina Van Pelt, "Gays Are More Prone to Substance Abuse," *Insight* (5 November 1990): 53.

82. Bell and Weinberg, table 21.12, 450–451.

83. Barbara Leigh, Mark Temple, and Karen Trocki, "The Sexual Behavior of U.S. Adults: Results from a National Survey," *American Journal of Public Health* 83, no. 10 (October 1993): 11403–11404.

84. Tom Smith, *American Sexual Behavior: Trends, Socio-Demographic Differences, and Risk Behavior*, GSS Topical Report, no. 25 (University of Chicago, IL: National Opinion Research Center, December 1996): 6, 7.

85. David McWhirter and Andrew Mattison, *The Male Couple* (Englewood Cliffs, NJ: Prentice-Hall, 1984), 3.

86. Paul Cameron, "Homosexuality and Child Molestation," *Psychological Reports* 58 (1986), 327–337, as quoted in M. Maddoux, *Answers to the Gay Deception,* 62–63.

87. Nicholas Zill, Donna R. Morrison, and Mary Jo Coiro, "Long-Term Effects of Parental Divorce on Parent-Child Relationships, Adjustment, and Achievement in Young Adulthood," *Journal of Family Psychology* 7 (1993), 91–103.

88. Thomas Verny and John Kelly, *The Secret Life of the Unborn Child* (New York: Dell Publishing, 1981), 50.

89. Ibid., 12–13.

90. Monika Lukesch, "Psychologie Faktoren der Schwangerschaft" (Ph.D. dissertation, University of Salzburg, 1975), as quoted in Thomas Verny, *The Secret Life of the Unborn Child, 47.*

91. Dennis Stott, "Children in the Womb: The Effects of Stress," *New Society* (19 May 1977): 329–331.

92. Leanne Payne, *The Healing of the Homosexual* (Westchester, IL: Crossway Books, 1984), 21.

93. Nicolosi, *Reparative Therapy,* 145.

Chapter Four—Process of Healing: Four Stages of Recovery

1. R. Bly, *Iron John: A Book About Men* (New York: Vintage Books, 1990), 72–73.

2. E. Moberly, *Homosexuality: A New Christian Ethic* (Greenwood, SC: Attic Press, 1983), 38.

3. Jan Frank, "Stages of Recovery" (Speech presented at PFOX Conference, Fairfax, VA, March 7, 1998).

4. Joseph Nicolosi, *Reparative Therapy of Male Homosexuality* (Northvale, NJ: Jason Aronson Inc., 1991), 199–200.

5. Interview with Dr. Chrisopher Austin at the Family Life Center, Austin, TX, December 9, 1999.

6. D. Byrd, "Understanding and Treating Homosexuality," seminar presented at the Therapeutic Seminar, Washington, D.C., March 13, 1998.

7. Walter Trobisch, *Love Yourself* (Downers Grove, IL: InterVarsity Press, 1978), 8–9.

8. Irving Bieber et al., *Homosexuality: A Psychoanalytic Study of Male Homosexuals* (New York: Vintage Books, 1962), 220.

9. Nicolosi, *Reparative Therapy,* 103–104.

10. Douglas Weiss, *The Final Freedom* (Fort Worth, TX: Discovery Press, 1998), 34.

11. Nicolosi, *Reparative Therapy,* 34, 105.

12. E. Kaplan, "Homosexuality: A Search for the Ego-Ideal," *Archives of General Psychiatry* 16 (1967): 355–358.

13. John Gray, *What You Feel, You Can Heal* (Mill Valley, CA: Heart Publishing, 1984), 86.

14. Steven Stosny, *Treatment Manual of the Compassion Workshop* (Gaithersburg, MD: Compassion Alliance, 1995), 17.

15. Granger Westberg, *Good Grief: A Constructive Approach to the Problem of Loss* (Philadelphia, PA: Fortress Press, 1973).

16. Bly, 118–119.

17. Moberly, 46–47.

18. Robert Moore, *Rediscovering Masculine Potentials,* four cassette tapes (Wilmette, IL: Chiron, 1988).

19. John Pierrakos, "Love, Eros, and Sex" seminar (Seven Oaks Conference Center, Madison, VA, December 7, 1996).

20. Bly, 25.

Chapter Six—Therapeutic Tools and Techniques

1. Ronald Richardson, *Family Ties That Bind* (Vancouver, Can.: International Self-Counsel Press, 1984, 1987), 92–93.

2. Sunny Shulkin and Nedra Fetterman, "The Couples Journey," presented at the AAMFT National Conference, Baltimore, MD, 1995.

3. Eugene Gendlin, *Focusing* (New York: Bantam Books, 1981), 173–174.

4. Barbara De Angelis, *Making Love Work* (Baltimore, MD: Inphomation, 1993), 63.

5. Lucia Capacchione, *Recovery of Your Inner Child* (New York: Simon and Schuster, 1991), 16.

6. Michael Popkin, adapted from *Active Parenting Handbook* (Atlanta, GA: Active Parenting, 1983), 23.

7. David Seamands, *Healing for Damaged Emotions* (Wheaton, IL: Victor Books, 1981), 60.

8. Martha Baldwin, *Self-Sabotage* (New York: Warner Books, 1987), 23.

9. Napoleon Hill, *Think and Grow Rich* (New York: Fawcett Columbine, 1937), 50, 68.

10. Harvey Jackins, *The Human Side of Human Beings: The Theory of Re-evaluation Counseling* (Seattle, WA: Rational Island Publishers, 1978).

11. Harville Hendrix, *Getting the Love You Want: A Couples' Study Guide* (New York: Harper Perennial, 1988), 119.

12. George Leonard and Michael Murphy, *The Life We Are Given* (New York: Putnam, 1995), 8.

13. Exodus 34:6–7. *New Oxford Annotated Bible.*

14. Jane Myers Drew, *Where Were You When I Needed You Dad?* (Newport Beach, CA: Tiger Lily Publishing, 1992), 6–8.

Chapter Eight—Anger: Accessing Personal Power

1. Steven Stosny, *Treatment Manual of the Compassion Workshop* (Gaithersburg, MD: Compassion Alliance, 1995), 13–15.

2. M. Welch, *Holding Time* (New York: Simon and Schuster, 1988), 46.

3. M. Welch, *Holding Time: Intensive One-Day Seminar,* audio cassettes, 1996.

4. R. Bly, *A Little Book on the Human Shadow* (New York: HarperSanFrancisco, 1988), 48.

5. R. Bly, *Iron John: A Book About Men* (New York: Vintage Books, 1990), 8.

Chapter Ten—Touch: The Need for Bonding and Attachment

1. Ashley Montagu, *Touching: The Human Significance of the Skin* (New York: Harper and Row, 1986), xiv.

2. Jane Warner Watson, *My Little Golden Book About GOD* (Racine, WI: Golden Books Publishing, 1956).

3. Earl Wilson, *Counseling and Homosexuality* (Waco, TX: Word Books, 1988), 35.

4. Paul Brand and Philip Yancy, *The Gift of Pain* (Grand Rapids, MI: Zondervan Publishing House, 1997), 157.

5. John Gottman, *Why Marriages Succeed or Fail . . . And How You Can Make Yours Last* (New York: Simon and Schuster, Fireside, 1994), 143.

6. Montagu, 38.
7. Laurie Weiss and Jonathan Weiss, *Recovery from Co-Dependency: It's Never Too Late to Reclaim Your Childhood* (Littleton, CO: Empowerment Systems, 1988), 97.
8. Montagu, 126.
9. Ibid., 54.
10. George Howe Colt and Anne Hollister, "The Magic of Touch," *Life* (August 1997): 53–62.

Chapter Twelve—Mentoring: Restoring Love

1. Gilbert Herdt, ed., *Rituals of Manhood: Male Initiation in Papua New Guinea* (Berkeley, CA: University of California Press, 1982), 121.
2. Harold Bloomfield, *Making Peace with Your Parents* (New York: Ballantine Books, 1983), 9.
3. M. Welch, *Holding Time: Intensive One-Day Seminar*, audio cassettes, 1996.
4. Patricia Love, *Hot Monogamy*, Sounds True Audio Tapes, No. 2, Side A. 1994.
5. Michael Popkin, adapted from *Active Parenting Handbook* (Atlanta, GA: Active Parenting, 1983), 23.
6. Ashley Montagu, *Touching: The Human Significance of the Skin* (New York: Harper and Row Perennial, 1986), xiv.
7. Ibid., 28.
8. Ibid., 97.
9. Ibid., 146.
10. Earl Wilson, *Counseling and Homosexuality* (Waco, TX: Word Books, 1988), 61.
11. John Gottman, *The Heart of Parenting* (New York: Simon and Schuster, 1997), 143.
12. Montagu, xv.

Chapter Fourteen—Healing Homophobia: A Positive Response

1. Marshal Kirk and Erastes Pill, "The Overhauling of Straight America," *Guide Magazine* (October–November 1987), 7–14.
2. Peter Freiberg, "Gay Budgets Near $100 Million," *Washington Blade* 30, no. 29 (16 July 1999): 1.
3. Ronald Bayer, *Homosexuality and American Psychiatry* (Princeton, NJ: Princeton University Press, 1987), 3–4.
4. Joseph Shapiro, Gareth Cook, and Andrew Krackov, "Straight Talk About Gays," *U.S. News and World Report* (5 July 1993): 46.
5. Felice J. Freyer, "Officials Say Being Openly Gay Isn't a Detriment," *Providence Journal-Bulletin* (21 November 1999): 1A.
6. Michael Swift, "Speaking Up for the Homoerotic Order," *Gay Community News* (February 1987): 15–21.
7. Platform of the 1993 March on Washington for Lesbian, Gay, and Bi Equal Rights and Liberation, Program Guide Project, April 1993, 16.
8. Luther Emmet Holt, *The Care and Feeding of Children: A Catechism for the Use of Mothers and Children's Nurses* (New York: Appleton-Century, 1935), as quoted in A. Montagu, *Touching*, 148–149.
9. John Broadio Watson, *Psychological Care of Infant and Child* (New York: Norton, 1928), as quoted in A. Montagu, *Touching*, 150–151.
10. A. Montagu, *Touching: The Human Significance of the Skin* (New York: Harper and Row Perrenial, 1986), 152.

Chapter Sixteen—A Final Thought

1. Robert Dreyfuss, "The Holy War on Gays," *Rolling Stone* (18 March 1999): 40.

Glossary

Attachment—an emotional bond between parent and child

Attachment/Holding Therapy—A technique for working with couples, parents, children, siblings, and other relatives. Through attachment/holding therapy with family members, much of the past can be healed and healthy attachment created or restored.

Behavioral and Gesture Reeducation—A process to help men inherit more masculine behaviors and women more feminine behaviors.

Bibliotherapy—Study of literature, i.e., causes of same-sex attractions, healing of homosexuality, nature of sexual abuse, and other issues in recovery.

Bioenergetics and Core Energetics—Therapeutic body work through which the individual expresses anger in a healthy way, learning to release pent-up bodily tension and pain, getting down to deeper emotions and needs, and becoming more grounded and centered in the body.

Bisexual—Having sexual attractions to both sexes.

Bonding—A strong attachment between a child and parent.

Breathwork—A deep-breathing technique to move repressed tension and memories from the unconscious to the conscious level, bringing healing and release.

Cognitive Therapy—Techniques for understanding faulty thinking/negative self-talk and learning new skills to correct the cognitive distortions.

Contracts—Agreements to help individuals fulfill assignments. Discipline is an area of weakness for many coming out of homosexuality, as implicit in the condition is insufficient bonding with the same-sex and/or opposite-sex parent. Making contracts to do homework assignments and other tasks is very useful. Accountability is important.

Enmeshment—Inappropriate intimacy, engulfment, a crossing of boundaries, usually referred to in a parent-child relationship.

Family Systems Therapy—Understanding the transgenerational dynamics of the family system by constructing a family history, seeing the bigger picture, and discovering how the individual is related to and influenced by the entire family system.

Friendships—Attachments between friends. Establishing healthy same-sex friendships is critical to healing out of homosexuality. Four kinds of friendships: 1) heterosexuals who know about the struggle and are supportive; 2) heterosexuals who don't know about the struggle and are good friends; 3) fellow overcomers; and 4) mentors.

Gay—A homosexual person who accepts his/her same-sex attractions. A political term coined by the Homosexual Movement.

Guilt—Feeling bad for doing wrong or going against one's belief system or an accepted set of values.

Inner-Child Healing—Another name for the unconscious. Inner-child work helps the individual learn to identify thoughts, feelings, and needs of the past and present.

Homosexual—The experiences of having sexual attractions for the same sex; having same-sex attractions.

Introjection—The process of internalizing messages, especially from parental and authority figures.

Meditation and Affirmations—Meditation is quieting the body, soul, and spirit, and learning to listen. Affirmations are words that enhance value and self-worth. It is wise to practice both on a daily basis.

Memory Healing and Neuro-Linguistic Programming—A process of going back to past memories, reexperiencing what happened, and this time reframing and healing the experience. This helps the individual disassociate from the problem and associate with the solution.

Mentoring—Process through which a mentoring model fulfills unmet homo-emotional and hetero-emotional love needs. The client is in the position of adult-child and the helper is in the position of the mentor.

Non-Gay Homosexual—The experience of having unwanted same-sex attractions; ego-dystonic.

Opposite-Sex Attachment Disorder (OSAD)—An attachment deficit between a child and the opposite-sex parent.

Psychodrama—A technique used in group sessions, having people recreate the family system or any other situation that caused harm. Here the client relives the experience and then is able to release repressed emotions.

Repress—To unconsciously bury feelings.

Role-Play/Gestalt Therapy—A technique whereby the client may speak to parents, siblings, perpetrators, himself, and anyone that caused him pain, by having other people play these roles.

Same-Sex Attractions—Sexual attractions for the same sex.

Same-Sex Attachment Disorder (SSAD)—An attachment deficit between a child and the same-sex parent.

Shame—Feeling bad for being wrong; a deep sense of unworthiness.

Suppress—To consciously bury feelings.

Therapeutic Massage—A technique to help release many repressed wounds in the body and bring healing and openness. Through therapeutic massage, the individual receives healthy touch.

Transactional Analysis—A paradigm of ego structure incorporating the adult, parent, and child.

Voice Dialogue—A technique for discovering one's inner family, or sub-personalities. It is also a method to uncover lost, or disowned, parts of the self.

References

Etiology and Treatment of Same-Sex Attractions

Kronemeyer, Robert. *Overcoming Homosexuality.* Farmingdale, New York: Macmillan Publishing Co., Inc., 1980.

Nicolosi, Joseph. *Healing Homosexuality: Case Stories of Reparative Therapy.* Northvale, NJ: Jason Aronson Inc., 1993.

——. *Reparative Therapy of Male Homosexuality.* Northvale, NJ: Jason Aronson Inc., 1991.

Satinover, Jeffrey. *Homosexuality and the Politics of Truth.* Grand Rapids, MI: Baker Books, 1996.

Siegel, Elaine. *Female Homosexuality: Choice Without Volition.* Hillsdale, NJ: The Analytic Press, 1988.

Socarides, Charles. *Homosexuality: A Freedom Too Far.* Phoenix, AZ: Adam Margrave Books, 1995.

Socarides, Charles. *Homosexuality: Psychoanalytic Therapy.* Northvale, NJ: Jason Aronson Inc., 1989.

Prevention

Lively, Scott. *Seven Steps to Recruit-Proof Your Child.* Keizer, OR: Founders Publishing Corp., 1998.

Schmierer, Don. *An Ounce of Prevention.* Nashville, TN: Thomas Nelson, 1998.

Wyden, Peter and Barbara. *Growing Up Straight: What Every Thoughtful Parent Should Know About Homosexuality.* New York: Stein and Day, 1968.

Children and Adolescents

Rekers, George A. *Handbook of Child and Adolescent Sexual Problems.* New York: Lexington Books, 1995.

Zucker, Kenneth, and Susan Bradley. *Gender Identity Disorder and Psychosexual Problems in Children and Adolescents.* New York: Guilford Press, 1995.

Christian and Jewish Books on Healing Homosexuality

Austin, Christopher, *Cleaning Out the Closet A Step by Step Approach for Christian Men Exiting from the Homosexual Lifestyle.* Nashville, TN: Power Source Productions, 1998. (1-800-331-5991)

Bergner, Mario. *Setting Love in Order.* Grand Rapids, MI: Baker Books, 1995.

Bulka, Reuven, *One Man, One Woman, One Lifetime: An Argument for Moral Tradition.* Lafayette, LA: Huntington House Publishers, 1995.

Comiskey, Andrew. *Pursuing Sexual Wholeness.* Lake Mary, FL: Creation House, 1989.

Consiglio, William. *Homosexual No More: Practical Strategies for Christians Overcoming Homosexuality.* Wheaton, IL: Victor Books, 1991.

Dallas, Joe. *Desires in Conflict.* Eugene, OR: Harvest House, 1991.

Davies, Bob, and Lori Rentzel. *Coming Out of Homosexuality.* Downers Grove, IL: InterVarsity Press, 1993.

Harvey, John. *The Truth About Homosexuality: The Cry of the Faithful.* San Francisco, CA: Ignatius Press, 1996.

Konrad, Jeff. *You Don't Have to Be Gay.* Newport Beach, CA: Pacific Publishing House, 1987.

Moberly, Elizabeth. *Homosexuality: A New Christian Ethic.* James Clark & Co., 1983.

Payne, Leanne. *The Broken Image.* Wheaton, IL: Crossway Books, 1981.

Saia, Michael. *Counseling the Homosexual.* Minneapolis, MN: Bethany House Publishers, 1988.

Wier, Terry. *Holy Sex: God's Purpose and Plan for Our Sexuality.* New Kensington, PA: Whitaker House, 1999.

Wilson, Earl. *Counseling and Homosexuality.* Waco, TX: Word Books, 1988.

Worthen, Frank. *Steps Out of Homosexuality.* San Rafael, CA: New Hope, 1984.

Personal Stories of Transformation (Christian)

Howard, Jeanette. *Out of Egypt.* Tunbridge Wells, Kent, Great Britain: Monarch/Regeneration, 1991.

Paulk, John. *Not Afraid to Change: The Remarkable Story of How One Man Overcame Homosexuality.* Mukilteo, WA: WinePress Publishing, 1998.

Paulk, John and Anne. *Love Won Out: How God's Love Helped Two People Leave Homosexuality and Find Each Other.* Wheaton, IL: Tyndale House Publishers, 1999.

Parents, Spouses, Family Members, and Friends

Anderson, Wendell and Nancy. *Family Manual.* Minneapolis, MN: Eagles' Wings Ministry, 1991.

———. *Wives' Manual.* Minneapolis, MN: Eagles' Wings Ministry, 1991, 1997.

Arterburn, Jerry. *How Will I Tell My Mother?* Nashville, TN: Thomas Nelson, 1988.

Davies, Bob, and Anita Worthen. *Someone I Love Is Gay: How Family and Friends Can Respond.* Downers Grove, IL: InterVarsity Press, 1996.

Johnson, Barbara. *Where Does a Mother Go to Resign?* Minneapolis, MN: Bethany House Publishers, 1979.

Weiss, Douglas. *Partner's Recovery Guide—100 Empowering Exercises.* Forth Worth, TX: Discovery Press, 1997.

White, John. *Parents in Pain.* Downers Grove, IL: InterVarsity Press, 1979.

Wright, H. Norman. *Loving a Prodigal: A Survival Guide for Parents of Rebellious Children.* Colorado Springs, CO: Chariot Victor Publishing/ Cook Communications, 1999.

Homosexual Movement

Bayer, Ronald. *Homosexuality and American Psychiatry.* Princeton, NJ: Princeton University Press, 1987.

Dannemeyer, William. *Shadow in the Land: Homosexuality in America.* San Francisco, CA: Ignatius Press, 1989.

Lively, Scott, and Kevin Abrams. *The Pink Swastika: Homosexuality in the Nazi Party.* Keizer, OR: Founders Publishing Corporation, 1995.

Maddoux, Marlin, and Christopher Corbett. *Answers to the Gay Deception.* Dallas, TX: International Christian Media, 1994.

Magnuson, Roger. *Are Gay Rights Right?* Portland, OR: Multnomah Press, 1990.

Rekers, George A., Editor. *The Journal of Human Sexuality.* Carrollton, TX: Lewis and Stanley, 1996.

Reisman, Judith, and Edward W. Eichel. *Kinsey, Sex and Fraud.* Lafayette, LA: A Lochinvar-Huntington House Publication, 1990.

Rueda, Enrique T. *The Homosexual Network: Private and Public Policy.* Old Greenwich, CT: Devin Adair Company, 1982.

GENERAL HEALING

Affirmations

Block, Douglas. *Words that Heal: Affirmations and Meditations for Daily Living*. New York: Bantam Books, 1988.

Cognitive/Behavioral Therapy

Alberti, Robert, and Michael Emmons. *Your Perfect Right: A Guide to Assertive Living*. San Luis Obispo, CA: Impact Publishers, 1995.

Burns, David. *The Feeling Good Handbook*. New York: Plume, 1990.

———. *Ten Days to Self-Esteem*. New York: William Morrow, 1993.

Cloud, Henry, and John Townsend. *Boundaries*. Grand Rapids, MI: Zondervan, 1992.

McGee, Robert S. *The Search for Significance*. Houston, TX: Rapha Publishing, 1990.

Schwartz, Jeffrey M. *Brain Lock: Free Yourself from Obsessive-Compulsive Behavior*. New York: Regan Books, 1996.

Young, Jeffrey, and Janet Klosko. *Reinventing Your Life*. New York: Dutton Book, 1993.

Emotional Abuse

Gorodensky, Arlene. *Mum's the Word: The Mamma's Boy Syndrome Revealed*. Herndon, VA: Cassell, 1997.

Love, Patricia. *Emotional Incest Syndrome: What to Do When a Parent's Love Rules Your Life*. New York: Bantam Books, 1990.

Diet

Sheats, Cliff. *Lean Bodies Total Fitness*. Arlington, TX: The Summit Publishing Group, 1995.

Family of Origin

Richardson, Ronald. *Family Ties That Bind*. Vancouver, Can.: Self-Counsel Press, 1987.

Grief Work

Westberg, Granger. *Good Grief: A Constructive Approach to the Problem of Loss*. Philadelphia, PA: Fortress Press, 1973.

Worden, J. William. *Grief Counseling and Grief Therapy: A Handbook for the Mental Health Practitioner.* 2nd ed. New York: Springer Publishing Company, 1991.

Inner-Child Healing

Capacchione, Lucia. *Recovery of Your Inner Child.* New York: Simon and Schuster Fireside Book, 1991.

Illsley Clarke, Jean, and Connie Dawson. *Growing Up Again: Parenting Ourselves, Parenting Our Children.* New York: Harper Collins Publishers, a Hazelden book, 1989.

Levin, Pamela. *Becoming the Way We Are.* Deerfield Beach, FL: Health Communications, Inc., 1988.

Pollard, John. *Self-Parenting: The Complete Guide to Your Inner Conversations.* Malibu, CA: Generic Human Studies Publishing, 1987.

Taylor, Cathryn, L. *The Inner Child Workbook.* New York: Putnam's Sons, 1991.

Weiss, Laurie and Jonathan. *Recovery from Co-Dependency: It's Never Too Late to Reclaim Your Childhood.* Littleton, CO: Empowerment Systems, 1988.

Whitfield, Charles. *Healing the Child Within.* Deerfield Beach, FL: Health Communications, Inc., 1987.

Inspiration

Hill, Napoleon. *Think and Grow Rich.* New York: Fawcett Columbine, 1937.

Warren, Neil Clark. *Finding Contentment.* Nashville, TN: Thomas Nelson Publishers, 1997.

Memory Healing

Bennett, Rita. *Making Peace with Your Inner Child.* Old Tappan, NJ: Fleming H. Revell Company, 1987.

Carter Stapleton, Ruth. *The Gift of Inner Healing.* Waco, TX: Word Books, 1976.

Payne, Leanne. *The Broken Image.* Grand Rapids, MI: Baker Books, 1981.

Seamands, David. *Healing for Damaged Emotions.* Wheaton, IL: Victor Books, 1981.

———. *Healing of Memories.* Wheaton, IL: Victor Books, 1985.

Men/Women Differences and Marital Relations

Gottman, John. *Why Marriages Succeed and Fail: And How You Can Make Yours Last.* New York: Simon and Schuster, Fireside, 1994.

Gray, John. *Men Are from Mars, Women Are from Venus.* New York: Harper Collins, 1992.

———. *Mars and Venus in the Bedroom.* New York: Harper Collins, 1995.

Hendrix, Harville. *Getting the Love You Want: A Guide for Couples.* New York: Harper Collins, Harper Perennial, 1988.

Kriedman, Ellen. *Light His Fire.* New York: Dell Publishing, 1989

———. *Light Her Fire.* New York: Dell Publishing, 1991.

Love, Patricia, and Jo Robinson. *Hot Monogamy.* New York: Plume, Penguin Group, 1994.

Moseley, Douglas and Naomi. *Dancing in the Dark: The Shadow Side of Intimate Relationships.* Georgetown, MA: North Star Publications, 1994.

Parrott, Les and Leslie. *Saving Your Marriage Before It Starts.* Grand Rapids, MI: Zondervan Publishing House, 1995.

Tannen, Deborah. *You Just Don't Understand: Women and Men in Conversation.* New York: Ballantine Books, 1990.

Sexual Abuse

Allender, Dan. *The Wounded Heart: Hope for Adult Victims of Childhood Sexual Abuse.* Colorado Springs, CO: NavPress, 1990.

Frank, Jan. *A Door of Hope.* San Bernardino, CA: Here's Life Publishers, 1987.

Sexual Addiction

Carnes, Patrick. *Don't Call It Love.* New York: Bantam Books, 1992.

———. *Out of the Shadows.* Minneapolis, MN: CompCare Publications, 1983.

Laaser, Mark. *Faithful and True: Healing the Wounds of Sexual Addictions.* Grand Rapids, MI: Zondervan Publishing House, 1996.

Schaumburg, Harry W. *False Intimacy: Understanding the Struggle of Sexual Addiction.* Colorado Springs, CO: NavPress, 1992.

Weiss, Douglas. *The Final Freedom.* Fort Worth, TX: Discovery Press, 1998.

Spirit Liberation

Anderson, Neil T. *A Way of Escape: Freedom from Sexual Strongholds.* Eugene, OR: Harvest House Publishers, 1994.

Fiore, Edith. *The Unquiet Dead.* New York: Ballantine Books, 1987.

Therapeutic Techniques

Baldwin, Martha. *Self-Sabotage.* New York: Warner Books, Inc., 1987.

Berne, Eric. *Games People Play: The Basic Handbook of Transactional Analysis.* New York: Ballantine Books, 1964.

Gendlin, Eugene. *Focusing.* New York: Bantam Books, 1981.

Hellinger, Bert. *Love's Hidden Symmetry: What Makes Love Work in Relationships.* Phoenix, AZ: Zeig, Tucker & Co., 1998.

Jackins, Harvey. *The Human Side of Human Beings: The Theory of Re-evaluation Counseling.* Seattle, WA: Rational Island Publishers, 1978.

Lowen, Alexander. *Bioenergetics.* New York: Penguin, 1975.

Pierrakos, John. *Core Energetics.* Mendocino, CA: LifeRhythm, 1986.

Stone, Hal and Sidra. *Embracing Ourselves: The Voice Dialogue Manual.* Mill Valley, CA: Nataraj Publishing, 1989.

Touch/Bonding/Attachment/Holding Therapy

Colton, Helen. *Touch Therapy.* New York: Kensington Publishing Corp., Zebra Books, 1983.

Joy, Donald M. *Bonding: Relationships in the Image of God.* Nappanee, IN: Evangel Publishing House, 1999.

Montagu, Ashley. *Touching: The Human Significance of the Skin.* New York: Harper & Row, Perennial Library, 1986.

Thevenin, Tine. *The Family Bed.* Wayne, NJ: Avery Publishing Group, Inc., 1987.

Welch, Martha. *Holding Time.* New York: Simon and Schuster, 1988. VideoTape Series: *Welch Method Attachment Therapy*, 1999. (1-888-447-6872 or www.marthawelch.com).

International Resources for Healing Homosexuality

International Healing Foundation
Tel. (301) 805-6111
Web: www.ComingOutStraight.com
Healing seminars, consultations/evaluations, counseling, speaking engagements, resource materials. Richard Cohen, M.A., Director.

Positive Alternatives To Homosexuality (PATH)
Web: www.pathinfo.org
International coalition of organizations helping those with unwanted same-sex attraction.

National Association for Research and Therapy of Homosexuality (NARTH)
Tel. (818) 789-4440
Web: www.narth.com
Scientific organization of professional therapists who assist those with unwanted same-sex attraction. Call for local therapists. Joseph Nicolosi, Ph.D., President.

People Can Change
Web: www.PeopleCanChange.com
Great web site for stories of change, online support groups, and information about men's weekend seminars (Journey Into Manhood).

Exodus International
Tel. (407) 599-6872
Web: www.exodus-international.org
Umbrella organization for more than 100 ex-gay Christian ministries in America and worldwide. Alan Chambers, North American Director.

Jews Offering New Alternatives to Homosexuality (JONAH)

Tel. (201) 433-3444

Web: www.jonahweb.org

Jewish organization offering support for strugglers, family, and friends. Arthur Goldberg and Elaine Berk, Co-Directors.

Parents and Friends of Ex-Gays and Gays (PFOX)

Tel. (703) 360-2225

Web: www.pfox.org

Support groups for family members and friends. Regina Griggs, Executive Director.

Regeneration Books

Tel. (410) 661-0284

Web: www.regenbooks.com

Book ministry of Exodus International.

Courage

Tel. (212) 268-1010

Web: www.couragerc.net

Catholic ministry for those with unwanted same-sex attraction. Encourage is for family and friends. Father John Harvey, O.S.F.S., Director.

Evergreen International

Tel. (801) 363-3837 or (800) 391-1000

Web: www.evergreeninternational.org

Mormon ministry (Latter Day Saints) for strugglers, family, and friends. David Pruden, Executive Director.

Powerful Change Ministry Group

Tel. (770) 210-4034

Web: witnessfortheworld.org

African American coalition of Ex-Gay Christian ministries. D. L. Foster, Executive Director.

Transforming Congregations

Tel. (302) 945-9650

Web: www.TransformingCong.org

United Methodist ministry for strugglers, family, and friends. Karen Booth, Director.

One by One
Tel. (585) 586-6180
Web: www.oneby1.org
Presbyterian ministry for strugglers, family, and friends.

Inqueery
Web: www.inqueery.com
Addressing same-sex attraction issues in public schools. Chad Thompson, Director.

Homosexuals Anonymous (HA)
Tel. (610) 779-2500
Web: http://members.aol.com/hawebpage
Christian-based support groups for those with unwanted same-sex attraction. John J., Director.

Additional Web Sites

www.newdirection.ca/research—Showing the efficacy of changing from a homosexual to heterosexual orientation
www.healinghomosexuality.com—Adventure In Manhood
weekend seminar
www.mygenes.co.nz—Dispelling the "gay gene" myth
www.realityresources.com—Helping those with transgender issues
www.drthrockmorton.com—Updates about healing unwanted same-sex attraction
www.janellehallman.com—female therapist helping woman with unwanted same-sex attraction
www.ojc.de/dijg/index.php—German/European organization
www.odwaga.oaza.pl—Polish organization

Resource Materials

Audio Tapes/CDs

Healing Homosexuality

MEANING AND CAUSES
The underlying meaning and causes of same-sex attractions are presented. The many factors that may lead an individual into a homosexual orientation are clearly described. This tape is an excellent introduction for anyone interested in the subject of same-sex attractions.

PROCESS OF TRANSITIONING
This presentation describes what to do in order to transition from homosexual to heterosexual. A complete treatment plan for transitioning is detailed in a four-stage model of recovery. This program has helped many men and women come out of homosexuality.

THERAPEUTIC TOOLS AND TECHNIQUES
This presentation describes how to do it, a step-by-step guide to successfully work through each stage of recovery. Practical tools and techniques are explained in detail. A list of books and workbooks are recommended.

AFFIRMATIONS AND MEDITATIONS
This tape consists of several wonderful affirmations and meditations to use each day to aid in accomplishing and achieving your desires and dreams. The affirmations and meditations are on such topics as healing gender identity, building self-confidence, healing relationships, and achieving your goals.

HEALING YOUR INNER CHILD AND MEMORY HEALING

Healing Your Inner Child is a meditation on recapturing and liberating your true self. The concept of "inner child" is explained.

Memory Healing is about resolving painful experiences of the present and past through guided imagery.

Book for Family and Friends

GAY CHILDREN, STRAIGHT PARENTS:
A PLAN FOR FAMILY HEALING

Finding out that a loved one has homosexual desires may be confusing and painful. This book offers practical suggestions for family members and friends whose loved ones experience same-sex attraction. You will learn how someone with same-sex attraction thinks and feels, and what you can do to help them heal.

Video/DVD

COMING OUT STRAIGHT

This presentation will help people understand the basic causes of same-sex attractions and the process of transitioning from homosexual to hetero-sexual. Topics include:

- Meaning and causes of same-sex attractions
- Process of transitioning from homosexual to heterosexual
- Current statistics and research on homosexuality
- Agenda, strategies, and goals of the homosexual movement
- Positive ways to promote change

This presentation is excellent for schools, colleges, universities, religious institutions, and mental health facilities.

To order materials:

Tel: (301) 805-6111
Web: www.ComingOutStraight.com

TELECONFERENCING CLASSES

There is hope for healing homosexuality! People can change their sexual orientation. Now you can receive personal coaching and guidance from an internationally recognized expert in sexual reorientation therapy. Educator, author, and psychotherapist Richard Cohen will share with you the wisdom gained through his journey out of homosexuality and years of experience helping others make the change.

Teleconferencing Classes are available for 1) Family & Friends, 2) Strugglers, and 3) Therapists/Clergy/Educators. Each class lasts 1½ hours with 30 minutes teaching and 60 minutes question and answer session/personal coaching. Each course has nine classes held over a three-month period of time. *You may join the course anytime.*

Through these courses, family members and strugglers will receive practical guidance and build a loving network of support with others in similar situations. Therapists and clergy will receive education about the causes and treatment of homosexuality, and direct supervision for individual cases.

Call for information/brochure or find out more online at:
www.ComingOutStraight.org

Index

Numbers in *italics* indicate figures and exhibits.

athletic inclination, 45, 46
athletics, 117, 128
  avoiding, 56
  fear of, 42
attachment
  disorder, 27, 37. *See also* Same-Sex
    Attachment Disorder
  lack of, 73, 184
  manifestation of unmet needs for, 39
  strain, 27, 37, 150
Attachment/Holding Therapy (Welch),
  14, 94, 117, 149–50, 156–58,
  165, 166. *See also* holding
  inappropriate for unsafe families, 157
attraction to people with similar characteristics, 126
Austin, Christopher, 70, 121–25, 163
authoritarianism, contraindicated with
  Same-Sex Attachment Disorder, 71
autosuggestion, 129, 149

B

Bailey, John M., 19–20
Balaban, Evan S., 21, 23
Baldwin, Martha, 131, 145
Barnhouse, 24
behavior, imitation of opposite-sex parents', 35
behavioral changes, 162–63, 184
behavioral genetics, misunderstanding
  of, 23
behavioral reeducation, 117, 167
behavioral therapy, 66–76, 108–9, 121
Bennett, Rita, 159
Bible, 30, 158, 177, 191
bibliotherapy, 71, 116, 121
Bieber, Irving, 24, 34
Big Lie Theory, 47, 48
bioenergetic exercise, 78
bioenergetic methods, 8, 175–77
bioenergetics, 79, 87, 91, 95, 116,
  152–53, 156, 159–60, 162,
  165, 181
bioenergetic work, 59, 82

Bioenergetics (Lowen), 152
biological predisposition, studies of,
  18–24
bisexual, 18, 43
Blake, William, 173
blaming, 17
Bloch, Douglas, 131
Bly, Robert, 3, 63, 89
bodily attributes, 41–43
body, disconnection with, 55–56
body-image wounds, 28, 41–43, 70, 87,
  156, 218, 222–23
  healing, 118
Boundaries (Cloud and Townsend), 206
boundary setting, 187, 206
Bowen, Murray, 71–72
Bowlby, John, 37
Bradley, Susan J., 35
Brand, Paul, 185
breaking through defense detachments,
  as adult-child, 213
breathing, 153, 156, 159
breathwork, 153–54, 165
Broken Image (Payne), 159
Brown University, 20
building skills, 133
Burns, David, 81, 82, 133, 134, 135,
  222
Byrd, Dean, 32

C

caffeine, abstaining from, 70, 123
Capacchione, Lucia, 82, 146–47, 181
Carlson, Richard, 133
Catholic Community Services, 13
Catholic Ex-Gay Ministry, 70
Catholic Parent's Ministry, 70
change, desire for, 66
character armor, 84, 86
child, parentifying in mentor relationship, 205
childhood
  core beliefs of, 88–89
  memories, 112

diet, 67, 70, 118, 128, 154, 163

"Difference in Hypothalamic Structure Between Heterosexual and Homosexual Men, A" (LeVay), 18–19

Dimock, Patrick, 43

disassociation, 81

discipline, 117

disorders, 86–87

divorce, 87

  caused by projection of past resentments, 94

  factor contributing to Same-Sex Attachment Disorder, 50

  rate of, 48

Don't Sweat the Small Stuff and It's All Small Stuff (Carlson), 133

drawing with nondominant hand, 82, 104, 147, 148

dread, 139

Drew, Jane Myers, 159, 166

drug abuse, 48

dysfunctional thoughts, accelerated by caffeine, 123

E

early infancy, imprinting during, 36

eating disorder, 181

eating healthy, 123

education, 116, 121

  in mentor relationship, 205–6

educational system, 46, 47

ego structure, 117

Einstein College of Medicine, 19

Ellis, 24

e-mail outreach, 70

Embracing Our Selves (Stone and Stone), 150

emotional dependency, 174

emotional growth, arrested at time of neglect, abuse or abandonment, 214

emotional healing, 118

emotional incest syndrome, 34

emotionally based condition, 25, 26–27

emotional makeup work, 162

emotional map, 140–41

emotional processing, 59

emotional recovery work, 155

emotional reprocessing, need for, 161

emotional tools and techniques

  for grounding, 141–52

  for hetero-emotional wounds, 165–66

  for homo-emotional wounds, 156–63

  for transitioning, 127–28

emotions

  open expression of, 124

  suppression of, 186

enmeshed, 95

enmeshment-abandonment issues, 212

entertainment industry, 46, 47, 73

environmental factors, 20, 23

epinephrine, 86

escape mechanisms, 77

etiology of same-sex attractions, 156

Evergreen International, 70, 256

exercise, 67, 70, 75, 81–82, 117, 123, 128, 154, 163

ex-gay ministries, 8–9, 11–12, 43, 69, 128

EXODUS International, 11, 69, 196, 255

expectations, 135

experiencing value, as adult-child, 215

Exploding the Gene Myth (Hubbard and Wald), 22–23

expressing needs, as adult-child, 212–13

eye-hand coordination, 45, 128

F

falling in love, as adult-child, 213

false memory syndrome, 147

false self, 84, 86, 145, 151

family, as support network, 67, 68

family constellation, 117, 156, 160, 165

family discord, 3

family dynamics, 28, 40–41

family history, 116, 171

About the Author

Richard Cohen, M.A., a psychotherapist and educator, is one of the leading experts in the field of sexual reorientation and the author of *Coming Out Straight: Understanding and Healing Homosexuality*.

Cohen is the director of the International Healing Foundation (IHF), a non-profit organization he founded in 1990. Based in the Washington, D.C. area, IHF provides educational programs, consultation/supervision, and healing seminars for individuals, families, therapists and clergy. As director, Cohen travels extensively throughout the States and Europe making presentations on marital relations, communication skills, parenting skills, sexual reorientation and healing from abuse and addictions. He is a frequent guest lecturer on college and university campuses, and at therapeutic and religious conferences.

Cohen holds a Master of Arts degree in counseling psychology from Antioch University and a bachelor's degree from Boston University. He is an adjunct faculty member at Washington Bible College. He has worked in child abuse treatment services, family reconciliation services, general counseling and support groups. For three years he worked as an HIV/AIDS educator for the American Red Cross.

As an expert in sexual reorientation therapy—both as a counselor and through his own personal experience transitioning from homosexual to heterosexual in the 1980s—Cohen has been interviewed by newspapers, radio, and television media, including appearances on *20/20*, *Larry King Live*, and *The O'Reilly Factor*. Board president of Parents and Friends of Ex-Gays and Gays (PFOX), he is also cofounder and vice president of Positive Alternatives To Homosexuality (PATH), and a member of the National Association for the Research and Therapy of Homosexuality (NARTH). In addition to academic papers and his book, *Coming Out Straight*, Cohen authored *Gay Children, Straight Parents: A Plan for Family Healing*. Both titles are available in numerous languages.

Cohen lives in the Washington, D.C., metropolitan area with his wife and three children.

For information about consultations, counseling, teleconferencing classes, healing seminars, supervision, and resource materials, please contact:

Richard Cohen, M.A., Director

International Healing Foundation

P.O. Box 901

Bowie, MD 20718

Tel. (301) 805-6111

Fax (301) 805-5155

Email: IHF90@aol.com

Web: www.ComingOutStraight.com